The Strange Deaths of
President Harding

Robert H. Ferrell

University of Missouri Press
Columbia and London

Copyright © 1996 by
The Curators of the University of Missouri
University of Missouri Press, Columbia, Missouri 65201
Printed and bound in the United States of America
First paperback printing, 1998
All rights reserved
5   4   3   2   1   02   01   00   99   98

Library of Congress Cataloging-in-Publication Data

Ferrell, Robert H.
    The strange deaths of President Harding / Robert H. Ferrell.
      p.   cm.
    Includes bibliographical references and index.
    ISBN 0-8262-1202-6 (pbk; alk. paper)
    1. Harding, Warren G. (Warren Gamaliel), 1865–1923—Public
opinion.   2. Presidents—United States—Biography—History and
criticism.   3. Public opinion—United States.   I. Title.
E786.F47   1996
973.91'4'092—DC20   96-31838
                                                         CIP

♾™ This paper meets the requirements of the
American National Standard for Permanence of Paper
for Printed Library Materials, Z39.48, 1984.

Text Design: Stephanie Foley
Jacket Design: Kristie Lee
Typesetter: BookComp, Inc.
Printer and Binder: Thomson-Shore, Inc.
Typeface: Minion

Contents

Preface		vii
Acknowledgments		ix
1	Death at the Palace	1
2	The Poison Theory	30
3	The President's Daughter	50
4	Scandals	105
5	Aftermath	134
6	Conclusion	166
Notes		169
Bibliography		187
Index		195

Preface

Fifty years ago a young college student was driving back from Columbus, Ohio, to Bowling Green in the northern part of the state, near Toledo, with a car full of friends, and approached the outskirts of Marion. There he saw against the leaden sky—snow covered the ground, and it was late afternoon—the rounded top of the Harding Memorial. Not a car was in sight, and he turned into the memorial grounds, irreverently driving down the wide sidewalk to the presidential tomb. Stopping, he identified it to his friends, and everyone laughed.

At that time it would have seemed impossible that this same student would write a book about President Warren G. Harding.

The passage of the years can change one's mind, and the pages that follow seek not merely to set out the decline and fall of Harding's reputation, and to point out what caused it, but also to argue that Harding has deserved better from history. His fate does not seem at all fair. Beginning in 1948 historians and political scientists and other presidential experts have taken part in half a dozen and more polls in which they have grouped presidents according to ability and achievement. They have divided them by categories—great, near great, above average, average, below average, and failure. Every time Harding has been in the failure category, and not only there but at the bottom of that category as well. This judgment surely is in error. He may not have been a great or near-great president. But should he not stand at least above three or four other holders of the presidency whom even the slightest student of the presidents can name?

During the lifetime of the nation's twenty-ninth president his reputation was very high. Unlike his predecessor, Woodrow Wilson, who was yet living at the time of Harding's death, and whose intellectuality, and beyond that, whose coldness, had not made him a figure of affection, Harding invoked the admiration of his fellow citizens. He was tall, over six feet, and handsome—he looked like a president. By all accounts he was a kindly man, genuinely interested in people. He possessed not an iota of self-importance, and his smile warmed everyone he met. He shook hands every day with a line of visitors, often several hundred, that formed at the door to the executive offices to the west of the White House. He told a protesting assistant that he had asked for the votes of his countrymen and was not about to ignore them thereafter, and besides, he said, he enjoyed meeting the American people, seeing them in the pleasure they took in meeting their president.

In conducting the public business, Harding proved a considerable success. He created the Bureau of the Budget, the Veterans' Bureau, presided over a dramatic reduction of the federal debt, and in foreign affairs arranged separate peace treaties with the former enemy nations and the calling of the Washington Naval Conference. Unlike his predecessor, he made strong cabinet appointments. His cabinet members admired him, including Secretary of Commerce Herbert Hoover who later became president. Vice President Calvin Coolidge saw nothing to object to, although he once told his friend, the Boston dry-goods store owner Frank W. Stearns, that he was not certain he would want to entrust the public business to individuals who played poker.

When Harding passed on, there was an outpouring of grief comparable to that accorded the death of President Abraham Lincoln in 1865. As Harding's funeral train crossed the country from San Francisco to Washington, and thence to Marion for burial, millions watched it go by and sang the president's favorite hymns.

Then, within a very short time, all this was gone, replaced by the harshest of criticism.

Students of the Harding era will notice the use of the title, albeit slightly modified, of the book by Gaston B. Means, *The Strange Death of President Harding*, which was published in 1930.

Acknowledgments

Many thanks to the archivists of the University of Massachusetts at Amherst—Ute Bargmann, Michael Milewski, and Linda Seidman— for their assistance with the papers of Dean Albertson; to the former librarian of Indiana University, Cecil K. Byrd, presently an associate of the Lilly Library, for commenting on a draft of the following chapters; Robert F. Byrnes, my former department colleague, who made copies of the Ray Lyman Wilbur Papers at the Hoover Institution in Stanford, California; Kenneth W. Duckett, former manuscript curator at the Ohio Historical Society, who offered wonderfully helpful advice on the Harding Papers; Barbara Floyd, Judith Friebert, and Robert A. Shaddy, archivists at the University of Toledo, for the Randolph C. Downes Papers; Matthew Fulgham and Rodney A. Ross of the Center for Legislative Archives, National Archives, for the records of the senate hearings on the Veterans' Bureau in 1923–1924; James N. Giglio, biographer of Harry M. Daugherty, for information about Harding's attorney general; Gene M. Gressley, for the Francis Russell Papers at the American Heritage Center, University of Wyoming, Laramie; Milton F. Heller Jr., son-in-law of Vice Admiral Joel T. Boone, for assistance with the Boone Papers in the Library of Congress; John K. Hulston (member of the Missouri bar and fellow Truman historian), Timothy E. Gammon (his partner), and Thomas B. Grier (attorney-at-law in Bensalem, Pennsylvania) for the case of *Britton v. Klunk* of 1931; Frank K. Lorenz of Hamilton College, who copied Samuel Hopkins Adams's papers pertaining to President Harding; John Lukacs, for reading the manuscript and sharing his unsurpassed knowledge of twentieth-century history; Dale C. Mayer, Dwight M. Miller, and Timothy Walch of the Herbert Hoover Library in West Branch, Iowa, for collections pertaining to Harding; Judge Charlton Myers, Trella Hemmerly Romine, and John D. Telfer—former president, current president, and director, respectively, of the Marion County Historical Society—for many courtesies; D. F. Shaughnessy, for a most thorough reading of the manuscript; Ann Sindelar and Kermit J. Pike of the Western Reserve Historical Society for assistance with the name "G. H. Harvey"; Robert Freeman Smith of the University of Toledo who sent a calendar of the Downes Papers and reminisced about his late colleague; Jerry L.

Wallace of the Regional Archives System, National Archives, for bibliographical suggestions; and Archivist Beverly Watkins of the National Archives's Great Lakes Region branch in Chicago, who found the case number of *Britton v. Klunk* and thereby made that file and an associated file available.

Beverly Jarrett, director and editor-in-chief of the University of Missouri Press, took an interest in the project from beginning to end, as is her wont, and her enthusiasm makes everything easier. A thank-you also to Jane Lago, managing editor. Annette Wenda edited the manuscript with extraordinary ability to turn up error and to straighten confusion; I much appreciate her fine work. Two anonymous readers of the press require special thanks. One of them was so anonymous that I discerned the style of John Milton Cooper Jr. of the University of Wisconsin, and thank him in his anonymous guise.

Betty Bradbury put the typescript, much corrected, on the word processor, and had reason to remember John Cooper's citing to me the advice of Bernard DeVoto to Catherine Drinker Bowen, "Run this through your typewriter again."

Lila and Carolyn, as usual, helped in ways too numerous to mention.

The Strange Deaths of President Harding

1

Death at the Palace

President Warren G. Harding died at the Palace Hotel in San Francisco on August 2, 1923. That his basic physical problem was cardiovascular disease should have admitted of no doubt. To use the description of his personal physician, Dr. Charles E. Sawyer, it was this trouble that allowed the president "to pass over the last rapids on his way to Eternity." Perhaps the earliest evidence, or at least the earliest clear evidence, that he was suffering from cardiovascular disease appeared in 1916 when the then senator visited his brother, Dr. George T. Harding II, a cardiologist in Columbus, Ohio, who tested his blood pressure. "I called upon my brother while in Columbus," Harding wrote Sawyer in Marion. "Blood pressure test scored 160. He thought this was greater than it ought to be, but I think that is about normal for me, so I shall not give it any considerable worry."[1] It thus was apparent well before his death that his systolic pressure was moving upward, beyond the safe range that might be defined as 140 or less. By the time he became president it had reached an alarming 180. Years later, in the 1970s, two cardiologists published a much noticed article that said people with hardworking traits—individuals who work incessantly, push with their lives, and never seem to rest—were describable as "type A" and were therefore at greater risk of developing cardiovascular problems. Early in his life Harding displayed such traits. His sister Charity Harding Remsberg wrote after her brother's death that as a youth he was large and strong, and "we thought him able to carry out anything he would undertake. He was taught to work at a very early age. The chores of a family home fell upon him as he was eldest and a boy." When only fourteen he spent vacation days from school helping neighbors thresh grain, working with the men. He did the plowing on the farm and much of the orchard work. When the Toledo and Ohio Central Railroad was being constructed he worked with a team, for the railroad's engineers paid extra for men with teams. Charity

1

Remsberg thought he overworked at too early an age and remembered nights he sometimes was too tired to rest. "He would drive those horses all night long, for we could hear him in his slumber."[2]

Another indication of a type A person was presence of cardiovascular disease among close relatives. Several of his close relatives died of the disease.

In youth Harding suffered from what was diagnosed as a problem of nerves, or nervous breakdown. He visited the Battle Creek Sanitarium in Michigan several times: in 1889 (two days); 1894 (twenty-nine days); again that year (dates unknown); 1897 (similarly); and 1903 (seven days).[3] Whether these illnesses had any connection with cardiovascular disease is impossible to say. In his adult years Harding moved to Marion, then a bustling town of several thousand inhabitants, fifty miles north of Columbus. There he purchased a newspaper, the *Marion Star*. As the town grew into a city, the *Star* prospered. Life in Marion admittedly was more complicated, one might say faster, than in the village of Blooming Grove, near which Harding was born, in Caledonia where his father had been half-owner of a local sheet, the *Argus,* and in Iberia where he attended an academy, what later would have been described as a high school, Ohio Central College. But surely, even in Marion, Harding's life must not have been subject to heavy pressures, and this may be the explanation for the virtual disappearance of any concern for physical problems until after he entered national politics. He served two terms in the state senate at the turn of the century, one two-year term as lieutenant governor, and entered the U.S. Senate in 1915.

As he told his brother, he gave no attention to blood pressure. He later confided to the assistant White House physician, a U.S. Navy doctor, Joel T. Boone, that when his pressure was high it was a sign he was not working hard enough. "In Ohio," he said, "my doctors used to get after me about my high blood pressure and tell me not to continue making campaign speeches, but every time I went campaigning it always went down; so I don't know if I ought to pay any attention to the advice to not make any speeches when you say I shouldn't, because I inherited it; it doesn't worry me."[4]

But the White House proved quite another experience for the newspaperman and politician. When he came into the presidency in 1921 he found the work far more confining than he had anticipated. It was almost exhausting, even though he had spent the preceding six years as senator from a populous state and knew what it meant to deal with constituents in person or through letters and then, when back in Ohio, attend functions and make speeches. The sheer volume of White House work undoubtedly did him no good, physically speaking, as it encouraged him (and he hardly needed encouragement) to overwork. After the world war the prominence of the federal government in the lives of Americans had not lessened. The work of the president increased, so one of the White House secretaries told Dr. Boone. Rudolph Forster had been in the White House since the time of William McKinley and estimated that the presidential workload was five times greater than when the Spanish-American War occupied the then president. He said it was many times greater than during the era of Theodore Roosevelt—when to observe the peripatetic activities of "T.R." was to make any White House newspaper reporter subject, some observers thought, to a headache: the president after McKinley had seemed that busy. William H. Taft when in the White House never worked very hard. Nor did Woodrow Wilson, at least before American entrance into the war; he worked three or four hours a day and took long and frequent vacations. It was Harding, Forster said, who discovered real busyness.[5]

Harding's correspondence testified to his activity and so did people who watched him. It was possible to contend that he did not manage well, that he had little experience with the work of a large and top-level office and did not know how to handle it. The White House, some people said, was not his newspaper. In opposition to such a theory was the statement of Forster, who ought to have known, and the president certainly agreed with his assistant. In the second year of his administration he wrote his Marion friend and next-door neighbor George B. Christian Sr., "Our days are full here, and as time goes on our duties instead of lessening, seem to increase." He wrote a golfing companion, Henry P. Fletcher, that "matters have been rather strenuous of late and have riveted me to my job." The White House chief usher, Irwin H. (Ike) Hoover, admittedly no neutral observer, who in his memoirs, *Forty-Two Years in the White House,* said he considered Harding a "sport," wrote that he worked all the time.[6]

With all the work came increasing tiredness. A reporter for the *St. Louis Post-Dispatch,* Charles G. Ross, who many years later would become President Harry S. Truman's press secretary and was his paper's Washington correspondent, wrote toward the end of 1922, "The President has aged perceptibly during the last 18 months. There is more gray in his hair, more bagginess under his eyes . . . After a long cabinet meeting he sometimes looks extremely tired." That winter Harding told his brother-in-law Heber H. Votaw, "I am not well, Heber." Votaw suggested he go to a hospital, and the president said that word would get out and the stock market would go down.[7]

Parenthetically let it be said that two physicians later testified that they knew Harding was in cardiovascular trouble and that his problems were so serious they expected him not to live out his first term. But it is difficult to know how much credence to give their testimonies, since although they both made the comments to friends at the time, their warnings passed into print long after Harding died. When President Ray Lyman Wilbur of Stanford University, former dean of the Stanford University Medical School, who was present in Chicago at the 1920 Republican National Convention, learned that Harding would receive the nomination (Wilbur was hoping that his Stanford friend Herbert Hoover would get it), he declared the intelligence impossible and told his informant, one of the leading Ohio politicians, "It doesn't seem possible! Anyone who knows the situation from a medical standpoint realizes that Harding could not last through the trials of a single term. He is not a well enough man to live through four years of the punishment that a president must take. Just to look at him you can see that he has cardiovascular disease and high blood pressure!" His friend answered, "If what you say is so, then we'll just have to pay a little more attention to who goes in for vice president. It is going to be done." The only trouble with this testimony is that Wilbur dictated it in 1944 (and may have been thinking, although the dictation does not reveal the point, of the then president, Franklin D. Roosevelt, whose cardiovascular disease was similarly serious). Wilbur's remarks were published in 1960. After Harding was elected, the New York cardiologist Emanuel Libman saw a full-page photograph of Harding in the Sunday *New York Times* and told two Washington friends, Eugene and Agnes Meyer, later owners of the *Washington Post,* that the president-elect looked unhealthy and that he did not believe he would finish his term. This commentary was not made public until 1939 and then in garbled form.[8]

On August 1, 1923, or thereabouts, Harding's sister Mrs. Remsberg told Malcolm A. Fraser, an acquaintance, just before she left to see her brother, ill in San Francisco, that he was in deplorable condition because of heart trouble. The acquaintance was a representative of Orange County and about to attend a meeting in Los Angeles to make plans for receiving the president when he went south from San Francisco. "Tell the Committee," the president's sister said, "to make no plans until they learn of a change for the better in Warren's condition. He has had bad heart trouble for several years and I fear he is on his deathbed at San Francisco. I am taking the train tonight to be with him." Mrs. Remsberg lived in Santa Ana and spoke over the telephone to Fraser. The latter did not reveal the conversation until 1939.[9]

It is an unfortunate fact that Harding's personal physician at this time, and until his death, was hardly qualified to make the diagnosis privately offered by Wilbur and Libman or perhaps guessed at by Charity Remsberg. In Marion, Dr. Sawyer was well known as the proprietor of a successful hospital, the Sawyer Sanatorium, located in splendid quarters at what the doctor called White Oaks Farm on the outskirts of the city. He was a small, wizened man, with a conspicuous goatee, and his patients including the presidential couple put much faith in him and his prescriptions. The latter often took the form of "a dose of soda water at least three times a day" together with two pink pills left on the dresser, or little yellow tablets, flat white tablets, and green medicine in a bottle.[10] The faith the doctor inspired came because of his confident, ebullient personality. He was a homeopath, and his patients may have expected more gentle treatment from him than from more conventional physicians, for he would be more diagnostic, more analytical (although many homeopaths practiced in those days and their prescriptions were not so carefully noticed by their patients, who considered them medical, just as those of any physician).

But beyond the analysis was Sawyer's confidence, which was infectious. He once set it out on a card, sent at Christmas 1916 to his grandson, in which he enclosed a coin that would buy a ticket on the Railroad of Progress, from his Marion farm to Prosperity, Worthy Man's Land, Universe. Stopovers were allowed at Good Health and its substations, Exercise, Rest, Recuperation, Good Cheer, and Smile. Also Achievement and its suburbs, Energy, Enthusiasm, Resolution, Determination, Opportunity, and Ambition. Satisfaction and its Burroughs, Accomplishment, Influence, Prestige, Honor, and Renown. A ticket holder would be able to carry the following baggage: Hope, Good Cheer, Joy, Courtesy, Confidence, and Self-respect, each without limit. Owing to an embargo of practical experience the following baggage was prohibited: Suspicion, Complaint, Dissatisfaction, Fault-finding, and Blues. It was a one-track railroad, Grandfather Sawyer told young Warren.[11]

This was Harding's physician, appointed the president's physician in 1921 virtually by the president's wife whom Sawyer had brought back from near death not long before the Hardings went to the White House. Mrs. Harding informed her husband that if "Old Doc" did not accompany them, she might die in Washington. The president installed him in the army medical corps, with the instant rank of brigadier general—which may not have been much more instant, so regular physicians in the army and navy in Washington whispered to each other, than the raising by Harding's presidential predecessor, Wilson, of Lt. Comdr. Cary T. Grayson to the rank of rear admiral a few years before.

Sawyer, one might add, took much pleasure in his Washington role. He was not a self-important man or a stupid man and possessed a large fund of common sense, but he had come suddenly to Washington, late in his life, and found the capital's ways, the attention directed to people close to the president, difficult to resist. A White House employee of long standing wrote in his memoirs, a bit uncharitably, that Sawyer liked to strut and talking to newspapermen was like strutting. He watched him during Sawyer's first day at the White House, dressed in his brigadier general's uniform, walking back and forth next to the executive offices, with photographers running after him taking pictures. Remonstrating with the photographers, whom he knew well, about wasting film, he learned from their responses and impish grins that they had no film in their cameras and were, they said, exercising the general, watching him strut.[12]

It was unfortunate that not merely Sawyer but the Marion physician's assistant during the Harding administration, Dr. Boone, was unable to discern the meaning of Harding's tiredness. Boone took up his duties as physician aboard the presidential yacht *Mayflower* and as Sawyer's assistant in the autumn of 1922. An observant man, also methodical, he was to provide a massive amount of information for later historians. Upon his death many years after Harding had passed on, in 1974, he left a diary, an oral history, a huge unpublished autobiography, and a massive collection of correspondence, all

all testifying to what he thought and observed during the course of a long and very distinguished career in which he traversed the U.S. Navy's ranks to vice admiral. He saw action in Haiti in 1916, in the world war at Saissons with the marine brigade of the Second Division when he won the Congressional Medal of Honor, afterward serving in the White House during the administrations of Harding, Coolidge, Hoover, and (for a short time) Franklin Roosevelt, and in World War II was fleet medical officer in the Pacific and at war's end the first American to go ashore in the Tokyo Bay area.

Like Sawyer, Boone was a homeopath, having graduated from Hahnemann Medical College in Philadelphia in 1913, but there the similarity between the two physicians ended, for Boone was a much younger man and much better trained. A descendant of the famous frontiersman, he had grown up in modest circumstances in Pennsylvania and after medical school joined the navy. The diminutive (he was 5'6") lieutenant commander took up his Washington duties with the same thoroughness with which he approached everything else. When in his first weeks he became acquainted with President and Mrs. Harding he gave them the best care he could, as much attention as he was capable of. Noticing the president's tiredness he worried about it and later might have wondered if it related to the illness that developed at the end of the Alaska trip. If so, he never made mention of it, though Harding's tiredness and increasingly high blood pressure could have had a connection, and cardiologists in later years surely would have remarked these two symptoms. All this, to be sure, had no connection with ptomaine poisoning, which was what Sawyer at first diagnosed as being Harding's trouble in San Francisco, or for that matter poisoning of any sort.

Boone worried about a cold the president caught in mid-January 1923 that worsened and verged, the physician thought, on influenza. According to the listing of daily events in the mansion by Ike Hoover, Harding remained in his room from Tuesday, January 16, through Sunday, January 21. Twice the assistant White House doctor stayed overnight, looking in on the president every two hours.[13] Even after Harding returned to his desk there were no engagements until the following Friday, January 26, when the cabinet met. Boone thought the cold could have been a form of influenza; it was obstinate, and its effects lingered, "causing considerable and persistent fatigue." "I might observe," he wrote years later in his autobiography, "that influenza toxemia definitely affects the musculature of the heart, which accounts for a lot of the fatigability that accompanies it and follows it."[14]

During this persistent illness Florence Harding worried, as she wrote relatives and friends. She told her sister-in-law, Dr. Harding's wife, perhaps in knowledge that her brother-in-law was a cardiologist, that "Of course you know Warren is under the weather. It took some effort to get the President of the U.S. on his back." She did have him where, she hoped, "we can accomplish something for his recovery." He still had a fever and weakness, and she believed that if he stayed in bed a few days more it would do him much good. Two days later she told her friend Evalyn McLean, wife of the *Washington Post*'s publisher, that "Mr. Harding is up today with his clothes on." He looked fine in the face but was weak and wobbly, for the "aftermath of grippe" was far more annoying than the disease. After a few more days she wrote another friend that his convalescence had been slow, but "he is really better and is back in the office today." The attack, of whatever it was, lingered into February, and Florence Harding wrote on February 5 that after a siege of three weeks "I take notice that he seeks a couch every day after lunch for a few minutes, which convinces me that he is not at par yet, although he does not say much about it." Sawyer and Boone remonstrated with him, telling him he needed to take things easy for a while, but he said he had had very little illness in his life and, as Boone put it, "really did not know how to give in to himself when he felt below par." Boone remembered that he was "most cooperative in carrying out prescribed therapy, except in the matter of getting adequate rest."[15]

By late February 1923 it was plain to the president's physicians that his stamina was flagging, that his will was strong, indeed almost indomitable, but something physically was holding him back. It was something long-term, for weeks had passed and he only became more tired. At this juncture they allowed him—they really had no governance over him, he was his own man, as everyone who saw him knew—to go on a trip to Florida, in the company of a group of friends, and if anything the trip must have given him even less rest than the duties of the White House, duties that as Forster said were increasing so rapidly.

The plan was to go by train to Ormond where the presidential party would board the *Pioneer*, the houseboat of Evalyn McLean and her husband, Edward, and journey from place to place, seeing the sights and playing golf when possible. The plan sounded fine, but carrying it out was not easy. For one thing, Boone heard that life on the *Pioneer* was unpleasant, that the boat, though sizable, almost as wide as the *Mayflower* and 130 feet long, allowed too much togetherness and did not permit sufficient privacy. For another, the *Pioneer* grounded several times on sandbars. And last, the president forced the pace; the vacationers' boat trip lost its purpose of leisure, turning into a busily moving boatload of people who passed along the Florida waterways from golf course to golf course, as quickly as possible. The women in the party were able to stay behind and rest, but the men were constantly on the move.

The trip aboard the *Pioneer* was something Boone did not observe but only heard about. He received the special task of watching over Attorney General Harry M. Daugherty, whose health was poor.

All this—the extraordinary duties of the presidency, the marked illness of the president in January–February 1923, the (in terms of rest that the president needed) fast-paced Florida boat trip—preceded the trip the president planned for midsummer, the journey by train and ship to Alaska and back.

Prior to the Alaskan trip there was a notable sign of the cardiovascular trouble that the president was suffering from, and one of the members of the White House Secret Service detail, Col. Edmund W. Starling, learned about it from the president's valet. One day Maj. Arthur Brooks took Starling aside and said, "Colonel, something is going to happen to our boss."

"What's the matter?" Starling asked.

"He can't sleep at night," was the response. "He can't lie down. He has to be propped up with pillows and he sits up that way all night. If he lies down he can't get his breath."

Starling thought this was what was known at the time as "high stomach." A cardiologist would have defined it as cardiac asthma, in which the heart of the sufferer is unable to pump blood out of the lungs, so the blood puddles there, making breathing difficult. It is possible to relieve the heaviness, the lack of breath, by putting the patient in a sitting position, allowing fluid to gravitate to the abdomen. An individual with this malady breathes more easily and can sleep only until he or she slides down in bed. Cardiac asthma is an ominous sign.[16]

Harding's golf game was affected, and the president said to Starling, "Colonel, why after playing eleven or twelve holes do I drag my feet and feel so tired?"

"You are working too hard," the colonel responded. "You need a vacation. Why don't you confine your game to nine holes until you rest up?"

"Hell!" the president said disgustedly. "If I can't play eighteen holes I won't play at all!"[17]

Harding similarly wrote George Christian that he had shortness of breath while playing golf.[18]

During these crucial months the president's physician did not worry. "The presidential family," Sawyer wrote Boone in April, "are in very good condition. . . . They both are doing splendidly. In fact, I have never known them to be better since coming to Washington than they seem to be now." Sawyer was visiting in Marion when he wrote Boone this intelligence.[19]

There is no possibility that Florence Harding saw the above communication from Sawyer to Boone, but it is clear that on the forthcoming trip she wanted more medical assistance than her Marion physician could provide. She told the president, who said to Boone, "That's it. You are going along."[20] If Boone was not worried sufficiently about Harding's health, he was indeed worried about the president's wife, because she had had another and very serious bout with her kidney disease in the autumn of the preceding year, and after his inclusion in the presidential party he quietly arranged that the naval transport USS *Henderson*, then at the Brooklyn navy yard, designated to make the presidential trip (the *Mayflower*'s draft was too shallow), take on board a coffin.

Florence Harding at this juncture was thinking of the president, and on the Sunday prior to departure, she and Colonel Starling were at the First Baptist

Church in Washington and had arrived late and were waiting for the opening prayer to end before being seated. She asked the colonel, "You are leaving soon to make arrangements for the trip?"

"On the twelfth," Starling said.

"I want you to promise me something," she said. "Wherever we are to stop I want the doctors, General Sawyer and Captain [she meant Lieutenant Commander] Boone, as close to the president's room as possible. . . ."

She looked at him steadily. "You understand?" she asked. "Are you sure you understand? It is not for myself that I want this done but for Warren."

"I understand," he said.[21]

2

Given what preceded the Alaska trip, the signs of impending physical trouble, it was clear that the president's death in San Francisco was no sudden development, no crisis for which some speculative cause was possible. There had been every evidence of a rapidly developing crisis in the president's physical condition. The fateful trip was only a logical end to what preceded.

The purpose of the trip was very clear in the president's mind, for it was to set out what he proposed the government should do for the people of the United States. Mrs. Harding earlier had written a friend that the people of the West did not know they had a president, and she wanted her husband to show himself to them, which doubtless was some part of the presidential plan although the trip was also intended to accomplish far more than that. The Harding biographer Robert K. Murray, a first-rate scholar, has pointed out that the speeches along the way were excellent statements of purpose and if taken together set out an entire program on which not merely the American people could have instructed their congressmen to secure legislation but a program on which Harding could have stirred his countrymen and run for reelection the next year as well.[22] Harding's Marion friend Malcolm Jennings received advice from a correspondent that it would not be wise for the president to speak, as press dispatches said he would, about foreign relations and organization of the nation's railways. "These issues," wrote William R. Clarke, a westerner, "are as popular here as mad dogs. He ought to talk American manhood, less graft in the next war, better conditions for the agricultural producers, and give some hope and counsel, etc. Then he would ring twelve." Jennings passed the letter to Harding, who in reply was outspokenly frank.

> I fear Mr. Clarke is greatly lacking in confidence and has a bargain sale appraisal for the President. However, that does not greatly disturb me. It might be pleasing to Mr. Clarke to have me address him with an Old

Glory talk and appropriate related remarks, but if his vision were as broad as is necessary in planning the Presidential speaking tour he will have to get off the one subject and say some things relating to the problems of government which we are facing day by day.[23]

The president's plan was admirable, much to his credit, but he was hardly up to it physically, as became evident. Boone in his papers described in detail what happened once the presidential party left Washington at 2:00 P.M. on June 20, 1923, a very hot day—ninety in the shade it was reported—over the Baltimore and Ohio Railroad, arriving in St. Louis the next day, thence to Kansas City and points west to Tacoma where the *Henderson* waited to take the president to Alaska. Harding left tired and must have become more so as he encountered thousands of people who lined the tracks to wave or, if there were short stops, see him go out on the back of the presidential car, the Superb, and say a few words. At longer stopovers city officials and reception committees greeted the party, automobiles conveyed them through the principal streets, a reception was held in the lobby of a hotel, after which he would dine, motor to where he was to deliver an address, then drive back to the train. Nor did the president get any rest between stops, for governors, senators, and congressmen joined the party to accompany him through their electoral districts.

There were two special expeditions. To keep Sen. Reed Smoot of Utah in good humor the president and his party rode horseback through clouds of dust to obtain a glimpse of what was to be Zion National Park. Afterward the president was exhausted. He was forced then to endure Yellowstone Park. At the park there was a platform, reached by steps, and Dr. Sawyer told the superintendent not to ask the president to go up the steps. Harding, he said, had not felt too well the night before.[24]

The plan was to cross the country by rail and after the Alaska trip return by ship from California via the Panama Canal. Harding knew the reason for that, as he told Jennings: "This will avoid the excess of speech-making incident to two rail trips across the continent."[25] But even one rail trip was too much, and Boone remembered that when the party went to the hotel in Tacoma he saw Harding talking with his advance man, Walter F. Brown, postmaster general in the Hoover administration, and with "great emphasis" telling Brown he could not stand such a heavy schedule, adding that if necessary Brown should make a whole new schedule. "Unless it is radically modified and changed in many respects following my Alaskan visit," the president said, "it will kill me. I just cannot keep up such a pace without dire consequences to me." Boone thought Harding said this in part so Boone could hear him—the president made no effort to keep the conversation private.[26]

The trip to Alaska aboard the *Henderson,* which involved a presidential party of sixty-seven people, fortunately turned out to be relaxing, perhaps because unlike the transcontinental journey the Alaskan requirements were almost entirely celebratory and there were not many people with whom to celebrate. The entire population of Alaska was sixty thousand, half of whom were Indians. There were ten towns in Alaska, the largest being the territorial capital, Juneau, population two thousand. Harding and the group could stroll about, and the presidential speeches could be casual utterances, with concern only that they made general sense to the accompanying newspapermen who themselves were more interested in the trip's varied sights.

The voyage was delightful, with what was called "Harding weather." On the second day at sea not a cloud was visible, and the *Henderson* seemed to float along at twelve knots, gliding over a calm, narrow channel with towering cliffs that were snow capped or covered with green dwarf pines. Here and there the channel widened at mouths of rivers. Bays and coves lined the water's edge, with little picturesque islands that forced the ship to change course and detour to port or starboard.

The first stop was at the village of Metlakatla, and the proceedings there set the pace. The president was met by Indians, including Edward Marsdon, who had studied at Marietta College in Marietta, Ohio, before taking a theological course at a university in Cincinnati. So wrote Ernest Chapman, a Baltimore and Ohio Railroad police captain, who accompanied the Harding party on the entire Alaska trip. Marsdon was a musician, having worked his way through college tuning pianos. He also had a good voice, and he and his charges sang and played, among other selections singing parts of *Hallelujah* and other oratorios, according to Captain Chapman. Marsdon had adopted a daughter named Marietta, whom he intended to send to Marietta College.[27]

The rest of the trip went similarly. Ketchikan was a primitive place, with fifty automobiles and three miles of roads, the principal mode of transportation throughout southeastern Alaska being motorboats. The population of whites at Ketchikan was more in evidence than the natives and had erected welcoming arches, and the native band from Metlakatla came over to join in the celebration. At Wrangel (population one thousand, mostly natives, who did not seem as far advanced in civilization as those at Metlakatla) the party saw the totem poles, some of them 150 feet high, others as small as one inch. Juneau's main attraction was the glacier, sixteen miles out of town. The governor's house was a large white building on an eminence above the harbor and resembled the White House, with large white columns. At Anchorage the party saw Mount McKinley, even after eleven at night, 150 miles away. From Seward to Fairbanks, the group traveled aboard a special train. A Dodge speedster on steel wheels followed the train. It fascinated Mrs. Harding who rode in it most of the afternoon.

All along the way, by ship or rail, members of the presidential party enjoyed themselves. At a little store along the railroad from Seward to Fairbanks, Secretary of the Interior Hubert Work purchased a big plug of chewing tobacco, and the president unwrapped his parcel, eyes lighted with amazement, and said, "I haven't seen Star tobacco for a great, great many years." Harding and Work each cut themselves big pieces and began chewing. Aboard ship things were equally relaxed. Seventy-five moving picture films had been taken along and were shown in the dining room. The president viewed them through a window as he stood on deck smoking his pipe. The U.S. Navy Band was aboard and played during luncheon and dinner hours, and people got up and danced. Mrs. Hoover asked Boone to teach her to dance, which he did. Evenings passengers could hear the Hardings, Sawyers ("Mandy and the doctor," as they were known to the Hardings), and other Harding intimates singing old tunes such as "Maggie" and "Genevieve."[28]

Mrs. Harding momentarily worried Boone when she took ill in Fairbanks where medical facilities were extremely limited. He remembered the casket he had quietly stowed in the *Henderson.* Fortunately the symptoms—they were of the old malady, nephritis—subsided after she went by train back to Seward and soon was safely aboard.

Nothing really untoward happened, and everything went well after the president finished the transcontinental rail trip and the *Henderson* left Tacoma, until on the way down from Alaska the ship stopped at Vancouver. There Harding took part in a parade, held a reception at a local hotel, and resumed serious speeches. The tiredness returned, becoming evident when the president was at the Shaughnessy Heights Golf Club. An observer watching the first presidential visit to Canada, marked by the day-long visit, might have noticed that he did not finish his golf game but walked carefully from the sixth to the seventeenth hole. Boone was in the second foursome when the president played. Harding at one point was looking for a ball. Boone strolled over and cheerily called to him, "How are things going, Mr. President?" He said, "Not at all well, Boone. I just can't get on my game today. I don't feel too well." Boone talked to him as he was dressing to leave the club and he still did not feel well, did not know what it was, thought he had some gastrointestinal upset. Boone suggested he go to the hotel and rest. Harding demurred, as there was a speech that evening.[29]

The Vancouver visit was unsettling, and Boone told Sawyer what Harding had said. That evening Brooks, the valet, whom Boone considered a very wise man, told him he and Sawyer should hold the president down, or "He will break. He is hurrying too much." All that night Harding was ill, and he looked drawn the next morning.

The ceremonies before and during the Seattle visit nearly prostrated the president. The ship passed through dense fog, arriving in early afternoon, several hours late, just in time to review the massed ships, more than fifty, of the Pacific Fleet and endure a series of twenty-one-gun salutes as the ships passed by. As the *Henderson* approached the city, Boone overheard Mrs. Harding say to her husband, "Oh, Warren, please cancel our going ashore. You are not physically up to it since you were sick last night." He answered, "Of course, I would not disappoint that great outpouring of humanity, many of whom have traveled far and wide to come and see their president. I would not disappoint them for anything, Florence. Of course, we are going to go ashore."[30]

After arrival at the dock and welcoming ceremonies had come the parade, during which the president waved to tens of thousands of people, raising his hand high, doffing his hat. Sawyer and Boone rode in cars behind the presidential car and observed the constant movement of the president's right arm. Each time Boone sought out the president he would ask how he was. The answer: "I am tired. Of course, I am thrilled with this reception and I wouldn't want to have missed a moment of it!" There were several speeches, including a long oration, written in large part by Secretary of Commerce Hoover, given in the stadium of the University of Washington before forty thousand people, with the president standing in the hot sun. Auditors noticed that he delivered the address listlessly. The topic was Alaska, and he confused the name, reading it as Nebraska. At one point he dropped the sheets of the address, which sprawled across the platform, but Hoover who was nearby managed to retrieve and sort them.

The day at Seattle would have exhausted a well man, but for Harding it was an ordeal, for after thinking that his program in the city had been abbreviated because of his late arrival he discovered it only had been telescoped, meaning that a luncheon planned by the local press club was in fact held even though the time was that for a dinner. After the meal, which the president was observed as hardly touching, he spoke with graceful references to his audience for perhaps twenty minutes and sank into his chair for the meeting's final moments. At the train, prior to leaving (the rest of the trip into California was to be made by train), he found a crowd of well-wishers and suitably bade them farewell and clambered back into his private car from the observation platform. Boone was standing immediately behind him as he made the talk from the car, and held the screen door open for him when he came in. He remembered the scene indelibly forty years later when he recalled it for his autobiography. "He took his straw hat. He threw it across the car. He said, 'Doctor, I'll tell the world that one Warren Harding has had a most strenuous and fatiguing day and he is an exhausted man.'" With that he went to his compartment where Brooks was waiting to put him to bed.[31]

It was after Seattle that the president's advisers decided he had had enough and canceled a stopover in Portland, sending the train straight down to San Francisco. It was necessary to change engines at Grants Pass in Oregon, and it was there that Sawyer and Work—the secretary of the interior in private life had been a doctor—spoke of ptomaine poisoning. En route from Vancouver, Sawyer had thought Harding had ptomaine poisoning, this from eating crabs taken aboard ship at Sitka as a gift from the citizens. Harding himself had mentioned this possibility to the mayor of Vancouver. According to Sawyer, the attack had no serious aspects. All the president needed was a short rest to bring him back to normal. When Sawyer made this announcement he was seconded by Work. The latter declared he was not sure the problem had been crabmeat but rather something, he was uncertain what, that had been in a can. "I will not say," he remarked, what the item of food was, "for otherwise I might depress the price of the canned product." He said that all the consumers of this unnamed food in the presidential party had recovered, and the president had almost recovered.[32]

At Grants Pass the president's private secretary, George B. Christian Jr., son of the president's Marion neighbor, explained the decision to go to San Francisco as the need of a few days of rest to refresh the president. Members of the party said no consideration had been given to abandoning the schedule thereafter, which called for the voyage on the *Henderson* southward from San Diego, via the canal, to the East Coast. Christian said that nothing in the president's condition was alarming.

Everything thereafter was downhill. The first night on the train Sawyer and Mrs. Harding had stayed up with the president, who was violently ill. Sawyer somewhat casually told Boone about the problem the next day. On the *Henderson* there had been an altercation between Boone and Sawyer when at Harding's request Boone had lanced the president's infected finger. Boone thought the president had asked him rather than his personal physician because Sawyer's eyesight was poor. Sawyer had taken offense, and the younger man presumed he had not asked for help with Harding the first night on the train from Seattle because of this incident. But when Boone found out how ill Harding really was, and spoke with Secretaries Work and Hoover about it, the three went to see Florence Harding and arranged for Boone to take her place with the president that next night, and Sawyer's too, for both needed the sleep.

The second night out of Seattle, Boone made the discovery that came too late to save Harding's life. The discovery had nothing to do with ptomaine poisoning. Like the scene inside the president's private car after Harding walked in after saying good-bye to the crowd in the Seattle station, that second night out, watching the president, was unforgettable. As he sat there, just outside the stateroom, hour after hour, Harding was restless and uncomfortable. His breathing was heavy. The doctor heard the continuous pounding of the train wheels on the tracks, jumping one joint after the other. In the middle of the night the train stopped, perhaps for water, at what Boone thought was Redding, California, and there was silence, and Harding was awake. Boone thought it was a good time to take his blood pressure. He did not like what he found, for it was lower than he had ever taken it. He knew about Harding's high pressure and had heard the president's explanation of how it was in the family and did not matter and that when Harding went out campaigning it went down. This time it was too low—something had happened. He opened the president's pajamas, had him lie on his back, and percussed his chest. He found the left border of the heart well to the left of normal, almost midway between the usual left border and the right axillary line of his left chest. The heart sounds were muffled with irregularity as he heard them and noted them through his pulse. The president had a dilated heart.[33]

Just as Boone made the discovery of dilatation the train began to move, picking up speed quickly and making considerable noise, and he could no longer continue his examination, but when morning came he informed Sawyer and then Work. Hoover was brought in, and Christian, and members of Harding's staff who worked with the railroad, and the train was directed to the San Francisco yards rather than the station, together with a request for an ambulance to be brought up to the observation platform.

In preparation for arrival in the yards, Boone and Sawyer told the president not to get dressed. He scowled and said nothing, but unbeknownst to them called Brooks and dressed himself, and appeared fully clothed, with his hat, ready to walk off the train. "Don't think for a minute," he told the doctors, "that I am going to receive the governor of the sovereign state of California and the mayor of our host city, San Francisco, in pajamas! That I shall not do. I will not be carried off this train!"[34]

A photographer caught the president walking down the steps of the observation car, clad in morning dress and hat. Alighting, he shook hands with the mayor and one or two other officials and walked a short distance to a limousine, stepping into the back seat with Mrs. Harding. Upon arrival at the Palace Hotel on Market Street the president got out of the limousine and walked up the steps. A photographer took what was to prove Harding's last picture as he was going up the steps.

The president passed through the lobby and took an elevator to the ninth floor. Beyond the view of onlookers he walked to the presidential suite and entered it. An assistant at once closed the door.

3 ———

Outwardly nothing seemed amiss. But that was not what insiders saw. When the president arrived on the ninth floor it turned out that the presidential suite was far from the elevator, down one long corridor, then down another. Boone, following the president, was very concerned. After Harding entered the suite and walked into the bedroom he threw his arms up in the air and fell across the bed with all his clothes on. His hat fell off and rolled on the floor on the other side of the bed. The doctors, shaken, saw he was so exhausted they made no attempt to undress him and let him lie there for some time before Brooks removed his clothes and put on his pajamas.

General Sawyer received a large group of newspapermen in a room at the hotel that afternoon and explained that there was nothing serious about the president's condition. He admitted that Harding was suffering a "violent case of ptomaine poisoning." Sawyer that afternoon was not altogether clear. He explained that crabs in Alaska frequently were tinctured by heavy copper deposits. This phase of copper poisoning, he said, usually did not become apparent until a week or ten days after eating the crabs. But to the correspondent of the *New York Times* he offered another interpretation of what ailed the president, which he said was exhaustion. It was the matter of casting off the poison from the crabmeat that caused the tiredness. "The first stage comes when one is tired out." The effects of tiredness might pass with a simple rest—hence the rest being taken at that moment by the president. "The second stage is extreme fatigue." This was a difficult stage, for patient and physician had to combat the exhaustion. "In the third stage, which is prostration, we must await developments before we can know if the body is casting off the poison." This last stage seemed to display an element of uncertainty, as if the presidential physician was uncertain how to assist his patient in the casting off.[35]

From that juncture, Sunday afternoon, until the fatal Thursday evening, stories about the president's condition gradually changed, from the diagnosis of food poisoning to pneumonia, with an underlying possibility of a stroke. The president's physicians at first numbered three: Sawyer, Boone, and Work. The secretary of the interior, one should add, had been a neurologist and psychiatrist and had held the presidency of the American Medical Association. On Monday two consultants joined them. Dr. Wilbur, an internist, in 1923 was not merely president of his university but also president of the American Medical Association. Wilbur chose the other consultant, Dr. Charles M. Cooper, a distinguished San Francisco cardiologist.[36]

On Monday, Sawyer befuddled the correspondents as he had the previous day yet prepared them for something more serious. He spoke of the president's toxic condition, which created a liability for complications affecting almost any organ in the body. He said Harding's heart had been working at fifty beats above normal. He did not give the number, the systolic pressure, and if he was calculating normal as the president's normal, which a bulletin on the following Thursday related was a systolic pressure of 180, he may have been saying the systolic was 230, which would or should have been alarming, indeed desperate in that day long before the time of blood pressure pills and other medication, not to mention heart pumps and surgery. At that point he carefully repeated himself: "The liabilities are such as would come from an increase in the toxic condition of the President's system, and complications caused by the inability of some of the organs to function." He spoke of something becoming serious because it was becoming dangerous, not that it was dangerous. An X ray showed congestion, the complication he most feared. The president's heart was overstrained, presumably from fighting the toxic effects of the congestion.[37]

The Monday bulletin at 10:30 A.M. put the case more tersely: "While his condition is acute, he has temporarily overstrained his cardiovascular system by carrying on his speaking engagements while ill." This must have meant the speeches in Seattle. What happened during them, perhaps on the occasion when the president dropped the pages of his address during his speech in the stadium, the bulletin chose not to say.[38]

Such were the first two days at the Palace Hotel in San Francisco, in which the pronouncements of Sawyer dominated newspapers, yet if a reader combined the words of Sawyer with the words of the Monday morning bulletin he or she could see a shift from homeopathic formulas and the jollities of the country doctor to something more modern, with stress not on toxic effects and behind them the consumption of crabmeat but on the cardiovascular system. The full team of physicians was changing the diagnosis from what one might describe as the nineteenth century to the twentieth.

As if in confirmation of the physicians' new concern, on Monday pneumonia set in. The physicians administered digitalis and caffeine. Dr. Wilbur who was writing the bulletins told Hoover, who asked, that Harding's chances were "Not one in ten." Monday night marked the president's worst period since arrival in San Francisco. Pneumonia in the 1920s was deadly serious, as it carried off patients in ways incomprehensible to a later generation accustomed to drugs not then available. The reporters that swarmed about the Palace got their cue, and next day's newspapers spoke of a black night and related that for the first time the president's doctors had used the medical word so feared at the time, "grave."[39]

Tuesday morning the inveterate willingness of physicians treating important patients reasserted itself, willingness to put the best face on medical conditions, and the bulletin of 9:00 A.M., July 31, said, "There has been no extension of the pneumonic areas, and the heart action is definitely improved." The bulletin at 4:00 P.M. related the same points, "The President has maintained the ground gained since last night." And what the physicians did not say to cheer readers throughout the nation, the reporters or their copy editors arranged, for a caption in the *New York Times* said, "Everything Looks Promising for the Patient's Full Recovery From Illness." Tuesday evening Sawyer took reassurance from an hour of sleep that Harding managed: "The President has just had a sleep of more than an hour—the most refreshing and satisfactory sleep since his illness began."[40]

Wednesday was up and down, no basic change. The first bulletin related the president fairly comfortable after "a few hours" of sleep, with less labored breathing, little cough, exhaustion but maintaining buoyancy, his normal buoyancy. The 4:30 P.M. bulletin found the president resting "after a somewhat restless day." He had sought to consume two boiled eggs and suffered indigestion; two were too many, for he had been eating only a single egg. For a while his fever came down to normal. As Wilbur related two months later, in an article in the *Saturday Evening Post,* Harding that day jested with his physicians. When his wife asked if his feet were warm, and one of the doctors asked the president, he responded, "This is no time to get cold feet."[41]

It was on Wednesday that Harding felt so much better, according to newspaper reports, that he suggested he leave San Francisco for Washington the following Sunday, that is, a week after he had been put to bed at the Palace Hotel. Apparently the reports were accompanied by talk that Harding had been meeting his advisers and discussing administration matters. "But this man has been a sick man," said one of the doctors. "He is not capable of transacting any business." As Dr. Sawyer explained that day, "We can never tell what sideshows may develop. By that I mean that unexpected complications may turn up, such as indigestion or nervousness, which are always probable in such a case as this." Sawyer remained confident, again speaking privately to the New York Times correspondent: "I think I may say that he is out of danger, barring complications."[42]

On Wednesday, August 1, Wilbur said privately that the chances had turned around and were now estimated to be nine in ten. But that afternoon when the doctors told the president his lungs had cleared remarkably well he said, for he knew his real trouble, "I am not so much worried about them, but what about this dilatation of my heart?"[43]

An interesting aspect of Harding's confinement, as compared with later presidential illnesses in which the question if not of succession then of temporary replacement of the chief executive by the vice president arose immediately, is that in the somnolent 1920s the issue never even arose. Not merely was Harding far away from Washington, almost as far as he could have been, short of journeying to Alaska or Hawaii, but Vice President Coolidge had ensconced himself in rural Vermont, in Plymouth Notch, across the road from his birthplace, in the house of his father, Col. John Coolidge. The homestead was not in the village of Plymouth, known to local people as Plymouth Union, but up a narrow road that ran through a gorge for a mile, to a plateau on which were three houses, a general store, a cheese factory, and a church. The Notch had no telephone. Coolidge seems never to have thought he should return to Washington and spent his days in farm tasks, not seriously, for he was photographed in a business suit, cutting away at a rotten place in a tree, piling hay into a wagon. He was a canny politician, and he may have been watching the scene in San Francisco with if not anticipation then deepest personal interest, but if he did so there was not the slightest outward sign. Presumably newspapers were brought up to the Notch each day, yet he made no serious comments. On Wednesday, the day before he became president, he was quoted as saying, "I have never had any doubt of his ultimate recovery." A reporter told him of a proposal to establish an "assistant to the president," and Coolidge said that would not work, there was only one president.[44]

Everything came down to the fatal day and evening, Thursday, August 2, 1923. The first bulletin at 9:30 in the morning said the president had had several hours of restful sleep and expressed himself as feeling "easier," which must have meant better. And then a reassurance that was to bring criticism upon the physicians: "While recovery will inevitably take some little time, we are more confident than heretofore as to the outcome of his illness." At 4:30, close to the end, the doctors related that "The President has had the most satisfactory day since his illness began." Harding did feel better but told his sister Mrs. Remsberg that he was tired out: "It isn't anything I have eaten. I thought I could stand anything but I find I can't. I am worn out, can't stand the heavy responsibilities and physical work too." Two hours before his death he talked on the telephone with Jennings and was cheerful and said he felt "out of the woods" but repeated, "I am so tired, so tired."[45]

There was a strange preliminary, during which Boone was present. Mrs. Harding was reading to her husband an article about Henry Ford in the *Dearborn Independent*.[46] The president had been very quiet, thoroughly relaxed, but suddenly stiffened, a frightened expression came on his face, and he turned pale. He broke out in a profuse perspiration. Sawyer, sitting by the bed, took his pulse without moving. One of the nurses, Ruth Powderly, got up from her chair, as did Boone, and both moved over to the president. The nurse felt his pajamas, which were wringing wet. Harding said, "I don't know what happened to me, a very strange, sinking feeling that I have never experienced before." He started to become restive, and Boone told him to keep very, very quiet. "But I'm so damn wet!" Harding said. The nurse took a Turkish towel, removed his pajamas, dried him off, and put on another pair. After a little while he said, "Florence, please go on with your reading. I don't know what happened to me. It was a very strange experience. Came on unbeknownst to me, now I feel perfectly comfortable, as though I had never had such an experience. Absolutely, I feel perfectly comfortable. Please go ahead with your reading, Florence." His color came back, his pulse returned to what it had been. All seemed normal.

After this odd behavior by the patient, Boone thought he might be able to leave the sickroom and go out on the street, take a short walk, get some air. He asked Sawyer if it would be all right. Night and day he had been in the president's room and did not take a bath or change clothes until Thursday afternoon. Not a soul "spent as many moments, hours, and days with him as I did at San Francisco." He thought the president was better. He knew that someone, a physician or one of the two nurses, would be in the room all the time. Nurse Powderly said she was going to be there, and Harding said, "I want Florence to go on with reading."

Boone went out, observed Gen. John J. Pershing at the cigar stand looking over the newspapers, went out on the street, and came back.

Then came the crisis. Actually it had happened while Boone was out on the street. As he went up the elevator he thought he heard someone calling his name several times. As he got out, a newspaperman appeared from nowhere into the hallway, and someone said excitedly, "There is Doctor Boone, there's Doctor Boone!" With that he ran down the hall.

As he entered the room Mrs. Harding "grabbed me hysterically, shook me by the shoulders, looked me in the eye with a very startled expression, and said: 'Doctor Boone, you can save him, you can save him! You can bring him back! Hurry, hurry, hurry!' "

Boone took a look at Harding and instinctively knew he was dead. To make Mrs. Harding feel better he raised the lids of the president's eyes, touched both corneas, then replaced the eyelids to the closed position. He stood erect and took Mrs. Harding in his arms. She looked stunned as he said, shaking his head, "No one can save him, no one can restore him to life. He is gone!"

He asked Sawyer and the nurse what had happened. Sawyer told him that just a few minutes after Boone had left, the president had a terrible seizure, shook the bed violently, his body quivered, the color left his face, all in the twinkling of an eye. The seizure departed just as fast as it came, and he was dead.[47]

4 ———

Secretary Hoover was the first person to arrive at the presidential suite, and when he came out he appeared to be stunned by grief, tears running down his cheeks, unable to speak.

A minute or two after the president's death an assistant manager rushed into the hotel's Rose Bowl Room where a dinner dance was in progress. He raised a hand and stopped the orchestra and explained why. The dancers gathered in little groups, then took their wraps and left.

The newspapermen had an engagement to meet General Sawyer at 8:00 P.M., when he was to tell them how the president was progressing. Instead one of the White House messengers said there would be a bulletin, and in a few minutes they received it, on thin white paper. It gave the astounding information that the president was dead.

In reporting Harding's death the Associated Press obtained a "scoop" on its competitor news services through the enterprise of two of its reporters, one of whom was the later well-known press secretary of President Roosevelt, Stephen T. Early. Early and E. Ross Bartley, his fellow AP reporter, had engaged a corner room on the eighth floor of the hotel, directly below the presidential floor, and the two took turns going up the nearby fire escape and surveying the scene. Early was a decisive, imaginative reporter, firm jawed, not the sort to leave any strings untied. Bartley was similarly endowed, a quick-witted sort. On the evening of August 2, Early had just replaced Bartley and looking down the upstairs corridor saw Mrs. Harding come out into the hall. As he remembered many years later,

I ran down the stairway to my room. Mr. Paul Cowles was the Chief of the San Francisco A.P. bureau at that time. He had had the foresight to have a telegrapher stationed in the room where Bartley and I lived. The telegrapher had cut into a trunk A.P. transcontinental line. I dictated a series of bulletins to him, slugging them E.O.S. In the A.P. this meant "extra ordinary service." E.O.S. copy could be used by A.P. papers at any time regardless of whether they were afternoon or morning members. These bulletins told of Mrs. Harding's sudden appearance, her cry for the doctors, the confusion that prevailed where all had been calm and peaceful up to that time.

He ran back up the stairway, and all he needed was confirmation, which he soon received. The president's secretary, Jud Welliver, was looking for a stenographer, found one, went into a room, and dictated the official announcement of the president's death, this without closing the door. For Early it was down the fire escape again and into the room and another bulletin that had a half-hour lead on all his competitors.[48]

In New York the first news of Harding's death was a bulletin from the *New York Times,* displayed on the north side of the Times Building. A small knot of people stopped to read it, and in a few minutes their number was in the hundreds. Cabarets and hotel dining rooms emptied out. At the Hotel McAlpin the music and dancing stopped with a brief announcement. A man in evening dress was coming out of the Montmartre, at Fiftieth Street near Broadway, and the doorman accosted him, holding a paper before his eyes. "Don't show it to me," was the response. "It can't be true."[49]

Papers the next day, August 3, told the story in banners: "PRESIDENT HARDING DIES SUDDENLY; STROKE OF APOPLEXY AT 7:30 P.M.; CALVIN COOLIDGE IS PRESIDENT." The *New York Times,* like many other newspapers, carried long black lines separating all its stories, even those not dealing with the president's death. The front page story was heartbreaking: "The Chief Executive of the nation, and by virtue of his office and personality, one of the world's leading figures, passed away at the time when his physicians, his family, and his people thought that medical skill, hope and prayer had won the battle against disease."[50] The disease was conquered, the fire was out, but after seven days of silent suffering a stroke of apoplexy without an instant's warning, before physicians could be called, members of the official party summoned, and remedial measures taken.

Papers carried eulogies from at home and abroad. Secretary of State Charles Evans Hughes, solemn, dignified, the first member of the cabinet, said, "No words can express the grief into which we are plunged by this calamity. The nation has suffered an irreparable loss. A quiet, brave, strong leader has fallen. . . ." Not only was the president an able and faithful public servant, Hughes said, but also one of nature's noblemen; true-hearted, generous, he left a rare example of gentleness in high office, conscientious and unselfish devotion to public duty. The *Times*'s editorial stressed the late president's private attractiveness, his simplicity. It closed on the need for confidence, that the foundations of the Republic had been laid too deep and broad to be loosened even by such a shock as Harding's death.[51]

On this day after the president's death the physicians in San Francisco measured for their countrymen what had happened. They felt they had done their best, if with an intensely saddening result. The preceding spring, they pointed out, the president had been confined to bed with influenza, followed by a few night attacks of labored breathing. He had suffered abdominal pain and indigestion, some pain from a feeling of oppression in his chest. "For some years his systolic blood pressure had ranged about 180, and there was evidence of some arteriosclerosis, enlargement of the heart and defective action of the kidneys . . . We all believe," it concluded, "he died from apoplexy or the rupture of a blood vessel in the axis of the brain near the respiratory center." A bulletin signed only by the consultants, Wilbur and the cardiologist Cooper, explained that "the heart was enlarged, and probably the blood vessels which carry its nutriment thickened."[52]

After the death of the principal occupant of the Palace Hotel, the president's assistants called in the undertakers, members of the firm of N. Gray and Company, who labored into the night, successfully they believed; one of them afterward published an account of their work in a professional journal.[53] On the morning of August 3 the body, enclosed in a rosewood-lined metal coffin, was taken from the bedroom to a drawing room of the presidential suite, and there in the late afternoon was held what proved to be the first of three funeral services. During the trip back to Washington, Mrs. Harding recalled the reason for the initial service. "I could not take him away without prayer," she said. "I believe in prayer." Officiating was the minister of San Francisco's First Baptist Church, who began with the words, "God is our refuge and strength." When he ended, Mrs. Harding said in a voice easily heard, which showed signs of emotion, "Amen." The room in which the service was held was streaming with late afternoon light, and the flowers gathered in various places did not seem funereal. The casket, not a heavy piece, was not ostentatious. The face of the president was calm. During the day Mrs. Harding had asked friends to look at the face of the president and called attention to the firm mouth. She said there was no hesitation there.[54]

Then began the long trip back to Washington and thence to Marion, "the saddest transcontinental trip in the history of the nation," with ceremony virtually all the way.[55]

As the coffin reached the entrance of the hotel there was a pause, and the U.S. Navy Band played the national anthem. The group moved forward toward the hearse, and the band began Chopin's "Funeral March." Immediately in front of the hearse was a sailor bearing the presidential flag, hung on its staff at half-mast, with a streamer of crepe from the top. Heading the cortege behind the hearse was a troop of the Eleventh Cavalry astride shining and well-groomed bays, carrying drawn sabers. Then came soldiers on foot, and marines brilliant in blue, with red stripes down their trousers. Then came the Thirtieth Infantry, whose officers wore bands of crepe on their arms. Several hundred bluejackets represented the navy. Following the servicemen were members of the cabinet, high officers of the army and navy including General Pershing, and leading city officials. With exception of the cavalry troop at the onset of the procession, everyone walked the three-quarters of a mile to the Southern Pacific Railroad Station except Attorney General Daugherty who had arrived in San Francisco to greet the president, only to learn of his death; he rode in an automobile. Vast crowds lined the streets between the Palace Hotel and the station, bowing to the dirge of the funeral band. The dirge and the clatter of cavalry on the pavement were the only sounds; all else was silent.

The scene at the station was equally funereal, with the platform decorated with shrubbery and a floral arch constructed around a window of the president's car, the Superb, from which the frame had been removed to allow passing the casket into the interior of the car, which itself had been decorated. Mrs. Harding remained at the hotel until the coffin was inside the train and then went to the station in an automobile with drawn curtains. Accompanied by Secretary Christian she walked through the station, lined on each side with thousands of people. The train started to move, and at that instant the arch of greens and flowers over the window through which the casket had passed was removed.

The train left the city at 7:15 P.M. on its long processional. Someone had thought to place the casket on a high catafalque so that it could be seen through the windows, and this was the memory, the view, that millions of Americans saw in their minds' eyes for the rest of their lives. The casket lay shrouded in a soft light, and at each corner stood a serviceman, two soldiers, a sailor, and a marine, each leaning on his rifle. At the outset members of the detail of sixteen men had decided to stand constantly, but Mrs. Harding instructed them to sit down while the train was between towns, and on approach to each town or crowd of people the guards immediately stood at attention.

Everywhere along the way the scene was practically the same, with people standing silently, men with bared heads. Former servicemen wore their uniforms and stood saluting, and if carrying flags duly lowered them. Civil War veterans thronged the stations, many of whom had seen the funeral train of Lincoln. Young men back from the world war were there, sometimes assisting the older veterans. At Stockton fifteen thousand people were at the station, and the city's bells had begun tolling a half-hour before arrival of the train, which was ten o'clock at night. Theaters, restaurants, and stores were closed. A silence hovered over the waiting crowd.

In desert areas there were memorable scenes, such as a cowboy faraway upon a hill, dismounted and doffing his hat. In farming areas men in the fields removed their caps. At places where the railway crossed highways, motorcars parked through the night so occupants could catch a glimpse of the coffin as the train rushed by.

As the train passed through Nevada, it received a wreath with the legend,

> His life was gentle and the elements
> Were so combined in him
> That nature might stand up and say
> To all the world, "This was a man."

At Cheyenne where thousands assembled, dust clouds blew in their faces, storm clouds broke while the train stood at the station, and wind drove the rain down upon them, but the men, women, and children stood their ground. When the train passed through Omaha at three in the morning the crowd totaled forty thousand. As it approached the city, the bluffs of the Missouri River were black with people; culverts similarly were jam-packed. At the station the throng was enormous.

Perhaps it was Chicago that gave the dead president the most memorable welcome. There the train was forced to proceed at a snail's pace, no faster than a man could walk, for fear of running over the people who filled the right-of-way. It was escorted above by five airplanes from nearby Maywood Field, and the planes had long mourning streamers flying in their wakes. The train crossed the city limits at 6:30 P.M., two hours behind schedule. As it neared the Kedzie Avenue station where city committees were waiting, a detective with flag in hand walked ahead of the locomotive to warn the crowds back, as they had surged onto the tracks despite efforts by two hundred uniformed police, railroad guards, and Secret Service men. This for a stop of only three minutes. As it passed through the city tugboat sirens took up the dirge, and there were thunderous reports of twenty-one-gun salutes. Not until South Chicago could the engineer open his throttle, and then only for a brief time, for ahead lay Hammond, Gary, and other stops. Estimates of the people who saw the train pass through Chicago varied, from three hundred thousand to a million and a half. In truth the people were impossible to count, but the latter figure seems likely.

Through this ordeal the president's widow held her head high, for after her husband's death she had said, "I am not going to break down." It was of course a saddening return trip from the West, as her husband had been so good-humored and so enjoyed the trip out to the coast. "It wasn't until our western trip," Mrs. Harding said in Chicago, "that I fully appreciated the nation's respect. Really, you know, when we were in Alaska I was electrified time and again by the murmur that so often rose as my husband stepped to the observation platform to face a waiting crowd. 'There he is!' the crowd would say. 'There he is!' " Mrs. Harding paused, then turned toward the room of the car where the president's body lay. "And now," she said, pointing to the flag-covered coffin, "there he is." Some people had likened the passage of Harding's body back to Washington to the trip through the nation's capital of the body of the unknown soldier, not quite two years before, the difference being that the soldier's widow, if there had been any, was unknown, whereas everyone could feel the anguish of the president's widow.

After the trip across Indiana the train turned down through Ohio, and one reporter claimed the crowds were "so close together as to virtually suggest an aisle of mourning extending across the entire commonwealth." All night people slept at stations or rested there, or in autos, or waited on lawns, to see the train pass. Many of them placed coins on the tracks and picked them up as souvenirs, flattened by the wheels that carried the body of their fallen leader. At some places the crowds sang softly the Baptist hymns of their dead president, as the cars slowly proceeded. Along the way, at every stop, floral offerings were taken aboard the train, and when it finally arrived at Washington there was a solid carload of them.[56]

The ceremonies at Washington were impressive in every way. The time of arrival was late, 10:25 P.M. on Tuesday. Borne on a caisson, the coffin passed through the streets along Pennsylvania Avenue to the White House, to rest in the East Room. A huge crowd watched at the concourse in front of the station, and people lined both sides of the avenue. Theodore Roosevelt Jr., assistant secretary of the navy, and his friend Sen. James W. Wadsworth of New York were among the spectators outside the White House.

> It was very impressive. The night was breathlessly hot. The streets were lined with people of all ages and all types. There was dead silence, with a hush you could almost hear. Finally down the dark reaches of the Avenue, under the motionless trees, came the sound of horses' feet, no voices, simply the noise of hoofs and the clatter of equipment. Then out of the dusk and shadows came a squadron of cavalry with white reins and the equipment sparkling an occasional gleam of light. The body was carried on a caisson and covered with a mass of flowers. Amid dead silence it was carried into the White House.[57]

Next day the scene followed virtually in reverse as the body was taken to the Capitol to lie under the center of the great dome for its second funeral service. Three presidents rode up the avenue that day, accompanying the dead president: his successor, Coolidge; Chief Justice William H. Taft, who had been president from 1909 to 1913; and Wilson, who despite his decrepitude (he was to die within a few months, in February 1924) insisted upon paying his respects.

A week and a day after Harding's death the final service was held in Marion, on Friday, August 9. The small city—its population numbered nineteen thousand—had been grief-stricken from the beginning, when the word arrived of what had happened. Church bells had begun tolling late in the evening of August 2, and the great courthouse bell added its resonance to the sound. The father of the president's secretary, George Christian Sr., had been asleep when his wife awakened him to say that the bells were tolling. This was the fourth time he had heard such a sound—the other three times were after the deaths of Lincoln, Garfield, and McKinley.[58] Nearly the city's entire population roused itself that night, people leaving houses and coming out on the lawns and into the streets. There was a stream of telephone calls to the two newspapers, the *Star,* which was the morning paper, and the evening *Tribune,* asking if the news that "The president is dead" was true.

Two of the friends of the president's father hastened to his residence, and Dr. George T. Harding broke into tears. "Boys, this is terrible," he said. "Warren has gone. He had the interest of his country at heart. There never has been a president since Abraham Lincoln that had the interest of the country at heart like Warren."

The obsequies at Marion were suitable to the city from which the president had come. The coffin was placed in the front room of Dr. Harding's house and outside stretched a long line of friends and neighbors. Thence they moved to the city cemetery, where there was a service, and the body was placed in a receiving vault, to await construction of a mausoleum that was not finished until 1927. No troops were in the procession that followed the body of the president, save the honor guard from the train. In that sense it was an ordinary Marion funeral. But it was impossible not to notice the many dignitaries, including the new president, the chief justice, and many others. The only other military mark during the procession to the cemetery, besides the honor guard, was the guns booming a parting salute, and with the final words a bugler sounded taps, the soldier's farewell.

5 ———

A single issue remains about Harding's death. This is that all five physicians present at Harding's last illness mistook the cause of death. The bulletin that night, August 2, signed by all the physicians, designated the cause as apoplexy, a word popular at the time, meaning a stroke. The final bulletin the next day, signed only by the consultants, Wilbur and Cooper, in an obvious effort to stand away from their government colleagues, to avoid any appearance that incompetent government physicians had outvoted them, repeated the designation. In actual fact, it is now clear that Harding died of a heart attack.

Cardiology was in its infancy in the early 1920s, and it is understandable why the president's physicians made their error—it was easy to do; most physicians would have done the same. At that time, 1923, the possibility of death through heart failure from a sudden blocking of a coronary artery by a blood clot after that artery had been narrowed by fatty deposits, the clot preventing cells in the heart from receiving oxygen-rich blood and nutrients, thereby destroying the heart muscle—understanding of what is now known as a myocardial infarction—was not then widespread. The first observation of a heart attack in a living patient had been made by James B. Herrick in 1910, when this remarkable Chicago physician saw a fifty-five-year-old broker who had eaten a moderate meal and suffered chest pain and acute indigestion and died fifty-two hours later. When the pathologist asked where to look for the cause of death, Herrick told him he would find a clot in one of the main arteries to the heart. Herrick published his observation and the pathologist's confirmation of it in a path-breaking article in the *Journal of the American Medical Association* in 1912, but the possibility of heart attacks in humans, as opposed to the well-known possibility of strokes, or apoplexy, did not catch on among physicians for a dozen and more years.[59] Herrick later said that his article "fell like a dud." He found himself going around the country attempting to inform physicians of what they simply refused to accept.

The defining difference between a heart attack and a stroke was the manner of death. In a heart attack the patient died almost instantly, which was what happened to Harding. A stroke required at least ten minutes. The other symptoms of a heart attack fitted Harding's case exactly—a heart attack patient may sweat profusely and be afflicted by nausea. In 1941 Dr. John J. Sampson of the University of California Medical School published an article titled "Changing Conception of Coronary Artery Disease" in which he compared the symptoms of a "Mr. X" with those of a known case of acute coronary artery occlusion and found them very similar. The historian Randolph C. Downes, a Harding biographer, wrote Sampson in 1961 asking if the physician was referring to Harding, and Sampson replied, "You were quite correct in assuming the case history of Mr. X was that of President Harding." Sampson said that in Harding's time the ability to diagnose coronary artery occlusion in a living person was confined to very few physicians, who commonly and erroneously diagnosed what they saw as acute indigestion.[60]

In looking into Harding's cause of death Downes got in touch with the first cardiologist to make a diagnosis of acute coronary thrombosis in a living person, Dr. Samuel A. Levine of Boston, who offered a remarkable testimony to what he remembered back in 1923, supporting what Sampson had written:

> During these days I felt convinced that President Harding had an acute coronary thrombosis with myocardial infarction. I felt so firmly about this that I suggested to Dr. Harvey Cushing, the celebrated brain surgeon, who was surgical chief at my hospital (Peter Bent Brigham Hospital), that we should telephone Dr. Sawyer who was President Harding's attending physician. After thinking this over, Dr. Cushing replied that it was not our business and that we should not interfere . . . None of the medical attendants knew about coronary thrombosis, or the patient never would

have been moved from city to city as he was during the illness. . . . [T]he entire illness was a coronary attack . . .[61]

Sampson and Levine were right, but so was Cushing in refusing to intervene, for a telephone call would have done little or no good. Levine's remark that none of the physicians was informed about myocardial infarction surely was correct. One must doubt if any of Harding's physicians had read Herrick's article of years earlier—or, having read it, would have believed it. Sawyer was a country doctor. When the president's valet, Brooks, took ill late in 1923, Boone noted with amazement that Sawyer's examination of Brooks consisted of placing his ear to Brooks's chest. Work, who helped Boone and Sawyer at the outset of Harding's illness on the trip to San Francisco, as well as during the next days, had been out of practice for many years. Of the consultants, Wilbur too was long out of practice. At a dinner party at Secretary Hoover's house in November 1923, attended by Wilbur and the journalist Mark Sullivan, the diners asked Wilbur for his diagnosis of Harding's death, and Sullivan recorded the response in his diary. Many years earlier, Wilbur related, Harding had had some kind of infection, presumably in or near his gall bladder, which impaired the kidneys and caused his heart to enlarge. While the doctors were with the president in San Francisco they received a telegram from Harding's father; Dr. Harding said that shortly after marriage his son had what was called a nervous breakdown accompanied by a low fever. Wilbur said this was probably the time when he had some kind of gall bladder infection. Harding's body, "to accommodate itself to the results of this infection, had set up a new balance, which balance was delicate and made Harding subject to the results of fatigue." Wilbur repeated the description offered in the final bulletins, that "the real cause of death was a constriction in a tiny blood vessel at the base of the brain, of a tiny nerve center there, which regulates the action of the heart and lungs." Interestingly, after describing Harding's pneumonia and labored breathing, and apparent recovery, Wilbur added, almost as an afterthought, what the president must have told his physicians in San Francisco, that shortly before he left the White House on the western trip he had had two or three attacks of severe pain in his chest during the night.[62]

The fifth member of the team, Dr. Cooper, had gone along with this diagnosis. A few days after Harding's death he wrote Wilbur that "Many physicians will naturally wonder whether the sudden ending was not anginal in character, they failing to understand that . . . the ending was definitely apoplectic in character."[63]

Boone never believed that Harding died of a heart attack. The historian Downes wrote him about the letter from Dr. Levine of Boston, which clearly irritated Boone who responded, "I knew Doctor Harvey Cushing. I would have been surprised that he injected himself in President Harding's illness unsought." When writing his autobiography he was reminded not merely of

Levine and Cushing but also of his colleague at San Francisco long before, Cooper. He had learned from Cooper's associate, Dr. Roger B. McKenzie, that Cooper changed his mind and came to believe that Harding died of a coronary occlusion. In the autobiography Boone related that he had talked with Cooper some time after the president's death and found him a delightful gentleman but that, as to Cooper's change of mind, he thought nothing was to be gained by questioning the accuracy of the diagnosis made in 1923, that it would not contribute anything to history.[64]

2

The Poison Theory

The first and most persistent of the attacks on the reputation of President Harding was the poison theory, the idea that Harding poisoned himself or that someone else, presumably his wife, poisoned him. Talk arose immediately after the president's death in San Francisco on August 2, 1923. E. Ross Bartley, the reporter who together with Stephen Early covered Harding's death at the Palace Hotel, wrote Dr. Boone about it in 1930, from Evanston, Illinois, where he then was living. He thought there were "thousands of persons" in his section of the Middle West who were "possessed with the idea that there was something strange and not quite all right in connection with President Harding's death." In their minds, he said, the possibility of poison ran all the way from blaming Mrs. Harding to belief that the president was poisoned by Catholics.[1] The theory has enjoyed a long life, down to the present day. It can still be heard in private conversation and frequently appears in print.

The poison theory has flourished for several reasons, all of them easily understandable. For one, Harding himself together with his personal physician had diagnosed the illness that began at Vancouver as food poisoning, and at Grants Pass the diagnosis became public. Sawyer blamed it on crabmeat, and Dr. Work was not so sure but thought it was a can of something. At San Francisco, Sawyer on Sunday afternoon spoke to the reporters of strange possibilities, which disappeared in bulletins by the president's team of physicians that spoke of pneumonia and other problems. The final definition of Harding's death was apoplexy, which as we now can see was wrong, caused by the elementary wisdom of the time about the difference between heart attacks and strokes. The medical explanations were, quite frankly, confusing, and introduction of the word *poisoning* encouraged the theory.

A second reason for the talk about poison was the failure, after Harding's death, to have an autopsy. Such a procedure would have dismissed the possibility of poison. The fact that Mrs. Harding did not want one was not taken in the way she meant it—that she simply did not want one. It was at once twisted into a support for the poison theory: of course she did not want one. Advocates of the theory could twist another fact, that the five attending physicians did not themselves think an autopsy was necessary. It was not difficult to contend that Dr. Sawyer, in league with Mrs. Harding, talked them out of it.

And last of the reasons for the rise and flourishing of the poison theory was two books—one a novel, the other a purported account of the truth surrounding Harding's death—that appeared respectively in 1926 and 1930. The novel was titled *Revelry*, its author the well-known and much regarded Samuel Hopkins Adams. The alleged piece of nonfiction was *The Strange Death of President Harding* by a former investigator of the Department of Justice, Gaston B. Means. It is true that no responsible author, then or later, save Frederick Lewis Allen in his *Only Yesterday*, published in 1931, believed the poison theory.[2] But it seemed so plausible as proposed by Adams and Means that it was impossible thereafter to put down.

1

The Adams novel was very well written, and its subject guaranteed a best-seller, with one hundred thousand copies in print. In its pages the author set out how a president of the United States with the attractive sounding name of Willis Markham, whose name resembled Warren G. Harding, poisoned himself. It was all by accident, because President Markham was a man without suicidal tendencies. But having taken the wrong pills from a bottle in a White House medicine cabinet he realized they would resolve his problem, about to be revealed, of involvement with the scandal of Teapot Dome.

Adams established his other characters as look-alikes of the principal figures of the Harding administration, and any reader of the time knew immediately whom he was writing about. The president's wife, Florence, whom he denominated Sara Belle, appeared in the novel somewhat smaller than life, as a virtual cipher, ill all the time, confined in a distant sanitarium. "His wife?" asked a woman who found Markham attractive. "As good as dead," was a senatorial answer. "She will be soon."[3] This device allowed introduction of a very pretty female character, formerly married, who conducted a salon in Washington and to whom Markham immediately was drawn. Adams had heard that the president—the real president, Harding—was attracted to women and made the most of his novelistic opportunity (and this, one might add, was some months before a former resident of Marion, Ohio, Nan Britton, appeared with a book, *The President's Daughter*, that made the most of another opportunity).

Adams's novel's female character was Edith Westervelt, a woman of the world as such individuals were described in the 1920s, quick witted, sophisticated, quiet, not dressed to attract. She had come upon the president of the United States late one night after Markham had spent the evening playing cards in a Washington hideout and decided to escape the Secret Service by bounding over a fence but failed to bound, landing on his face in an alley, whereupon Edith came along in her automobile, on her way home, and picked up the stranger.

The woman in the story found the president of the United States a strangely attractive person. "In her short but immensely varied career she had encountered every type of ruling personality but this." His shortcomings, "unbelievable simplicities and banalities," baffled her. The warmth and happiness of the man attracted her. She almost showed her excitement, which would have been contrary to the carefulness with which she lived. "My house is my house," she said to him. "Come when you like."[4]

After lending a touch of femininity to what was a political novel, Adams introduced what readers understood to be references to the Harding administration's irregularities. Edith Westervelt was walking down a passage in the White House and came to a half-open door, knocked, and with no response walked in. There against the wall "a big, fat, jauntily attired man was jammed in the deadly clutch of another and older man." The fat man's hands were clawing the air, his face purpling, breath cut off by the grip on his throat. The other man shook him side to side. "You yellow dog! You grafting crook! You've double crossed me—once—too often." It was President Markham shaking the novel's equivalent of what in real life a *New York Times* correspondent reported privately to his paper's owner, Adolph Ochs: he had come across Harding shaking the director of the Veterans' Bureau, Col. Charles R. Forbes, under the same circumstances, in the White House.[5]

To help make everything believable Adams introduced the president's niece, a fat young woman named Beryl Hartley, who invested money in land for herself and her uncle that soon revealed an oil well. This convenience the president accepted unquestioningly, justifying the name by which his associates knew him, "Easy Markham." Other similarities to Harding administration scandals were duly noticeable, such as Charles M. Madrigal who strongly resembled the real-life head of the Veterans' Bureau who stole his own organization blind by taking money for contracts for hospital sites and construction and for selling off hospital and other supplies at bargain prices. Charlie was double-crossed by his administration friends and shot while attempting to escape his prison guards, but his friend, Zoa Farley (who was to Charlie what Roxie R. Stinson—the star witness of a later Senate investigation—was to Attorney General Harry M. Daugherty's friend Jess W. Smith), saw the weaknesses in all the schemers and nicely, thirty thousand dollars from an emergency fund of the party, profited from their failures to cover their tracks.

All this was preliminary to bringing the subplots together in a denouement that eliminated, and vindicated, the president, who espied the "small phial of pellets" on the second shelf, remembered that one was the dose but had not been effective the week before, and so took two.[6] Thinking he might take a third later he carried the phial back to his nightstand. After he began to feel queerly, with a burn at the pit of his stomach, a severe pang, a wave of nausea and retching, a second fiery thrill, he switched on the light and looked at the bottle from which he had taken the pellets. There was time for an antidote. He called his doctor who came right up, but the president did not say he had taken poison, only that he did not feel well. As an intelligent if aging senator, in whom Edith confided, informed her after it was all over, the resultant solution was a martyr's death, not a suicide, for the former was heroic, the latter cowardly, and furthermore it would "wipe out the whole score" not only for President Markham but also for everyone else.

One novel, sharply drawn, can be worth dozens of bulletins by physicians, such as Harding's doctors released to reporters during the president's last days in San Francisco. Even Secretary Hoover, whom the Harding scandals never touched, and who was present at the time of Harding's death, believed what Adams the novelist had to say. Hoover read Adams's book in manuscript form and (so wrote a friend to whom he spoke and was keeping a diary) said it gave "a photographic account of all the scandals of the Harding administration, even of many things which are not known."[7] Believing, thus, was not difficult, even for people whose eyes had seen the enthralling event of the administration.

For those individuals who did not read *Revelry,* or perhaps for those who read it and desired more, the novel was made into a play and also a motion picture.

From the poison theory in *Revelry* it was easy to take belief one step further, to attribute the presidential poisoning not to ineptitude at the medicine cabinet, or decision to take an easy way out after reading the label on the bottle by the light of a bedside lamp, but to conclude that the hapless and shadowy Sara Belle of Adams's novel had undertaken a mercy killing, in part because she knew Teapot Dome was imminent and in part because she had learned of her husband's connection with Nan Britton. This was what Gaston Means did. He had met with Ms. Britton after publication of her book and had volunteered to assist her, offering his diaries. She demurred, uncertain both of Means and of his literary collaborator, May Dixon Thacker, sister of the author of *The Clansman,* Thomas Dixon, who visited her one day. Means nonetheless was grateful to Ms. Britton for giving him and Thacker interviews and showing the way with her book. He was so impressed he offered the post of publisher of his book to one of Ms. Britton's assistants, a young Harvard graduate named Maurice Fryefield. Ms. Britton's publishing company was the Elizabeth Ann Guild, named after her daughter. Her assistant probably was responsible for naming Means's publisher the Guild Publishing Corporation. For such reasons he confirmed Ms. Britton's story in his own book.

Means had reached the middle years of his life by the time he entered the Harding administration as an investigator associated with the chief of the

Bureau of Investigation of the Department of Justice, William J. Burns. The latter was the owner of a well-known detective agency. The investigator was a large, hulking man with an ingratiating baby face. He could take on the color of his surroundings, a quality that commended him to Burns; he could mingle with all kinds of people and invent plausible stories for the mingling. Burns found him useful. The connection of Means with the bureau was bona fide. It became the basis for his contentions in his book that he did this or that, carried out special investigations, was employed by the president's wife as a private investigator, had easy entrée to the White House, and on occasion—a notable occasion—saw the president face down his wife over Nan Britton.

Means's story began with his confidential arrangement with Florence Harding. He was not hesitant in relating it: "I know—as no other living person—the entire confidential story of the White House during those years."[8] As if to give his explanations a cachet of certitude he thereafter, on almost every occasion he claimed to have seen the president's wife, took the liberty to describe her, often in pitiless terms. She was not, he knew, a woman of great beauty. Five years older than her husband, of medium height, thin, sharp faced, she wore fanciful dresses in the manner of the day. She stood very straight and stiff, head and chin held high, clad in soft, flowered silk, lavender and gray. Or it would be a brownish-figured dress that looked like "upholstery goods," accompanied by a black-and-red Spanish shawl over her shoulders and a wide fringe that nearly touched the floor in front.[9] The dresses always came down low so as to hide her swollen (from kidney disease) legs and feet. Means (doubtless it was May Thacker, who had written for *True Confessions*) usually described her hair, arranged with studied care, each hair in place, waved by her hairdresser—as if the waves would subtract from her age. A black velvet band encircled her throat, so as to hide the wrinkles.

In describing Florence Harding, Means took care to give the telling details of age, especially her hands with "the pale white thinness . . . the interlacing of tiny blue veins, the nervous trembling—every mark of pitiless age." And again: "She was an old woman: withered, nervous, high-strung—tenaciously holding on to the illusion of youth and fooling nobody but herself."[10]

At the beginning of the administration, as *The Strange Death of President Harding* moved toward its denouement, the author drew the wife as possessed with endless ambition. The book appeared only a decade after women received the right to vote, through constitutional amendment, and the subject was also in the minds of readers who had heard that during the last months of the Wilson administration the wife of the ailing Democratic president had taken on the responsibility of governing the country, through controlling access to her husband's sickroom. The author insisted that the hope of Florence Harding was not to be the first lady of the land—for her the ceremonial role of hostess of the White House was altogether insufficient. She wanted to be the first lady of the world. "This is the age of woman . . . ," she allegedly told Means. "For

the first time in American history, a woman shall be recorded as a real factor—
a power—and not have to go by that insipid and uninteresting and moth-eaten
title: First Lady of the Land! Silly!"[11]

As the book established her plan it described her as a "Child of Destiny,"
relating that she herself had been told that by a fortune-teller. When she said she
thought the title of first lady silly, "The low chuckle with which she pronounced
the last word had nothing of mirth in it. It was more like the purring of a
female tiger, intent, threatening."[12] Some of the description must have been
May Thacker's, for even Means's dictation—he had told his story, he said, to
Ms. Thacker, who wrote it down—could not have risen to these heights.

Two advancing concerns then destroyed the vision that the president's wife
held of her own destiny, and Means with relish established them for his readers,
for when taken together with what he said was her intensity and her ambition
they set the scene for what would happen in San Francisco. The first concern
was the hold that the "gang" commenced to have over her husband, the
president. The second was her discovery, through the agency of Means, of
the affair between the president and Nan Britton.

The gang's machinations were in themselves very serious, for its members
soon were holding the president in their hands. Their hold was tighter and
tighter, ever more merciless. Harding had to sign papers put in front of him.
He was appearing like a hounded animal, tracked, his back against the wall. As
a Child of Destiny, his wife needed to discover some means by which she could
frustrate the infernal machinations of the gang, by snatching her husband away
from its members, putting him beyond their power to carry on their nefarious
practices.

Meanwhile the wife had commissioned Means to find evidence, any evidence, that her husband was maintaining a connection with "a girl named
Nan Britton from Marion." She knew there was danger in that direction, from
that girl. Means in his narrative remarked his surprise that when Florence
Harding said this, he then found her telling him the Nan Britton story. "I
became suspicious of this girl," the president's wife said,

> when she was but a child in Marion. She was a greatly over-developed child
> and wore extremely short dresses above the knees. It was not considered
> quite decent. And she was always doing everything on earth that she
> could—to attract Warren's attention. This overdevelopment tended to
> attract men—on the streets and together with her unusually short dresses,
> why she attracted attention of course and not in a very nice way. . . . And
> I could see from Warren's eyes and manner that this young girl affected
> him—by her very presence.[13]

After the above recital she told Means she thought Warren Harding was
incapable of having a child (by this time, 1930, a book published in Marion
in 1928 had offered the point, and Means used it for his own purpose). She

commissioned Means to prove to her that Harding could not be the father of this child.

To look into the possibility that the first lady was wrong, that Harding indeed was the father of Ms. Britton's child, Means took every measure, and among them was surveillance of the apartment in Chicago occupied by Ms. Britton's sister and brother-in-law Elizabeth and Scott A. Willits, and Ms. Britton's daughter whom they had adopted, and from time to time Ms. Britton. Without great difficulty for an individual of Means's talents he obtained access to the apartment and uncovered Ms. Britton's papers, including letters and diaries. When he took these materials back to Congress it required two or three days of intensive work to analyze them. To his delight, however, he saw that the president's mistress had kept everything. "One thing that impressed me most was the fact that Mr. Harding had been sending Nan Britton souvenir postcards for a great many years, since she was a child in Marion. Evidently, she had preserved every scratch of his pen."[14] Among other items he discovered jewelry that Harding had sent his mistress and her child. These items, every one of them, after his analysis of them, he passed to Florence Harding, together with written reports from the men who assisted him in his surveillance work. He brought everything to her apartment in the White House, and they spent several hours reading and discussing what he had found.

When the president discovered, as he did from his wife who confronted him with the issue, what Means had obtained, that is, proof of Harding's paternity, he was furious. Harding, Means said (and he heard the words from the lips of the president's wife), was coldly angry. She had wondered why she did not cry like other women, she was sure that any other woman would have cried, but she did not, and she said calmly to her husband, "What will you do with me?" Her voice, she told Means, was as firm as if she were inquiring the time of day.

"You can do—what you damn please—" was the presidential response.

Then Florence Harding began to plead. "Warren—Warren—think of our young love—" she said.

He would not let her finish. "Young love," he hissed, "our young love! Love! I never loved you. You want the truth. Now you've got the truth. Young love! You ran me down! God in heaven—young love—You ran me down—."

Florence Harding, who never cried, was nonetheless shocked by what her husband said to her. "Mr. Means," she told her investigator, "—those are the very words that President Harding said to me. The very words—to me, his wife,—for thirty-three years. Oh—it was a terrible scene. He was insane that night."[15]

On one occasion Harding appeared in the White House room where Means was conferring, and again there was a scene. He "whirled" on his wife, shook his clenched fist almost in her face, and said: "You have ruined me. You have ruined me! You and your contemptible detectives." Then he turned on Means.

"And as for you, you have been discharged and you'll be indicted in twenty-four hours. You will never again put your foot in the White House. And—I'll have those papers. I'll have search warrants—and you'll be under surveillance for the rest of your life—."

Means (or was it Ms. Thacker, his amanuensis, the contributor to *True Confessions*?) wrote that he made no response but looked the president of the United States straight in the eye. The president had said Means would never enter the White House again. "To be sure, that was my last visit to the White House during President Harding's life, but it was not so very many months before I entered its portals again. And then—President Harding was there,—lying in magnificent grandeur—in his gorgeous casket amid banks of flowers in the center of the East Room: a commanding figure even more regal and kingly looking in death than he had been in life."[16]

From the confusion that had reigned when the president and his wife were fighting over their marital past, and when Harding, according to Means, confronted him and wished him ill, order was restored, an order that created the scene in the East Room, after Florence Harding some weeks later heard of the suicide of Jess Smith, who lived in the attorney general's apartment in the Wardman Park Hotel in Washington. The suicide showed the president's wife that her husband's enemies, the gang, would stop at nothing. Her two difficulties with her husband—destruction of her dream of a triumphal tour of Europe by the machinations of the gang, together with her discovery of her husband's affair with Nan Britton—combined to make her see what was necessary to accomplish her mission as a Child of Destiny. When Smith on Memorial Day 1923 was found in the apartment of Attorney General Daugherty, apparently dead by his own hand but perhaps not, destiny made itself clear.

The president's wife told Means carefully, deftly, and cautiously but almost openly what she was about to do. "There is no length, Mr. Means," she said in her forthright, intense way, "to which I will not go . . ." She said she had discussed the matter, "held many councils of war" with General Sawyer, her physician and that of the president, and he stood solidly with her. The two of them could feel the icy chills of onrushing menace. "We see ahead of us terrible possibilities. And strange—irrelevant as it may seem to you,—Jess Smith's death removed the last vestige of hesitation and fear."

It was because of her new resolution that a trip to Alaska was being planned. The trip would enable her to fulfill her and the president's destiny. "*The President is to die first*. He will die in honor: the stars have so decreed."[17]

All that seemingly was necessary was for the occasion to present itself. The president's wife had brought General Sawyer into her plan. The plan involved no simple reaching into a medicine cabinet and taking out the wrong bottle of pills. It would be a deed accomplished without trace, without the slightest evidence left behind.

Means learned from the wife, after she had become a widow, what had happened in San Francisco. The death of Warren G. Harding was a quiet, almost simple affair as she remembered it and told it to her investigator who had provided her with the information she needed. "I was alone with the President . . . [the ellipses are in Means's book] and . . . only about ten minutes. It was time for his medicine . . . I gave it to him . . . he drank it. He lay back on the pillows a moment. His eyes were closed . . . He was resting . . . Then—suddenly—he opened his eyes wide . . . and moved his head and looked straight into my face. I was standing by his bedside."

As she paused, Means could not refrain from the question, "You think—he knew?"

"Yes. I think he knew. Then—he sighed and turned his head away—over— on the pillow. . . . After a few minutes,—I called for help. The papers told the rest."[18]

2 ———

The poison theory was announced by two authors whose bona fides were worth looking into—for they had announced a preposterous theory. The author of *Revelry* was born in upstate New York, where his father was a Presbyterian minister, his mother the daughter of a professor of theology. The son graduated from Hamilton College in Clinton in 1891 and went to the *New York Sun* as a reporter where he worked with a generation of "gentlemen journalists" including Arthur Brisbane, Jacob Riis, Richard Harding Davis, Will Irwin, and David Graham Phillips, all of whom learned their trade from the distinguished editor, Charles A. Dana.

Adams's career mirrored the interests of his time. In 1900 he was engaged by S. S. McClure for *McClure's* magazine, and over the next years found himself in the midst of the muckraking era, employed for a while by the principal muckraking editor. Ida M. Tarbell also was working for the able if mercurial McClure, taking on John D. Rockefeller and Standard Oil Company, Lincoln Steffens turning to the "shame of the cities," their vices and squalid political circumstances. Adams after a while moved on to *Collier's*, to write about patent medicines and medical quackery, and was credited along with Harvey Wiley and Upton Sinclair for passage of the Pure Food and Drug Act. The American Medical Association sponsored his first book, *The Great American Fraud*, in 1906 and made him an associate member in 1913.

An observer of his career might have remarked that he represented the coming-of-age of American journalism, a transition from the partisanship, sly or outright, and for the rest of it a tradition of largely factual reporting, that had marked newspapers and magazines from journalism's beginnings a century before. Some of the reporters of his generation proved able to go beyond muckraking to very considerable achievements in nonfiction. In later years Ida Tarbell wrote a remarkable history of the era from 1878 to 1898 titled *The Nationalizing of Business,* which was published in 1936. Others, as in Adams's case, turned to fiction, and as they removed themselves from reporting their qualities increased, for perhaps in their earlier work they had been more imaginative than correct in the recalling of details from the real, as opposed to the imagined, present day or past.

The muckrakers, whatever their later interests, were often very successful, and such was the case with Samuel Hopkins Adams. In the years before World War I he began freelancing and eventually was the author of fifty books and innumerable articles and short stories. An observer of his career wrote that he produced few lasting works, books that received critical acclaim.[19] But he was so able a writer that in a half century and more of writing he had only two stories that did not sell. Although he specialized in fiction, he published a biography of Daniel Webster, colorful if unreliable, and in 1939 published *Incredible Era,* an account of the Harding administration, of which more will be said later. Seventeen of his novels and stories became motion pictures, including *It Happened One Night,* with Claudette Colbert and Clark Gable. His last novel, *Tenderloin,* which was published posthumously (he died in 1958), was made into a Broadway musical.

Adams justified his career as a writer with some gentlemanly phrases that made sense—because, after all, he had to make a living. As he put it, after he went on his own as a writer he had to choose themes that would sell so that his work would permit a life of "freedom of thought, action, and mode of existence." When he wrote this description for a biographical dictionary of twentieth-century authors published in 1942 he added that he chose to live and work this way because he did so "in an era when individual choice, threatened as it is throughout an imperiled world, has never been so precious."[20] He may have been referring to World War II.

But he was commercial with his undoubted skills, and one suspects not altogether because he had to be. He wrote *Flaming Youth,* published in 1923, a book that in its title and subject gave lasting description, and celebration, to the sex and scandals and general looseness of young men and women after World War I. He published it under the pseudonym of Warner Fabian. "I knew it was a book that could make a helluva lot of money," he explained, "but I didn't want my own name on it." He cheerfully described himself as "a professional hack." He said he wrote "like a reporter—for pay."[21] If some of this description sounded like braggadocio—he was good and knew it, could write quickly and well and almost to order—he talked too much about money. He was proud that *Revelry* sold one hundred thousand copies. He failed to measure what might have been described as the responsibility that a writer of fiction as well as nonfiction should observe toward the reading public. If he touched upon history in a novel, however tangentially, it was incumbent upon him, so critics of *Revelry* believed, to keep to the truth, not to distort. He obviously never felt such a responsibility. Within three years of the death of a president he was willing to take advantage. Later, in *Incredible Era*, his nonfictional account, he wrote that if it could not be proved that Harding was not poisoned, for there had been no autopsy, the case might well remain a mystery, save for the fact that there were people in the presidential party of unimpeachable character. Dr. Sawyer was an old and devoted friend of the family; and there was Cooper, a San Francisco diagnostician; Wilbur, president of Stanford and a physician; a cabinet member, Work, a doctor of medicine; Hoover; and Boone, a war hero: none of these people, he observed, had ever subscribed to the poison theory, and Wilbur had informed him that it was impossible.

The other writer about the poison theory, Gaston Means, was an amateur at prose, compared to the talented Adams, but a far different figure in ways that Adams might have observed in his journalistic investigations but of course, in his own person, was never acquainted with. Means was an out-and-out scoundrel, in almost any way one might have imagined. J. Edgar Hoover, who knew him well, described him as "the greatest faker of all time" and "the most amazing figure in contemporary criminal history."[22]

He was born in 1879 into a respectable North Carolina family and when seven years old betrayed what he would do later in life when he stole almost three dollars from a box belonging to the Women's Missionary Society that his mother kept in the house. The son denied any connection with the money, and his mother accused a maid, whom she sent packing. Means later bragged about the affair. "I think," he said, "the sound of those coins in my pocket was the sweetest music I've ever heard."[23]

It is possible that the Women's Missionary Society money was something the youngster did not intend to take, and only later when he was an adult and into all varieties of misbehavior he fixed upon that episode as his beginning. Actually the beginning of his career may have come in 1912, from a physical rather than pecuniary circumstance that could have made him unbalanced. In that year he had fallen from the upper berth of a Pullman and landed on his head. The only awkwardness with this theory was that he not only sued the Pullman Company but also had the foresight, before the "accident," to take out accident insurance policies with several different companies.[24]

Not long afterward he became involved in the strange death of a wealthy widow with whom he had become friendly, Maude (Mrs. James C.) King. He had joined the William J. Burns detective agency and been assigned to protect her. He persuaded her to allow him to manage her affairs, transferred money to his own account, gambled in cotton futures, and decimated her fortune. In August 1917 she visited him in North Carolina. He purchased a gun and the next day persuaded her to walk with him into a woods "for target practice." She was shot in the back of the head, and Means was the only witness. Tried by a local jury, he was adjudged innocent, though gun experts testified that the widow could hardly have shot herself in the back of the head. Previously Means had maintained a connection with German agents who paid him to provide information on Allied purchases and shipping. With American entrance into the war this connection perhaps was embarrassing. He explained the death of Mrs. King by the fact of his betrayal of the German cause: German agents had shot her, intending to kill him.[25]

He entered upon the golden era of his career in October 1921, when he became an agent in what then was known as the Bureau of Investigation, the forerunner of the Federal Bureau of Investigation. For a short while Means was an employee. Unfortunately, when Attorney General Daugherty dismissed him in February 1922 he remained on the bureau's payroll as an informant. Both arrangements gave him a platform by which he could go into the shaking down of underworld figures involved in bootlegging. He claimed he could get government whiskey released from warehouses if the bootleggers would advance him the money to pay the "warehouse tax." Means's wife, Julie, later confessed that by the autumn of 1922 her husband was "hand in glove" with them. She recalled that on October 22 at the Hotel Vanderbilt in New York City a bootlegger gave him $5,000, two days later another gave him $11,500, and on October 31 another handed over $13,800. She estimated his take from bootleggers that fall as $50,000, and these sums were only for transactions she knew about.[26] He managed such accomplishments by making apparent telephone calls in front of his clients to such individuals as the bureau's head, Burns, holding the telephone close to his chest to conceal the fact that he was holding the hook down, and by talking to the clients about the need of the Republican National Committee for money to erase the deficit of 1920 and prepare for the campaign of 1924. "We have had many meetings— Mr. Daugherty, Mr. Burns, and the Republican National Committee, and we decided that the only way this money can be raised quick is in the liquor game."[27] His other method of producing satisfied clients was that when he did not do what he claimed he could, his suppliants almost never complained, for that would have involved confessions that they were taking part in illegal activities. Moreover, he always had special explanations. When one client called his house to inquire why the warehouse whiskey had not arrived, Means's secretary said he had been called to New Orleans with seventy-five men to investigate the Ku Klux Klan.

Means eventually got into trouble over his shakedowns of bootleggers. He engaged an assistant, Elmer Jarnecke, who was methodical and not very bright and mistakenly gave a receipt for the warehouse tax to a go-between for two wealthy New Yorkers who were vastly disappointed when Means failed to deliver. Two other New Yorkers desirous of eighty-eight barrels of whiskey paid a tax of $7,250, and they also were disappointed. A canny special assistant attorney general offered immunity for testimonies, and the combination of disappointments and jail-free statements overwhelmed these customers' natural bashfulness.

At that point Means was in difficulty not merely over the shakedown and the receipt, but the Bureau of Internal Revenue entered the picture and filed a lien against him for $267,614.40 for unpaid income taxes and penalties for the years 1921 through 1923.

Nor was bootlegging the only illegal interest of Means, for there was the glass-casket case. That problem had arisen when a company was organized in Altoona, Pennsylvania, to manufacture a casket that would permit people to see their departed loved ones in every possible way, as if they were lying on a bed asleep instead of enclosed and visible from the top down. Glass caskets went on display in several cities, and the company sought to interest bankers and the public. A group of salesmen pursued commitments and tried to make sales. But they made statements in letters that misrepresented the caskets, which had not been perfected. The federal government accused the casket entrepreneurs of using the mails to defraud. This accusation persuaded them to testify against Means in a trial, for Means had shaken them down for $65,000 by promising to quash their indictments.

While awaiting trial for the bootlegging and glass-casket charges he gave testimony in 1924 before a special Senate committee investigating Attorney General Daugherty; Means understandably had no love for Daugherty who had dismissed him. He referred darkly to graft in high places. He produced two large sacks containing "hour-by-hour" records of his investigative work. Not long afterward they disappeared; he said he had surrendered them because of an order from Sen. Smith W. Brookhart of Iowa, chairman of the committee, and exhibited the order, signed by the senator. It turned out he had forged the document, and he was subsequently indicted for forgery.

In 1925 he was convicted of the bootlegging charge and the glass-casket shakedown. In a long statement (which, typically, he refused to sign) he repudiated almost all of his testimony before the Senate committee. By this action he may have hoped to avoid long prison sentences for his two federal offenses. But the repudiation was to no avail, for in each case he was sentenced to two years in prison, the sentences to run consecutively, not concurrently, and received two fines of $10,000.

It was while he was in the Atlanta penitentiary that he met May Dixon Thacker who was interested in the rehabilitation of prisoners and who heard from Means how the Harding "gang" had sent him to prison because he knew too much. Believing what he told her, she became his collaborator on *The Strange Death of President Harding*. In 1931 she was to tell how she wrote the book, adding a particular or two showing how Means swindled her.

His connection with her was complicated, and no more open and above-board than any of his other actions of the time. After volunteering her services she found herself virtually on her own, finding that she had been "stalled along." She was "snatching material for the book as best I could." He talked with her a little about what Mrs. Harding had said to him and what on the notable occasion the president himself had said to him. For the rest of it she failed to obtain the diaries, letters, documents, and senatorial endorsements he promised her. Instead he gave her the three-volume senatorial hearings and told her she could believe anything in them. "What better or more authoritative documentary evidence could one want," he asked, "than the official reports of the testimony taken before the Senatorial Investigating Committee?"[28]

At this juncture Means, his wife, and their son disappeared. The book was published on March 20, 1930. Thacker had not seen him since August 4 of the preceding year. On April 16 he reappeared and said he had been busy. Earlier she had noticed that he had been living in style, first in a hotel in Washington, D.C., where he and the family occupied three rooms with two baths, then in a furnished house in Maryland where he had sported a chauffeur-driven limousine. It turned out that he had been employed by the National Civic Federation, investigating the activities of Communists in the United States, Canada, and Mexico, at one hundred dollars per diem. During his absence he had removed his family to Los Angeles.

May Dixon Thacker's disgust with the author of *The Strange Death of President Harding* turned into anger the year after publication. The disgust had begun when he gave her no help on the book other than to tell her stories about how well he knew Florence Harding and the president. It was her task to weave the stories into the book, using whatever sources she could get her hands on. "I had spent a year of the hardest work of my life on the book."[29] In its first weeks the book sold eighty thousand copies, which sales doubtless increased thereafter to a figure well beyond the sales of Samuel Hopkins Adams's book. How much of the money from the sales she received is uncertain, but it was probably not enough to pay her expenses, for which Means had paid her nothing in advance. She was given a final rude awakening when she called upon "one of the highest officials in Washington" who told her it was absolutely and positively an impossibility for Means to have entered the White House to see Mrs. Harding, as he had claimed in sixteen instances in the book. Then she learned of Means's affidavit about his testimony before the Senate committee.[30]

She had involved herself in a hoax and indeed was the virtual author of it. She took what little revenge she could by publishing the account of her undoing in the magazine *Liberty*.

Indefatigable in bilking thieves and innocents, Means went on to other things. He persuaded the daughter of Jay Gould, Mrs. Finley Shepard, to pay him thirty-two thousand dollars to protect her from the Communists, for Mrs. Shepard had spoken out against the Reds and feared they were all around her, waiting to kill her. They did not do anything to her.

In 1932 he entered into another enterprise that again proved his undoing. After the infant son of Charles and Anne Lindbergh was kidnapped, the

Hardings' friend, Evalyn McLean, sought him out, in hope that a criminal could catch a criminal and find the child. By coincidence, he said, he knew where the child was, and upon his request she gave him one hundred thousand dollars in one-hundred-dollar and fifty-dollar bills. He needed expense money, and she gave him an additional four thousand dollars. He and an assistant met the kidnappers in South Carolina and Texas. For the payoff he said he needed another thirty-five thousand dollars. Mrs. McLean went to the police, took him to court for grand larceny, and he was convicted and sentenced to prison for fifteen years. He said at the time and later that he had acted in good faith and given the first installment of the ransom money, the one hundred thousand dollars, to the kidnappers. The FBI dug up every foot of the yard surrounding Means's house and dug in the basement, looking for the money. Means died in prison in 1938. No one ever found the one hundred thousand dollars.

3 ———

Considering the books of Adams and Means, and their authors' personal interests and backgrounds—Adams and his erstwhile muckraking that had turned to surveying such subjects as flaming youth, Means who had become a con man and perennial crook—what little there was to the case of Harding's poisoning rested on the way in which they drew the nation's first family. As mentioned, Adams could not admit even to himself, much less to his readers, that President Markham was a suicidal sort. The president of his novel was a lovable, almost doglike figure who was not angry with anyone. Adams related that the pills in the medicine cabinet had come from Markham's friend, the attractive divorcée, who had kept them in her own cabinet until Markham found out about them and told her they had no business there and put them in his White House cabinet for safekeeping, whereupon he took them by mistake. It required a leap of imagination for Adams's mythical president then to resist any help from his personal physician, so readily at hand, available for the calling. But in a novel that was filled with both likely and unlikely events and personalities, the novelist skipped through the charade of Markham's making up his mind to die and turned to the event itself.

Any notion that Harding might have used poison to remove himself from Teapot Dome was not really believable. But then in considering the case for poisoning, speculators on President Harding's demise could choose Means's theory, involving Mrs. Harding.

Means's drawing of Mrs. Harding was of course a caricature. There is no evidence he ever met her. He was sufficiently observant, one might say malicious, to notice the difference in age between Florence and Warren Harding and make everything he could out of it, and for the rest of her portrait draw on his imagination and that of his collaborator.

The wife of President Harding was a woman of the world in a way Means would not have understood. Born in 1860, the daughter of the wealthiest man in Marion, she married a drifter named Henry (Pete) De Wolfe, who left her not long after she gave birth to a son. Returning to Marion from a nearby town, Bucyrus, she refused to live with her father and gradually made a new life for herself by giving piano lessons; she had studied at the Cincinnati Conservatory, then as later a considerable institution. After marriage to Harding, which her father violently opposed, she by all accounts assisted her husband greatly by handling the business end of the *Marion Star* and thus helped him become secure financially before he entered politics.

Mrs. Harding was no person to have accomplished the task Means malevolently assigned her. She was a woman of decisiveness and one must say of very considerable courage but had none of the qualities Means imagined. With great pride she watched her husband's reputation rise so rapidly that before he completed his first term in the Senate, the Republican National Convention in 1920 chose him as its presidential candidate. Thereafter he was a certainty for the presidency, given the discrediting of the Wilson administration because of failure of the Treaty of Versailles in the Senate; the country had tired of Wilson's calls for renewal and idealism, and Harding's political regularity together with the promise of "normalcy" was what the country wanted. She enjoyed the campaign, with a touch of innocence that was attractive. "No matter what comes into my life," she wrote Evalyn McLean, "I shall always regard this summer as one of the greatest epochs of all my life." She did her best for her husband and wrote an Ohio friend her thanks for a reception that suited the occasion: "I enjoyed the occasion immensely, and my heart is full of gratitude toward the splendid women of America everywhere, who have risen so nobly to meet in the right manner, the new responsibility which has recently come to them, but especially close are the women of Ohio, and I send to you in Akron my choicest greetings, and good wishes." Proud of Warren's nomination and campaign, she was even more proud of the victory. "The overwhelming victory," she opined, "places a staggering responsibility upon us—personally, and as a party; it is sobering in the extreme." She spoke of "tremendous undertakings," and when the president-elect rose in the Senate to address the upper house prior to his departure, she saw "the fineness of it all" that was "ennobling and thrilling." Withal she was not without humor, as when she wrote "Dear Louise" that "I am about the busiest mortal today on this globe . . . I can dictate now while doing a dozen other things, such as having my face artist, hair lady, manicure performer, interviewing the cook, holding telephonic political conferences, and getting ready to go to the White House."[31]

Boone saw a great deal of her and found her warm and friendly. She was not difficult to satisfy, and her favorite song was "The End of a Perfect Day," which the U.S. Marine Band included in every program at the White House. Her husband she described in correspondence as "W. G.," and he wrote of "Florence" but often playfully described her as "the duchess." In an early letter, in 1907, Harding signed himself as Jerry, and in the left-hand corner at the bottom he wrote, "Dictated by the Duchess." Christmas Day 1920, when he was president-elect, he wrote Mrs. George Christian Sr. and signed himself, "The Secretary to the Duchess of Ququa." When the president was through with his golf game he would tell Starling to "call the duchess" and tell her he was on his way. When someone wanted him to do something he might say, "I'll have to check with the duchess."[32]

Mrs. Harding liked to talk politics, and Boone often heard her express herself with vehemence and positiveness. He believed she had a "man's mind." Sometimes the couple disagreed, and the president would scowl, shut his mouth tightly, and if the disagreement was sufficient leave the room. The doctor never remembered hearing him scold Mrs. Harding.[33]

The president's wife had many superstitions, one of which amused the assistant White House physician. When Mrs. Harding was confined to bed, ill with the kidney disease that often afflicted her, Boone and a nurse were attempting to help her out of bed into a chair, and Boone saw a pair of white fur slippers under the bed, picked them up, and placed them on the bed. The patient sat up, this when he and the nurse thought she had no such strength, and said to him, "Do not ever place slippers on a bed! You ought to know that is very bad luck."[34]

Mrs. Harding while in the White House had come very close to death, and Boone and the other physicians who cared for her had managed to save her, and she may have saved herself by simple willpower. She was undoubtedly a strong-willed woman. In the autumn of 1922, shortly after Boone took up his White House duties, he commenced caring for Mrs. Harding during a bout of illness, a malfunctioning kidney, that nearly killed her, and learned that she possessed an indomitable will to live, the intensity of which may have communicated itself to people who knew her and, suitably twisted by Means, accounted for some of his imaginary dialogue. One morning at four o'clock Boone and Dr. Charles Mayo, who was consulting at the White House over Mrs. Harding's dangerous condition that perhaps was to require surgery, came down the hall of the White House's second floor; they had been up discussing the possibility of surgery, and because their patient was in great pain decided to go in and see her. She looked strangely at both of them. Boone saw her grip her two hands firmly, and after a few minutes he went back and investigated, to learn she had cut herself with her fingernails deeply, in both palms. Dr. Sawyer, also present, said mournfully, "Her last chapter is being written." Shortly afterward she took a turn for the better and later, when fully conscious, told her young navy physician what had happened. "Doctor Boone," she said, referring to the visit by Boone and Mayo, "I saw two indistinct figures standing at the foot of my bed . . . You seemed to fade away into the fireplace. I felt I was looking through the small end of opera glasses. When you were disappearing from my view, I knew that I was losing consciousness and I also knew that, if I did lose consciousness, I would die. I was determined not to die and that is the reason I squeezed my hands so firmly that I cut the palms, as you observed, until they bled." This "very kindly lady, as I found her to be," Boone wrote many years later, possessed a strong will and thus showed him how mind could triumph over matter.[35]

But kill her own husband? This was beyond belief. Her behavior when her husband died was full proof of that. When Harding suddenly passed on, Mrs. Harding was beside herself. Wilbur wrote privately afterward an account he included in his memoirs a quarter century later when Mrs. Harding long since was dead, in which he said it took nearly an hour to convince her the president was dead, and "it was pathetic to hear her call to her husband." When Boone arrived on the scene she dropped her head on his shoulder and sobbed, and the nurse took her into her bedroom and gave her sedatives and put her to bed.[36]

Means, let it be added, was far off the mark about Mrs. Harding in another respect, namely, that with one single exception at the beginning of the president's stay in the hotel, Harding never was alone, never by himself. The exception was so memorable the doctors saw to it that it never happened again. Shortly after Harding was put to bed on the first day in San Francisco, Boone slipped out of the room for a moment, and to his horror discovered upon his return that no one else was in the bedroom and the president had gotten out of bed and gone into the bathroom and gone to the toilet. He was helped back into bed and thereafter never left alone. Contrary to Means's account it would have been impossible for Mrs. Harding to have poisoned him. There were five doctors, two nurses, and the valet, Major Brooks. The senior nurse, Ms. Powderly, had cared for President Wilson during his illness and was chosen because of her experience in the White House. Her assistant, Sue S. Dauser, was the first woman to achieve the rank of captain in the regular navy. Both were taken on the Alaska trip because some of the men in Harding's party, Hoover and Work among them, had taken their wives, and this required nurses in the ship's infirmary. Years afterward Captain Dauser remembered the poison theory and wrote Boone in 1964 that "almost immediately after the tragedy, it seemed almost before the details were known, some fantastic and completely unfounded rumors started to circulate. Such impossible stories!" She retired to La Mesa, California, and a story in the *San Diego Union* on May 13, 1966, quoted her on the poison theory. "A story went around that Mr. Harding was poisoned in his room at the hotel. Just the other day someone from the University of Michigan wrote me about it. The story was utterly ridiculous. No one could have poisoned the patient because someone was with him every minute."[37]

Means did not say so, but it was an easy inference that after the president died Mrs. Harding, so it was said, poisoned Dr. Sawyer, who died a year later, suddenly, under the same circumstances as Harding. The presumption of the whisperers was that Mrs. Harding obtained the poison for her husband from Old Doc and therefore required his death. "Father's passing on," Sawyer's son, Dr. Carl Sawyer, wrote Boone, "was almost identical with that of his friend, President Harding." He had worked until almost the last minute, drove home, went to his office, felt a little bad, talked with his wife and son who sought to help him, felt better, and said he wanted to lie down and sleep but never awakened.[38]

But like Means's other speculations, there was nothing to this one. In the year between Harding's death and his own, Sawyer had very rapidly declined physically. Boone noticed the decline as he worked with him (for several months Sawyer remained in the White House as physician to President Coolidge). Boone observed an increasing irritability that sometimes made little sense, a sensitivity to supposed slights that showed a decline in Sawyer's faculties. Sawyer was constantly feeling unsure of himself. Coolidge worried him, and Boone felt the physician wanted to stay on but at the same time was unduly concerned about what Coolidge might think of him. Coolidge, as was his wont, was not very communicative, save to Boone, to whom the new president confessed he always felt better when General Sawyer was away in Marion. Sawyer told Work, who told Boone, that he might quit because Coolidge was always giving himself home remedies—he was a "self-medicator."[39] The old doctor's eyes were failing, and Boone had to catch his arm when the two of them were going down some street and came to a curb or when they tried to cross a street in traffic. Sawyer had to hold up close to his eyes anything he was trying to read. Boone took him to the best ophthalmologist in Washington, D.C., George B. Trible, who found marked signs of hardening of the arteries. Boone thought that in Sawyer's last months there were virtual personality changes, that he was losing his grip.

Sawyer died on September 23, 1924, and when Mrs. Harding attended the funeral it was clear that her health left much to be desired—and that the second assumption the whisperers drew from Means's novelistic account, that after Mrs. Harding took care of Sawyer she arranged her own death, had no basis in fact, unless it was the almost obvious evidence that Mrs. Harding was losing the will to live. At the funeral of her close friend, her physician for many years, the president's widow was excited and nervous, according to former senator Joseph S. Frelinghuysen, a family friend, in a letter to Coolidge. And behind that appearance she was simply wasting away. She had written Boone even before Sawyer's death that "The past week, particularly, has been, oh! so trying." She wrote on August 9, 1924, "Each day I have lived over those San Francisco days. The old adage that time softens grief is not true, so far as I am concerned, but I have had to meet it, and I have had to meet it somehow, some way." The anniversary passed, and not long afterward there was a return of the kidney trouble. Her enlarged heart added to the problem; in San Francisco at the hotel, when the funeral procession was forming outside and Harding's casket was being taken down to the street, Dr. Wilbur stood with her at a window watching the scene, gripping her arm, and could feel the beating of her enlarged heart. Boone was told that after she returned to Marion and took ill she went to bed and stayed there in the sanatorium at White Oaks Farm, that unlike her behavior in the White House two years before she would not fight back this time. Nature took its course, and on November 21, 1924, she died.[40]

3

The President's Daughter

Nanna Popham Britton was born in Claridon, Ohio, a village five miles east of Marion, in 1896. Within months of her birth the Britton family moved to Marion, where she grew up. Her father was a physician and may have become acquainted with Harding through the latter's father or may have met the owner of the *Marion Star* directly, because of the son's prominence. The daughter remembered that her father wrote humorous articles about country people he had met in his practice and that Harding printed them in the *Star*. When Dr. Britton died in 1913, his widow asked the by then leading citizen of Marion to help her find employment and keep her five children together. Harding arranged for Mary Britton to do substitute teaching in the local public schools.

Even before the death of her father, Ms. Britton seems to have fallen in love—if love is the correct word—with the editor of the *Star,* who was thirty years her senior. At one point her father rode on the streetcar with the editor and told Harding about it. The youngster kept campaign pictures of Harding on the walls of her room, was accustomed to stand across the street from the offices of the *Star* and gaze at the editor as he sat at his desk, and on one occasion when she and her older sister were driving past the Harding residence at 380 Mount Vernon Avenue and saw the editor and his wife sitting on the front porch the two of them turned their buggy around and went back, stopped in front, were invited up, and spent some time talking with the Hardings, during which Nan's sister in the way of youngsters "told on" Nan by relating that Harding's pictures were on the walls. Harding's retort was that he should give Nan a real picture of himself to put on the wall.

A schoolbook belonging to Nan, titled *A Progressive Course in English,* has survived, and throughout the pages are scrawled several dozen references to Harding. Judging from the book, any suggestion for a theme in English classes reminded the moonstruck youngster of Harding. On one page is an exercise for compositions, and in the proposed list of topics is: "Three Reasons why we Honor Washington." Next to it in pencil is the explanation, "cause he looks like Harding." Opposite a query on another page, "Who is the hero of Ivanhoe?" is the answer, "Harding." And a few pages later, "My Favorite Pastime," for which the answer is "Looking for Harding." Another proposed essay was "Why we Love St. Roger." The last two words of the proposed theme were crossed out, with the substitution of "Warren G. Harding." One of the teachers at Marion High School must have been a Mr. Cole. Opposite the declaration, "Men are not created equal," the same hand wrote, "Harding and Cole for instance. Cole is n.g." The owner of the book heard her hero speak: "Warren Gamaliel Harding speech in the opera house. It was great."[1]

After graduation from high school in 1914, Nan remained in Marion a year and then went to Cleveland where she stayed at the YWCA and worked at the George H. Bowman Company, a china store on the city's finest boulevard, Euclid Avenue. Her older sister, Elizabeth, meanwhile went to Chicago and from there wrote advising that two could live cheaper than one and inviting her to live with her, which offer she accepted, obtaining a position in Carson, Pirie, and Scott's china department. From there Nan removed to New York City to attend a business school. After completion of the school's course she wrote the then senator Harding asking for a recommendation for employment.

As a grownup the daughter of Dr. Britton was undoubtedly attractive. Thin and lithe, with a pleasant face, and a feeling for dresses and jewelry that was not ostentatious, she must have possessed a sort of small-town air that would have caught the attention of men in the city. The photographs in her two books—the one published in 1927, the other in 1932—were especially attractive when unposed, showing her standing outside a house or sitting at a desk typing; in them she seemed a warm-hearted young girl. In the posed portraits, with her hair bobbed in the 1920s fashion, dresses more formal and hence more severe, she appears hard, very much a woman of the time, too sophisticated, no longer the schoolgirl. But posed or unposed she was attractive and would have caught attention.

As Ms. Britton remembered what happened, she asked Senator Harding for a recommendation to Judge Elbert H. Gary of the United States Steel Corporation and obtained a position with the manager of the corporation's bureau of safety, sanitation, and welfare, C. L. Close. Following the recommendation and its successful outcome, she quickly saw more of the senator, for that summer when Harding next came to New York he invited her up to his room in the Manhattan Hotel where he had taken the only available room, the bridal chamber, a very lovely room, and when they had closed the door behind them they shared their first kiss. Her book said that they did not disturb the bed, which stood upon a dais, with furnishings in keeping with the general refinement of the room.

Of the descriptions that followed by the author of *The President's Daughter* there is no need to go into detail. Harding, she said, soon was telling her everything, including his early experiences with women. Because she herself had never been "possessed," she imagined that she was more interesting to him. Harding and she often talked, she wrote, of how wonderful it would be to have children, and in these discussions the senator told her frankly how he had wanted to adopt a child but "Florence" would not hear of it. He related his domestic unhappiness in no uncertain terms, the descriptions ending with the same words, "She makes life hell for me, Nan!" Knowing this, the younger woman did her best to make up for Florence's inadequacies. Part of the problem, she wrote, was that Mrs. Harding often was ill, and there was a time in 1918 when she was very ill. The senator told Ms. Britton of what he would like to do if his wife were to pass on—he would buy a place for the two of them in the country. "Wouldn't that be grand, Nan? You'd make such a darling wife!"[2]

Sometimes the former Marion resident journeyed down to Washington, but the couple found New York more congenial, for it was safer. Even then the senator was becoming prominent. He had given the keynote speech at the Republican National Convention in 1916, and his face was becoming known. Nonetheless she had gone down to the city, and she and Harding, she wrote, later decided that during a visit to the Senate office building one evening, which had not been a wise thing to have done because the rules governing guests were rather strict, their baby girl was conceived.

Elizabeth Ann Christian, as the physician in Asbury Park, New Jersey, filled out the birth certificate, was born October 22, 1919. Senator Harding was not present or nearby, and the mother gave the father's name as Edmund M. Christian, age thirty-two, and said he was in the U.S. Army serving in Europe.

Thereafter the question became where the child would live, for if with her mother it would not have been easy to work also. "Mr. Harding" mentioned the possibility of giving the baby to his sister in California, who unlike his other two sisters had children of her own. The mother gradually came around to the idea that Elizabeth Ann should go with her sister in Chicago, for whom she had named the child, and her sister's husband (by this time Elizabeth had married). The couple were musicians, and both held jobs, which meant the need for money to hire someone to care for the child, but Harding, the mother of Elizabeth Ann wrote, was quite willing to handle that problem and did so, and also made it possible for her sister's husband, Scott Willits, to spend some months in Prague studying with a Czech master of Scott's instrument, the violin.

Arranging the adoption by the Willitses, Nan wrote, cost more than anticipated, notably the instrument of adoption that made them the child's foster parents but the mother the guardian. Harding, she averred, thought the charge excessive, but paid it. Meanwhile, he advised her to save what she could, however small the amount, though he quickly added that he had plans for establishing a fund in a more substantial amount. In this matter she took little interest, for the time when she saw him was so brief "and I adored his kisses."[3] She did start a policy with the Prudential Life Insurance Company, for five hundred dollars, but she had little more than one hundred dollars paid on it when in 1923 she went to Europe and upon return dropped it.

During the several years of their friendship, as Ms. Britton described it, the couple met when possible, and during the presidency sometimes in the White House, apparently in the presidential office that looked out upon the mansion's grounds. Outside was the stalking armed guard, walking up and down, face rigidly to the front. The president told her that people nonetheless had eyes in the sides of their heads and that it was necessary to be very circumspect. A small closet in the anteroom, a place for hats and coats, otherwise empty, was available, and they many times repaired to it.

The problem with the affair, as she drew it, was that time was so short. At one point during Harding's presidency she invested in a lovely orchid negligee and ostrich-befeathered mules, which she thought she might have need of upon next seeing Harding, for he had intimated that he would visit her. The reader, she wrote, could be sure that this intimation from him had "set my heart beating wildly." But time was short, and the visit did not take place. The president, too, was so worried and distressed. She hesitated to raise the question of Elizabeth Ann. When she reluctantly did so, the answer was reassuring. "You must remember, dearie, that Mrs. Harding is older than I, and very probably will pass on before I go, and if she goes first, remember, I myself will adopt Elizabeth Ann and make her a *real* Harding!" At this juncture he said as he had before that she and the child were to have ample funds for as long as they both lived.[4]

The accountings of money from the senator and then the president, as given in the book, were considerable, quite generous for the times when annual incomes of $2,000 or less were common for professional people, despite the inflation that accompanied American participation in the world war and lasted until the boom collapsed in 1921–1922. According to Ms. Britton, Harding often sent $300 or $400 in a single letter, taking no care to register it, affixing a two-cent stamp. One time he gave her two or three—she could not remember—$500 bills. While in Marion shortly thereafter she visited friends for two weeks and kept the bills in a silver mesh bag. She had in mind to buy a coat, which would require most of one of the bills. All the while, as mentioned, he provided money for the Willitses. When in 1923 she contemplated an Armstrong Tour of France, he heartily endorsed the plan and enclosed $200 or $300 as a deposit, advised her to get her passport immediately, and said he would cover the balance.

All this came to an end when she was in a provincial French town and had a very bad dream. She had been conscious of something above her, to the left of her.

It seemed to be floating through the air. It was shrouded about with white clouds which seemed not to hide it from view but rather to protect it in its slow mount upward. *What* was I seeing! God! A coffin! A coffin draped with, and trailing about it, American flags, and heaped with red, red roses! . . . The whole, mounting majestically, lifted by an invisible force, upward, onward, protectingly shrouded by white, white clouds! So he had come to me! He had come in this way that I might be the first to know he was leaving this earth![5]

The book took its origin, derived directly, from the sudden death of Harding, for which Ms. Britton had no preparation, especially in a financial sense. She found herself afflicted by one financial trouble after another. Initially it was the trip, for it plunged her into debt. She had bought clothes and paid the regular tour expense of $525, and the president had only given her $200 or $300 for the cost of the tour and an extra $400. Before leaving she had borrowed $50 from a friend, a Danish sea captain, Magnus Cricken, whom in her book she named Angus Neilsen. From Europe she wired the captain for $200 more, which he sent immediately. She cabled for another $200 to await her at the American Express office in New York; this was most fortunate, because upon arrival at the pier she had barely enough to tip the stewards.

Captain Cricken had been paying court, and this resulted in a failed marriage. She told him that before marriage she needed a check for $25,000 or $30,000. Without hesitation he said he would provide a certified check the next day. He evidently was a man of means, and she married him without the check, only to discover after the wedding that he did not have the money. By January 1924 it was clear that the marriage was a "pitiful failure," and she left him a year later, by which time she was still in debt.[6]

In late 1925 she arranged to bring Elizabeth Ann from Chicago, where the child had been living with the Willitses, to New York, but the arrangement lasted only half a year. She had appealed to her English teacher at Marion High School, Abigail (Daisy) Harding, another sister of the late president, who provided money to supplement her own weekly salary of $35. Through Daisy Harding there was the possibility of more; she made contact with the president's brother, Dr. Harding, and on April 1, 1926, had a conference with him in Marion. She told Dr. Harding that she either must have support from the family or would have to appeal to the president's friends. Dr. Harding said he would consider her situation. His only response was to turn his sister against her, for the money from Daisy Harding virtually stopped.

It was in this crisis situation that she told her story to her superior at the Bible Corporation of America, where she was then employed. After her daughter was born she had moved back and forth between New York and Chicago, taking courses at Columbia University and at Northwestern University in Evanston, mostly working in stenographic positions. For a short time she took part in Harding's campaign in Chicago. In New York she was employed at the Town Hall Club, then at the Bible Corporation, where she was secretary to the corporation's head, Richard Wightman. In her book she denominated Wightman as Norman Pickway. He was a man of "ministerial mien," indeed a former minister, of medium height, regular features, and gray-white hair.[7] He was a man of acumen and sent her to a lawyer who told her she might possibly expect $25,000 from the Hardings, no more. She herself had fixed upon a sum of $50,000, approximately one-tenth of the estate that the dead president had left to his wife and his sisters and brother. To this she added the $2,500 necessary to free her from debt. She knew that at this time a drive for money by the Harding Memorial Association in Marion had yielded, from contributions of more than one million donors, two hundred thousand of them schoolchildren, funds to construct a mausoleum costing $783,108 to entomb the president and his wife, and believed that $50,000, which at interest would yield no more than $2,500 per annum, was not too much to ask. When she told her story, including these details, to Wightman, and despite the lower estimate made by the lawyer, the Bible Corporation executive was inclined to agree with his secretary.

It became evident that for Ms. Britton the most important duty of her life was to ensure a lifetime of happiness for Elizabeth Ann, and the book was the result. Moreover, she envisioned a situation whereby in the book, in addition to telling her story, she would present to readers the plight of all the illegitimate children in America, who because of the irresponsibility of their fathers, and because of the male-dominated laws of the country, were left without financial support and in reality without social support—for society visited upon them the errors of their fathers, refusing among other things to recognize that they should inherit part of their fathers' estates, just as children ordinarily would do. The book thus was more than a statement of her own cause; it was a statement of a much larger cause.

Ms. Britton was transfixed by her purpose. On August 30, 1926, there appeared in the *New York Times* a poem signed by Ninon Britton—she was unsure why the *Times* attributed such a first name to her—titled "The Child's Eyes," and it told of what she saw there:

> Sometimes her eyes are blue as deep sea-blue,
> And calm as waters stilled at evenfall.
> I see not quite my child in these blue eyes,
> But him whose soul shines wondrously through her.
> Serene and unafraid he was, and knew
> How to dispel the fears in other hearts,
> Meeting an anxious gaze all tranquilly:
> These are her father's eyes.
>
> Sometimes her eyes are of a tired gray-blue,
> Filled with the sadness of an age-old world.

> And then again my child's not in these eyes;
> These are the eyes of one whom grief assailed,
> Whom disappointment crushed with its great weight.
> Around his head a halo memory casts,
> Reflecting that refiner's fire which purged
> Him clean, and made him what he was.

In the autumn of 1926 the plan for the book unfolded, and Wightman and his wife, who maintained two houses in Connecticut, arranged for Ms. Britton to live with them for a month in December and work on it. The Wightmans sympathized with her story and sought to help her. They realized that in the writing she would undergo a sort of catharsis, that it would allow her to bring out the suffering of the past nearly ten years, the great hopes with which she had commenced this era in her life, and the tragic disappointment. They offered her every encouragement, and she worked in Wightman's study in the larger of the two houses, amid his books, a writer's room that itself gave inspiration. From half past eight or nine in the morning she worked until dinnertime. "The white pages piled up; the yellow carbon copies piled up. It was unbelievable!"[8] It was, as she wrote in her second book that bore the title *Honesty or Politics*, which was published in 1932, a comfort to be writing everything down, to be no longer under the necessity for silence and secrecy.

Wightman drew up a contract and made a series of visits to publishers in New York. The contract was the easy part, stipulating that he was to be his author's sole representative, sharing all profits on a fifty-fifty basis. Publishing the book proved far more difficult, for as Wightman passed from publisher to publisher he found that although they said the book would sell, they feared legal action or at the least that they would place themselves in a position of notoriety. One publisher, Boni and Liveright, had just brought out the novel *Revelry*, and the firm's telephones had almost jangled off their hooks, the volume of mail overwhelmed their offices, and they told Wightman they did not wish to involve themselves in another such hullabaloo.

The final arrangement was creation of a publishing house known as the Elizabeth Ann Guild. Wightman and his partner created shares in the guild, which they held, and borrowed money at an interest rate of 100 percent. A New York state delegate to the Republican National Convention in Chicago in 1920, Stephen U. Hopkins, supplied the major financing for publication. Wightman organized an office force of a dozen or more people to handle the publication and distribution and established offices at 20 West Forty-Sixth Street.

The enterprise was attended with success, though there were trials along the way. When the book was being cast in zinc plates and printed, before being sent to the binder, the Society for the Suppression of Vice, once headed by Anthony Comstock, arranged for the New York City Police to seize the plates together with the printed sheets. The guild got everything back, but it was anxious work. A dishonest employee secured a full copy of the book while in galley proof and offered it to a leading New York newspaper for $5,000. Fortunately the newspaper declined to make the purchase. The guild's legal counsel, Charles H. Wilson, proved untrustworthy and when dismissed presented a bill for "balance due for services" of $10,450. The guild protested his bill, and he attached 22,100 copies of *The President's Daughter,* then being produced by the W. B. Conkey Company of Hammond, Indiana. Because the attachment was served in this remote place it was necessary to settle the bill, which was done. A former manager of the guild, Richard H. Sears, and another attorney, L. Harding Rogers, moved to declare the guild bankrupt, but a federal judge, Francis A. Winslow, refused to appoint a receiver.[9]

Another worrisome development in midsummer of 1927, shortly after the book was off the press, was the appearance of a man at the guild offices who stated his interest in purchasing the plates and copyright and made an offer to Wightman of several thousand dollars. The man later declared he represented a group of Republican sponsors who felt the book would not assist their political party. As Ms. Britton described this effort, "A purchasing price for silence? It is a sad commentary upon the political ethics of this great republic."[10]

With such preliminaries and accompaniments the book at last was published. A few years later its author reflected her own satisfaction with this result. "Today," she related in 1932, "*The President's Daughter* holds a unique place in the book world."

> Unlike many short-lived best-sellers, there has been an unceasing demand for this book. Its theme has found tender response in the hearts of hundreds of thousands of readers, and it may be found in homes from far-off New Zealand to ancient Syria, from the Philippines to Alaska. It has been estimated that a million people in the United States alone have read *The President's Daughter.* Lending libraries, even in the most sparsely populated sections of the country, are daily replenishing their supplies of this book, which, it is reported, is all too quickly worn with much reading.[11]

The book's author was reminded of how the nation's grandfathers and grandmothers had talked about another book, *Uncle Tom's Cabin.* What Harriet Beecher Stowe had done to arouse the conscience of the American people to favor abolition of slavery, she herself was doing for abolition of an equally deplorable injustice. For combating the deprivation of innocent children of their legal rights she had established (independent of the Elizabeth Ann Guild) the Elizabeth Ann League, which was engaged in the purpose of reform (although it depended upon the guild for financing until it was strong enough through memberships and contributions to stand on its own). Its program was twofold. First it sought state and federal legislation "That on the birth of a child the name of the father be *correctly* registered in the public records, and that failure to do so shall constitute a criminal offense." Second, "That every child born in the United States of America be regarded as legitimate whether born within or without wedlock." President Harding was the author of a book of collected speeches, *Our Common Country*, in which a chapter was titled "What of Our Children?" The president had said that "If society has permitted the development of a system under which the citizens of tomorrow suffer real privation today, then the obligation is upon society to right that wrong, to insure some measure of justice to the children, who are not responsible for being here."[12]

2 ——

Much of what Ms. Britton wrote was believable, yet if looked at closely her books raised nagging questions. Consider her account of a series of meetings with Harding. Walking in the streets of New York, not to mention Washington, D.C., with a man of Harding's appearance—tall, distinguished, and obviously much older than the young woman who presumably was taking his arm—would have been dangerous for a senator in the years 1917–1921, at a time when newspapers were publishing photographs and filling Sunday papers with rotogravure sections containing more photographs than the newspapers of later years, with much more modern technology. Her point about meeting in New York, rather than Washington, did not make sense, for in both places they could have been recognized.

The existence of a liaison during Harding's Senate years would seem doubly impossible because the senator's assistants almost certainly would have learned of it—they often accompanied him. A close friend of Harding, E. Mont Reily, governor of Puerto Rico during the presidency, was grossly affronted by publication of *The President's Daughter* and made a public address to this effect, which was printed in the newspapers of Kansas City, where he lived. Shortly thereafter he received a letter from an attorney in the Bureau of Internal Revenue in Washington, W. Frank Gibbs, who had passed through Kansas City and read Reily's remarks. Gibbs wrote at length, and Reily included the letter in a later and unpublished account of his relations with Harding. Gibbs identified himself as a former member of Harding's senatorial office staff, who during the presidential campaign of 1920 was with Harding almost constantly. "I traveled with Mr. Harding on all of his campaign trips during that campaign." He had "never heard of a woman by the name of Nan Britton."[13]

As for the presidency, when the author of *The President's Daughter* said she had visited the president in his office, Reily offered the testimony of the doorkeeper at the executive offices for nearly thirty-five years, his friend Patrick Kenney, who told him he "*never* had heard of Nan Britton, and that he had *never* admitted any woman by such a name in to see or meet any president!" Kenney was certain of the fact. "I keep a record. I remember, and I know, and I also know that *no* strange woman ever came here to *see* President Warren G. Harding."[14] In event that Ms. Britton might have gone to the White House proper, rather than the executive offices, there was the testimony of Ike Hoover, who had come into the mansion during the administration of President Benjamin Harrison and left at the outset of the Franklin Roosevelt administration. Reily asked him about Nan Britton, and he bristled at the notion that she could have entered the executive mansion. "Nan Britton? No, there was never a gadabout by that name, or any other name, in the White House. Nan Britton is a liar."[15]

When one considers the possibility of meetings it is of even more moment that Harding by the mother's own account never saw the daughter. When the child was born in 1919 and Harding was still a senator, he never came to see her. During the Republican National Convention in 1920 in Chicago, when the mother was staying with her sister and brother-in-law, Harding, she wrote, refused to see the child. "I tried to persuade Mr. Harding to meet me some morning in the park so he could see her, but, though he pondered it all lovingly and said he was 'crazy to do it' as I was to have him, he never did." She supposed that a meeting at that time would have been unwise, but that is difficult to believe because at the outset of the convention Harding was by all accounts a "dark horse," believed to have no chance of the nomination, despite repeated announcements of Daugherty that he would be nominated. At least in the first days he could have made the effort safely, if he had wished. Another remarkable occasion when the president failed to see his purported child occurred in 1922, when the Willitses and Elizabeth Ann visited Washington, D.C., and one of Harding's sisters, Caroline Harding Votaw, arranged for them to tour the White House's public rooms. As the mother wrote later, "the President's own sister escorting the President's own child, unknown to her as such, through his home and grounds!"[16]

Then there was Ms. Britton's testimony to having received many letters from Harding. In her books she did not quote any of the letters, because at his request, she explained, she had destroyed them.

She was quite detailed in describing how they corresponded. She used a small-sized notepad, ruled, and always wrote with pencil. She placed the letters in a series of envelopes of graduated sizes, enclosing and sealing each letter as many as three times. Usually she addressed the innermost envelope to "Dean Renwick" so if a curious person went that far, it would give the impression that the purpose was to write someone else in Harding's care, the letter not meant for him personally. His own letters often were blue, of very tough fiber but not weighty. He often wrote them in the Senate during the conduct of official business. Nearly every Sunday morning she received a special-delivery letter, for which her landlady usually signed. "What glorious awakenings those

Sunday morning letters used to bring!" On Harding's side he had a drawer in his desk in the Senate office that he always kept locked, and he instructed his private secretary to destroy the contents if anything happened to him.

But, alas, the letters were all destroyed by their recipients. When Harding's purported friend was en route to Europe in the summer of 1923 she remembered reading the president's last letter as she stood at the rail of the deck, and after rereading the letter she tore it up. "I read it over slowly, then kissed it and tore it into bits. I tossed the bits out upon the billowing waves and watched the little white floating pieces as our boat sped along."[17]

The letters, the surviving correspondent remembered, were intimate and contained many "heart-revealments," and the correspondents hesitated to entrust them to the mails, and during the presidency sent them through intermediaries, one of them being a member of the Secret Service whom Ms. Britton in her books described as Tim Slade. After she visited Washington one time they decided that she should send her letters to the president's valet, Brooks. Slade she identified many years later, long after he had died. Brooks died in 1926.

Governor Reily's correspondent, Gibbs, who when working with Senator Harding saw him daily and opened his mail, never saw a letter from Ms. Britton and, as mentioned, never heard of her.

The White House mail was something else, and in that regard some of her letters did turn up, but in quite a different way from what she wrote in her book. In *The President's Daughter* she was troubled that she had lost a letter sent to Harding during his presidential term and said she explained to her friend Slade how she had addressed it and enclosed many snapshots of Elizabeth Ann and some of herself with the president's daughter. This was a strange happenstance and many years later received an explanation. When Slade was speaking with Elizabeth Ann's mother about the lost letter, according to her, he remarked that at the beginning of the administration he helped the president's private secretary, Christian, learn how the presidential office functioned, and at the outset someone else opened all of the president's mail. That "someone else" undoubtedly was the man in charge of the White House mail room, Ira R. T. Smith, an old-timer who started in the McKinley administration. Upon retirement in the Truman administration he moved to Santa Barbara and there cooperated with a professional writer to produce a book of his experiences.

Ira Smith remembered many humorous events in and about the mail room, but one matter he remembered as altogether unamusing: the reception of not a single Nan Britton letter but three of them. One morning, he recalled, not long after Harding became president, he was going through a huge accumulation of mail and came on a long envelope addressed to the nation's chief executive in slanting, feminine handwriting. "That envelope, I suppose, was one of the most explosive of the millions that I opened and read at the White House." It was postmarked New York, and although it had been written—as the postmark showed—before Harding was inaugurated, there had been such a backlog that

Smith did not get to it for weeks. The envelope had a long sheet that he glanced at hastily. Then he stopped and began reading carefully. The letter said that the writer was again appealing to Mr. Harding to do what the by then president had promised. It referred to earlier letters written him "and it made one thing very clear: The writer was calling upon the President to acknowledge that he was the father of her infant daughter. The letter was signed by Nan Britton."

The first letter, if Smith recalled it correctly, said that Ms. Britton was not only blackmailing the president but also all her claims in her books of seeing Harding during the presidency were imaginary because the blackmailing had started well before the presidency. It was of course possible that the writer of the letter that Smith was looking at had enjoyed a liaison with Harding, but it was also possible that she had never seen him and was only attempting to obtain money.

Smith in his narrative said he let the letter cool on his desk while he decided what to do and then took it around to Christian. "I think you'd better see this one, Mr. Christian," he said.

Christian read it through and became "a bit white" around the lips. "My God!" he exclaimed. "If the President finds out we opened this he will fire both of us!"

Knowing Harding's temper, Smith thought the comment an understatement. They both looked at the letter again and noted the slant upward toward the right-hand side of the page, the language indicating the contents perhaps had been dictated to or copied by the writer. "It was threatening, but stilted."

Christian hesitated a little and then tore the letter into strips, tore them again, and deposited them in a wastebasket. The two looked at each other silently and returned to their desks.

Two weeks after Christian tore up the Britton letter another similar letter arrived for the president. This time Smith did not even open it but tore it up and put it in the wastebasket. A third letter he treated the same way.

Years later he met Christian at a small White House ceremony during the Truman administration. Christian had gone blind but at once recognized Smith's voice and said, "Remember, Ira, when we tore up the President's letter?"

"I remember," Smith said. "You tore up the first one."

"Yes," Christian said, smiling, "I did. Good thing, too."[18]

No one thus saw any letters, save blackmail letters, and this fact raises what might have been Ms. Britton's purpose from the beginning—that having had an illegitimate daughter she obtained the idea of profiting financially from the experience, and the first way she thought of was to write letters to the man with whom she had a slight acquaintance when she was a schoolgirl. It is difficult to believe that the letters she claimed to have had from Harding ever existed. Her Victorian explanation of tearing up letters, because Harding asked her to, might not have been true. If she was concerned about money, and her two books so indicate, the thought could have occurred very early in a possible affair that a single letter containing heart-revealments, in her possession, would have constituted an insurance policy, making possible whatever she might ask of so prominent an American politician as Warren Harding.

Her statement that she did what she did for Elizabeth Ann was not altogether convincing. She had an arrangement for her daughter that was workable if awkward; her sister and brother-in-law had adopted the child. The mother wrote that she could not afford to keep the child, which forced her to ask the Hardings for money, but it was not absolutely necessary, save for a desire to have the child in New York.

Her campaign, for such it was, for recognition of the property right of her child did nothing for Harding's reputation. Perhaps the latter was dropping anyway because of *Revelry* and *The Strange Death of President Harding,* and the revelations of the administration scandals such as Teapot Dome, but her books did it great harm. This to the man with whom she said in her books she was deeply and irrevocably in love.

The stress of *The President's Daughter* on the need for a financial settlement seemed to say that her purpose was to obtain it any way she could. The introduction of that theme was artful, opened in terms of a settlement that the president intended. She hedged the issue by relating that the two of them were too busy making love to think of the details. Her account of Harding's generosity, if true, showed a marked admiration for what money might secure—child care for the Willitses, study abroad for Scott Willits, her trip to France—the latter at a time when trips abroad by the average American were quite unusual, for in the 1920s only comfortably fixed Americans could afford such travel.

The manner in which she presented her problem to the Harding family was almost crude, as crude as it might have been embarrassing. She appears to have used her high school friendship with Daisy Harding to confess to her former teacher that she had borne the president's daughter and commit the teacher to a virtual admission of the possibility by receiving money from her. If the sums Nan Britton listed were true, the president's sister gave more money than she, still a teacher and living in modest circumstances with her father, could afford. Then began the push for a meeting with Dr. Harding, Daisy's brother, to a point where, Nan wrote, Ms. Harding provided the money for her to visit Marion.[19] The sister must have felt that she had no other recourse. "How many people know this, Nan?" she asked. The former student told the president's sister that the Willitses knew, as did the Secret Service man Tim Slade.[20]

In relating how she sought money from the Hardings, the mother of Elizabeth Ann hesitated at nothing, even though it would hurt the reputation of the late president. From her narrative it might have appeared that she knew intimate details of the Harding estate, for she wrote that Daisy Harding mentioned her dead brother's debt of $90,000 due a brokerage firm for stocks the president had received but had not yet paid for. The firm, she related, had sued the estate, and the Harding lawyers settled for $40,000. This story, which was making the rounds in the 1920s, may not have been true. William Allen White told another story to Samuel Hopkins Adams in 1939: "Did you know that he was in the market up to his ears when he died and that they had to charge off a large sum, something comparable to $100,000, when he died? Nicholas Murray Butler told me that. He told it to a luncheon table full of editors so it's no secret. This Wall Street story could be obtained from a half-dozen quarters."[21] Butler, president of Columbia University, was an inveterate gossip, and White should not have retailed the account. For Ms. Britton the alleged indebtedness, however incurred, made her case with the Hardings appear more reasonable. She related that Dr. Harding and Daisy, and presumably Caroline Harding Votaw and Charity Harding Remsberg, had added the indebtedness to her own requirement of $52,500, and thought the result, if subtracted from the estate, too much.

After the unsatisfactory meeting with Dr. Harding she threatened the president's sister in a thinly veiled proposition that if "the matter" could not be settled in a reasonable time by the Hardings she intended to approach Slade in Washington, who by this time had left the Secret Service and become a broker, and that Slade had volunteered to raise a fund from "the anticipated generosity of Mr. Harding's closest friends."

"Why, Nan!" exclaimed Ms. Harding amazedly, "you would not approach *strangers,* would you?"

"I would do *any*thing to obtain fair treatment for Elizabeth Ann!"[22]

After she returned to New York, Daisy Harding wrote her that "your claim is one that any woman can make and get away with to a certain extent, and while it isn't, it might look like a complete case of blackmail."[23]

That spring of 1926, Nan Britton received a little more money from her former teacher, $125 in addition to the $685 she already had received, and with it came advice that she did not relish. The president's sister suggested that she move into the New York suburbs where it would be cheaper to live, though it would "necessitate your rising a little earlier." There followed the "astounding suggestion" that if she could not find a cheaper place to live she might better send Elizabeth Ann, then staying with her, to Grandmother Willits's farm in Illinois, which would have the attendant advantage of being in the country. Ms. Britton was outraged. "As though the mother of Warren Harding's child should have nothing to say, should acquiescently ship his daughter to people who were not relatives, simply because she would find there a welcome for her!"

Soon afterward Daisy Harding drew back from trying to assist Nan. The mother of Elizabeth Ann noticed that her former teacher, who by this time had married, signed the above-mentioned letter, "Hastily, A.V.H. Lewis." This was not the usual affectionate ending, "Lovingly."[24] In mid-June, Daisy sent another $40, signing her name as "Lewis." On July 2 another $40 was sent, without an accompanying note. At Christmastime a cashier's check came from Daisy, enclosed in an envelope with a formal Christmas card. Ms. Britton said she put the card and check away and kept them, never cashing the check. After her book came out she displayed the check to reporters.

What was evident was that the dead president's brother saw danger in his sister's giving money, and anyway she had sent all she could. Moreover, the demands were escalating. Dr. Harding sensed immediately the danger in any settlement with Nan, for it could not be permanent, only a prelude to requests for more. Correspondence with Daisy Harding was taking on the brittleness, the evidence of being dictated, that Ira Smith noticed in the letters that came into the White House mail room early in the Harding administration. Ms. Britton wrote Ms. Harding that "Now, without wasting any more time in explanations, I want to say that I am not at all unconscious of the fact that any publicity in connection with this would reflect upon the character and reputation of Mr. Harding. . . . Nevertheless, there are possibilities of its becoming an international scandal—and I am sure you will agree that we none of us want that." To Caroline Votaw and her husband, Heber, in Washington, where Votaw was president of the boards of parole and the superintendent of federal prisons, she wrote more sharply, with an edge to her words. She had offered to come to Washington, and the Votaws had refused to see her. "I shall expect to see one of you or both of you very soon. . . . If I do not hear from you to this effect, I shall proceed to go about in other ways to justify Elizabeth Ann's claim to being cared for by her father's people. . . . I shall certainly tolerate no conduct on your part which smacks of being ignored by you."[25]

In June 1926 she asked her sister Elizabeth and Elizabeth's husband, who were visiting, to take back Elizabeth Ann. She could not meet her rent and was asked to vacate her apartment, and gave it up for a single room and bath.

Lacking all proof of her claim upon the Hardings, and after attempting to face the family down, with some small success with Daisy Harding Lewis but none with Dr. Harding and his other sisters, she had failed with representations. She had threatened to solicit money from a group of Harding's close friends, but the Secret Service agent Slade may not have had sufficient acquaintance with them. This left what her employer at the Bible Corporation, a literary man, must have seen from the outset as the possibility of publication. The appearance in November 1926 of *Revelry*, a huge publishing success, may itself have been decisive.

And here, in the way in which Nan Britton and Wightman organized the Elizabeth Ann Guild and the Elizabeth Ann League, readers of the subsequent books might have raised further questions. The meetings in New York and Washington, the lack of love letters, representations that were becoming edgy, could have led to questions about the financing of these organizations.

The guild was the working organization for publication of *The President's Daughter*. A writer for the *New York Daily News*, John O'Donnell, on November 2, 1927, revealed that not merely Ms. Britton and Wightman were incorporators of the guild but also two other individuals. One was Robert M. Werblow of the Polygraphic Company of America, which made the plates for the book. With his brother, Henry, Werblow was sentenced in 1924 to serve from five to ten years in Sing Sing for having defrauded the Guaranty Trust Company and the Asia Banking Corporation of $139,000. They were released the next year after a court of appeals decided that the courts of New York had no jurisdiction, because while preparations for the crime were made in New York the criminal act itself was committed in London. Another incorporator of the guild was Richard Sears whose address was the Hotel Shelton. He was the former manager of the guild who with the guild's attorney, Harding Rogers, moved to declare the guild bankrupt. According to O'Donnell, Sears had engaged in promotion and stock selling, principally oil stocks. A man named Joseph Taylor, alias Young, described as New York's original daylight robber, with a record of three convictions and who was facing a life-sentence prison term at the time, said he was asked to join the group. "I've been a bandit and seen some mighty rough rackets," Young declared. "But after I understood the whole plan, I decided it would be safer for me to pass it up."

According to the O'Donnell story, Wightman was especially unreliable. Aged sixty in 1927, but looking ten years younger, bland and chubby, with twinkling blue eyes, he had been first a Methodist minister, later a Presbyterian. In 1903 he had resigned his pastorate at the Christ Presbyterian Church in New York. He began selling life insurance by mail. The scheme perished after the investigation into insurance practices in New York State by Charles E. Hughes, and Wightman thereafter wrote advertising copy and promoted organizations to advance the prosperity of such diverse commodities as apple gum, automobiles, movies, fountain pens, altruism, and real estate. In 1918 he married his second wife, his secretary, Patricia Margaret Street, in a ceremony that took place on the grave of Ralph Waldo Emerson in Concord, Massachusetts. Two years afterward the new Mrs. Wightman appeared on the front pages of metropolitan New York newspapers as the highly successful woman miner who went to New Mexico, invested $15,000 (one account said $65,000) in gold mines, and in a year developed the property to a value of $5 million. Wightman at the time was interested in selling stock in the mines. His wife's good fortune happened, she related, because a stranger, who turned out to be a New Mexican miner, stopped her husband in the Hotel Manhattan and congratulated him on his writings (he had published two inspirational books and a volume of poetry).

In a sworn statement one of the former employees of the guild, Earl Hauser Smith, said that he had worked with Ms. Britton and Wightman for months in the preparation of The President's Daughter. The rough outline had been mapped in Wightman's house in Saybrook, Connecticut. Wightman wrote the book. "There could never be any doubt in my mind as to who wrote The President's Daughter," Smith insisted. "Day after day during last April and May, while I was employed in the offices of the Elizabeth Ann Guild, Wightman was there closeted with Miss Britton." Smith alleged that he could recognize Wightman's writing anywhere, "just as I do in this book. He makes a peculiarly distinctive use of alliteration and coining compound words. He wrote remarkable advertising copy with his word and phrase wizardry in the national advertising agency where I was employed for years as art director." Smith pointed out that an epigraph in the book's front matter, "There is no such thing as concealment," was by Emerson. He remarked hyphenations, such as "love-child," and might have added "love-union," "convenience-father," "fact-story," "man-smell," "life-issues," "woman-change" (concerning Daisy Harding), and "health-time," and odd words such as "vicissitudinous," "disconcertion," "growingly," "conspicuity," "wroth," and other expressions usually not seen in the work of a beginning author such as "severalth time," "mental pandemonium," and "cynosure of the whole world."

As if to corroborate Smith's story, Patricia Wightman early in 1928 became the subject of articles in the New York press, typified by a caption in the *New York World* of March 3, "Nan Britton Book Spur in Wife's Suit—Harding Story Written by Her Husband, Mrs. Wightman Charges in Separation Action." Mrs. Wightman named the author of *The President's Daughter* in state supreme court as the principal cause for filing her suit. She said her husband had written the Britton book. "I feel I have the right," she said, "to oppose my husband's association with a woman of the admitted character of Nan Britton." She said her husband had been living in New York at the Hotel Shelton and had not been in Saybrook nor had she seen him since the previous August 12 and that she knew him to be constantly in Ms. Britton's company. In December 1926, she said, she read thirty-two pages of the manuscript and stopped, disgusted with not only the nature but also the literary style of the story. She urged her husband to have nothing to do with it because of its scandalous nature, but he had paid no attention. He feared Ms. Britton would quit him and engage another writer, so brought her to the Wightman house and maintained her there. She said that in addition to royalties her husband was receiving $175 a week as an officer of the Elizabeth Ann Guild. She asked to receive $500 weekly as a settlement.

Ms. Britton's book published in 1932 completely rejected the idea that Wightman wrote her book. Patricia Wightman, she said, had given signs of a spirit of hostility and irritability when Nan had been staying at the Wightmans' house. When her sister in Chicago sent a negligee and she mentioned to Mrs. Wightman that she wished she could give it to her, the answer was, "I only wanted to wear it when we go to the Riviera!" Both Wightmans were concerned about what was going into the book, but Patricia Wightman objected more. "Lots of things are true that we don't tell the public," the wife had interposed.[26] In regard to the action naming her as corespondent in the suit for separation, Ms. Britton had felt that her business manager needed to respond, and she was obviously unhappy with the time, more than a month, it took him to compose an affidavit of denial, which she immediately sent in facsimile to newspapers and national press associations, most of which gave it no notice. She wrote that she already had decided, the previous month, to dismiss him as her business manager.

Once written and published, *The President's Daughter* sold handsomely. It went on sale in the summer of 1927 and by November had sold more than 42,000 copies. By April of the next year sales were approaching 75,000. Its author said in her second book when she was relating that the book sold from New Zealand to Syria, the Philippines to Alaska, that sales by July 1931 were more than 110,000. The price was $5, very high for a time when books were selling for $2 or $2.50. Because of the book's notoriety, advertising was unnecessary; what the author said was a disadvantage was just the opposite. Because many bookstores would not stock the book, purchasers bought copies directly from the guild offices, and so it was not necessary to pay bookstore discounts—the guild kept the face price of each book it sold.

Ms. Britton's only serious regret about the book was that it was not made into a motion picture. She was sure the reason was the head of the Motion Picture Producers and Distributors of America, Will H. Hays, who before taking on the task of "cleaning up" the movies had been chairman of the Republican National Committee and Harding's postmaster general. For his perhaps dual reasoning in preventing *The President's Daughter* from being made into a movie, Hays earned her contempt. She ruefully remembered his movie-sized salary of $150,000 per year. She recalled the remark of the newspaper columnist O. O. McIntyre, who wrote of the film industry: "Hays has cleaned it up." She thought one should remove the "it."[27]

The reporter O'Donnell estimated in November 1927 that the guild's incorporators had netted $250,000 on the sale of 75,000 books. Ms. Britton's figures for sales did not reach that number until mid-April of the next year. She did not say where the money went, but she and Wightman each received in royalties (so Mrs. Wightman said in her separation suit) 45¢ per book, or by 1931 about $50,000 apiece. This in addition to salaries they took from their posts as president and business manager, respectively, of the guild. The other incorporators—Robert Werblow and Sears—too would have been paid. The delegate to the national convention in 1920, Hopkins, according to O'Donnell, put up $10,000 and would have doubled his money.[28]

The staff of the guild was a real question mark. Ms. Britton and Wightman made errors in choosing staff members—the guild's lawyer, the employee who tried to sell galley proof—and errors cost money. But the guild had too many employees for the (in those days) wondrously inexpensive task of publishing a book, and the incorporators might have offset their personnel errors this way. The guild's employees, apart from the league's typists (for which, see below), numbered thirteen in early 1928, and not merely an elevator operator and an office boy but a lawyer, an accountant, a publicity director, and others. Wightman placed his friends in the guild and according to his partner showed inattention to the work of his appointees. The author on her part employed her younger sister, Jeannette. Some of them, perhaps Jeannette, may have worked, but it is possible that most of them were ghost employees, their duties suitable for the telling in books, their function being the drawing of salaries that passed to the guild's two principal officers and the other incorporators.

The money that went into league work, almost all of which came from the guild from book sales, was surprisingly small, amounting to $12,000 in the years 1927–1931, according to Ms. Britton. In the first months when correspondence from unwed mothers poured in with requests for assistance, it was necessary to answer this correspondence, and five people were on the guild payroll doing league work. By May 1928 this clerical staff was down to two. This meant that the ultimate purpose of publishing *The President's Daughter,* which was to assist in raising the legal position of illegitimate children, received little more attention than to write letters. Had Ms. Britton wished to help the mothers of these children she might have spent much more money on the task. There was much to be done in this benighted era when unwed mothers were hustled off to abortionists or treated in their pregnancies like pariahs, when the Comstockery that she herself protested was in full course. Ms. Britton gave this deplorable scene only the slightest attention. O'Donnell disclosed that whereas in 1927 the guild had a bank account of nearly $50,000, the league's account was less than $500. In an interview at this time Ms. Britton said, "Of course, my chief interest in life is the success of the league and I shall undoubtedly make a contribution to it after my child is cared for." She intended to establish a trust fund for Elizabeth Ann. "After that is done I can use some of my money for the league."[29]

At about the time that O'Donnell of the *New York Daily News* was writing critically of the organization of both the guild and the league, a problem appeared in the choice of Margaret E. Rogers as one of six incorporators of the league. She was the wife of the attorney who had turned against the guild. She was visited by agents of the Children's Society who relieved her of her five children, two of whom were illegitimate. None of the children, whose ages ranged from three to fourteen, had attended school during the last four years. Her husband in an affidavit filed in children's court had complained that his wife had developed an attachment for a delicatessen clerk and also habits of intoxication. According to Rogers, the clerk made his home in the family apartment. Upon visiting the apartment, Children's Society agents found such a person there.[30]

3 ———

In the years after Nan Britton published *The President's Daughter* she did her best to support her statements of her relationship with the late president, and on three occasions there were inquiries into them. The first she encouraged in a lawsuit that came to trial in Toledo in 1931, this being *Britton v. Klunk*. In this instance nothing turned up to support her claim against the Harding estate.

The Toledo court case had its origin in a book published in Marion in 1928 by Dr. Joseph De Barthe, titled *The Answer*. Its author had been a resident of Marion for twenty years and was known there as a physician who had discovered a special "glandular treatment." At the time he wrote *The Answer* he was not well known beyond Marion, and the *American Medical Directory* for the years 1906 to 1927 does not contain his name. That fact may not mean much, for he could have become a physician earlier when almost anyone could practice the medical arts. Until the 1890s in Ohio (and doubtless other states had similar arrangements), all that was necessary to obtain a medical license was to register with the nearest probate court. De Barthe, it should be added, was an author of note, having written several books. As a young newspaperman in the American West he published the memories of a frontiersman named Frank Grouard, which became a western classic. The book was reprinted by the University of Oklahoma Press in 1958.[31]

As one might have suspected of an author with a western background, *The Answer*, being an attack on a book that the author did not like, was not freighted with an excess of diplomacy. De Barthe did not mention Ms. Britton by name, but referred to her as the Complaining Witness. Withal, the descriptions of her were probably libelous. On page 25 of the book he stated flatly, "An aggregation of sex perverts have been permitted to attack the reputation of the foremost citizen of the Republic in an attempt to impugn his motives and assassinate his character." He said the deed of villainy was "one of the most outrageous and flagrant scandals in existence and a criminal libel without parallel in our times." He wrote darkly of a great authority on the subject with which he was dealing, author of a book titled *Psychopathia Sexualis*, Richard von Krafft-Ebing, a German neurologist who lived from 1840 to 1902, who placed "all those suffering from abnormal mental manifestations in the category of degenerates." These words out of the way, the Marion author said he could cite "many instances from this book of the Complaining Witness to prove absolutely the degeneracy of the Complaining Witness were I so disposed." This was on page 33. Warming up, the physician-author announced on page 41, "The book which this author refers to as that of the Complaining Witness is so palpably criminally libelous and untruthful that no jury sitting on the matter should hesitate a moment in sending a verdict that would mean state prison to the perpetrators of it . . ." On page 173 stood another libel: "Would a normal flesh and blood mother cast the pestilence of a bawdy house upon her innocent offspring to gain her own financial independence?"

De Barthe on page 219 asked his readers what Harding would have thought, even in his present state. "Denied man's inalienable right of self-defense, I cannot but think that, if the marble sarcophagus wherein he lies was opened to our vision we should find implanted on that cold dead face a look of pitying incredulity . . ."

What may have counted more than a few critical words was the book's principal point, that *The President's Daughter* was an invention because Harding was incapable of being the father of a child—that he was, De Barthe asserted, sterile. De Barthe did not say where he learned this, but it may have been from the president's brother, Dr. Harding. Years later the biographer Downes learned that one of the president's physician nephews (there were three of them), Warren G. Harding II, possessed medical proof that the president was sterile.[32] He also could have heard this from Mont Reily, whose unpublished memoir related a conversation with Harding in 1920, just before the nomination, when Harding stayed with the Reilys in Kansas City for several days. Reily took him for an automobile ride, through one of the city's parks, and the two were talking about children and families "and he said something to me that I have never forgotten, and never shall." They were both sitting in the front seat, riding along, and he said,

> Reily, I have had a great sorrow in my life that the world usually doesn't know about, and it is this: I have never had any children. I have never been able to be the father of children, and no human in the world is as crazy about little folks as am I. I used to say to my wife in the long winter nights that I believed I would be the happiest man on earth if I had half a dozen little ones playing around my knee. But God ordered it otherwise.[33]

There might have been more to De Barthe's accusation than appeared on the face of it, for Reily after reading *The President's Daughter* felt certain that the author had gone to Marion in 1926 to meet Dr. Harding in part to discover what the president's brother knew about the sterility issue—for if the brother knew about it and was prepared to talk about it publicly, the book would have been baseless, unbelievable. Reily suspected its author scented this possibility from some source and needed to see how far she could go. She did inquire if the brother knew of a "particular physical trouble" the president had in early life. The brother refused to discuss the matter. Reily doubtless was thinking of mumps. Ms. Britton in her second book expressed her sorrow that she had not named the physical trouble in *The President's Daughter* and said she was not talking about sterility. It is possible that she had heard from some Marion friend, what was true enough, that the president suffered severely from hemorrhoids.[34]

Something had to be done about De Barthe's book, and Ms. Britton brought suit against the owner of the Hotel Marion, Charles A. Klunk, who had backed the book's publication, paid for its printing, and sold copies from a hotel newsstand. De Barthe had died in 1928. His antagonist delightedly informed readers of her second book that he had been intoxicated and fallen down a flight of stairs at the Hotel Marion, in which he was residing.

The suit was filed in December 1928 and did not come to trial until October 1931, in part because of the normal time lag between entering of a suit and trial but also because Ms. Britton's attorneys agreed with Klunk's attorneys that since President Hoover and former president Coolidge were to dedicate the Harding Memorial in Marion in May 1931, it would be wise to wait until after the dedication before scheduling such a trial.

The delay in bringing *Britton v. Klunk* to trial did not prevent Ms. Britton, shortly before the trial, from giving an interview to the *New York World Telegram*. The reporter evidently had asked if the childhood of Elizabeth Ann had been happy, and Ms. Britton answered that it had, with exception of an experience in Sunday school. A few old ladies at the school did not know what to do with the child. They were old-school people, like her own mother, who never felt it was right for her to acknowledge Elizabeth Ann's illegitimacy. Ms. Britton took the child away and gave her Bible lessons herself. The reporter asked the author of *The President's Daughter* if she would wish Elizabeth Ann to repeat her own experience and become an unmarried mother. Ms. Britton thought a moment and said: "It's a hard question to answer. I'm a rather conventional person myself, but I shouldn't want her to miss the love that comes only once in a lifetime. If she should do anything like that I believe she has enough inherited mentality to safeguard herself against doubt. I have a streak of courage myself. Perhaps some people might call it nerve, and I don't think my child will ever be slighted by anyone."[35]

At last, on Tuesday, October 7, 1931, *Britton v. Klunk* came to trial in federal district court in Toledo, John M. Killits presiding. It was a $50,000 suit against Klunk. Ms. Britton employed a Cleveland attorney, William Fish Marsteller, grandson of Cassius M. Clay, the famous Kentuckian. Klunk's principal attorney was Judge Grant E. Mouser Sr. of Marion, a one-time congressman and common pleas judge.

The proceedings in the courtroom should have been interesting, considering their subject, but unfortunately it is not possible to discover much about what happened. No stenographic record survived. In the case files presently in the Chicago branch of the National Archives there is evidence that a record was taken and transcribed. Probably Judge Killits kept it until he finished with the case—after it ended Marsteller moved for a retrial—and then somehow the record was lost, with the possibility that Killits destroyed it, because during the trial it was clear he considered the subject of the case lewd and degrading. The other reason it is impossible to discover much about what happened was that Killits was concerned for order in the courtroom and took measures that soon closed the trial to newspaper reporters until near its end. This problem began in a small way when the trial opened, for not merely Nan Britton but also Elizabeth Ann was in attendance. The twelve year old sometimes sat with her mother, the two fondling and kissing each other, or skipped around the courtroom telling anyone who would listen that she was "Elizabeth Ann, the president's daughter." After a day of this, Killits made it known that he did not want her in the courtroom. All the while there was another problem: the presence of high school girls who, Killits learned, were attending the trial, and on Friday, October 30, he barred anyone from the courtroom under the age of twenty-one, promising to hold violators of the order in contempt. "I can't believe that, despite the demoralizing features of our modern civilization," he said, "all the old-fashioned ideas of decency and self-respect are extinct."[36] The following Monday he closed the courtroom to all spectators. The courtroom was so crowded, the judge said, that the air became foul and it was difficult to get inside the room. Then, too, when people came to court only because of the filthy, lascivious, and wholly indecent testimony, and this had a bad effect on young people whose minds were still plastic, the court had the right to exclude everyone. Killits was thorough, excluding even the bailiff, doing so with some humor; he said the bailiff's absence would make little difference, because the bailiff was deaf. But closure otherwise made a difference because among other auditors he excluded reporters who thereafter could only mill around outside and try to learn what they could from participants. In the event they seemed not to have found out much, or may not have tried, and newspaper stories quickly thinned out.

From reading what remains of the court file it nonetheless is possible to discover the outlines of what went on in the courtroom, and here one of the more interesting developments was presentation by the plaintiff's lawyer, Marsteller, of two registers from the Hotel Imperial in New York, for July 30 and 31, 1917. In her book Nan Britton had written that on July 30 she and Senator Harding registered in a New York hotel.

> On July 30th, 1917, Mr. Harding came again to New York. He decided we could safely go to a hotel where friends of his in Washington had intimated to him that they had stopped under similar unconventional circumstances with no unpleasant consequences. This was on Broadway in the thirties. I remember so well I wore a pink linen dress which was rather short and enhanced the little-girl look which was often my despair. I waited in the waiting room while Mr. Harding registered. . . . The day was exceedingly warm and we were glad to see that the room which had been assigned to us had two large windows. The boy threw them open for us and left. The room faced Broadway, but we were high enough not to be bothered by street noises. We were quite alone. I became Mr. Harding's bride—as he called me—on that day.

Not long thereafter the couple was disturbed by the entrance of two hotel detectives, who gruffly asked the business of the occupants. The detectives withdrew upon learning that a United States senator had taken the room, because it was unlawful to detain a senator en route to Washington to serve the people. "We packed our things immediately and the men conducted us to the side entrance. On the way out Mr. Harding handed one of them a $20 bill. When we were in the taxi, he remarked explosively, 'Gee, Nan, I thought I wouldn't get out of that under $1000!' "[37] Hence Marsteller's submission to the court, which accepted the documents in secret session, of photostats of the two registers. Word of this submission was reported in the newspapers, but no details were divulged.

The documents, now in the files in Chicago, do not show the names of Harding or his alleged friend. They are thus inconclusive. In her book, Nan Britton wrote that she thought Harding registered the two of them under a pseudonym, which would have been likely. She thought he used the name of "Hardwick" or possibly "Warwick." There is no such name. There is a signature of "G. H. Harvey & wife Cleveland." The manuscript curator of the Ohio Historical Society at the time of accession of the Harding Papers in 1963, Kenneth W. Duckett, believes the handwriting is that of "the old philanderer himself." To the present writer's eye, the hand is not that of Harding. Daniel R. Weinberg of the Abraham Lincoln Book Shop and Gallery in Chicago, who was consulted on this matter, attests that "It seems to me that you are correct. The 'Harvey' on the register is close to that of Harding, but no cigar." Duckett suggested resorting to a Cleveland city directory for 1917 to determine if "G. H. Harvey" was a fictitious name. The Cleveland directory lists a "George A. Harvey," not a "G. H." George A. was a partner of Harvey Bros., dealing in real estate, leaseholds, building, and insurance, with offices in Cleveland's well-known (it is a remarkable building, yet standing) Arcade. Harding, checking in, might have signed the name of a friend, this Harvey, and given the wrong middle initial. Or as the alert reference supervisor of the Western Reserve Historical Society in Cleveland, Ann K. Sindelar, suggested, "G. H. Harvey & wife" might have lived in a suburb and signed themselves as being from Cleveland. The reader must judge from the present book's inclusion of the register page and, for comparison, a holograph Harding letter.[38]

One might ask why Marsteller submitted registers not containing Senator Harding's name. The registers supported the defense, not the plaintiff. Why did he not check them out first by privately approaching the Imperial's manager, Bryntav H. Brobst? It is possible that Marsteller was bluffing his antagonist, Judge Mouser. He took depositions not merely from Brobst but from the manager of New York's Columbus Circle Hotel, from whom he asked for registers for the entire period of a year beginning August 1, 1917. The Columbus Circle Hotel's manager, incidentally, gave an affidavit that his company destroyed its registers every three years. But the date when Marsteller, who perhaps was a bluffer (Judge Killits, who did not like him, thought him so), took the depositions was March 10, 1931, not long before dedication of the Harding Memorial, and could not Marsteller have been attempting to scare Mouser by making it appear he "had the goods" on the judge's client? More than that, he could embarrass all the residents of Marion who were on tenterhooks in anticipation of a presidential visit; nothing like that had been seen in the past eight years, since Coolidge's arrival for Harding's funeral. The very request for the registers could have moved Mouser to settle the suit. Even if only word of the request had gotten out, which for some reason it did not, it would have assisted his case.

If obtaining the registers was a ploy it failed, and when the case at last came to trial the plaintiff's lawyer could do little other than offer his client's book in evidence. Judge Killits allowed parts of the book to be read in court. The author asked to testify, but Killits refused, for he believed the book sufficed and that she would only repeat her allegations. The judge allowed her sister, present from Chicago because she was keeping Elizabeth Ann after the child's exclusion from the courtroom, to take the stand, but gave her only five minutes; what she said is unknown because of disappearance of any stenographic record.

The defense sought to make its case, as one of Klunk's lawyers, Donald D. Melhorn, told the jury, on only two points: whether the statements in *The President's Daughter* were true and whether the plaintiff had a fifty-thousand-dollar reputation in June 1928 when *The Answer* was published. The former was not provable. In regard to the latter, Judge Mouser called sixteen witnesses from Marion, including Dr. Carl Sawyer and Mildred Christian Roberts, sister of the late president's private secretary. Three high school friends of the plaintiff testified that they had heard nothing of her character until after publication of her book, which was quite generally read in Marion. William R. Martin (municipal judge of Marion), W. T. Jones (a contractor), and Edna Dutton (society editor of the *Star*) testified, and all said that after publication of *The President's Daughter* Ms. Britton's reputation was "bad."[39] Mary Catherine Hane testified that in high school Ms. Britton's reputation was not good, as a story was whispered that she had gone bathing in the nude. The witness did not say where this happened or whether the accused was alone or with other girls or whether boys were there. The witness admitted the story was purely gossip.[40]

While the witnesses from Marion testified to Ms. Britton's qualities, the subject of their concern sat quietly in court, attired in a flowing white blouse, brown knitted skirt, and a brown caracal wrap, set off with a small turban of the same color scheme.

In the final summations on Wednesday, November 4, it is not fully known what Marsteller said, though contrary to the original suit he said of the plaintiff that "She is in this lawsuit solely for vindication and for no money," and again, "I have stated to you that we are here not for money. . . . I pray to you that you bring in a verdict for the plaintiff . . . and give her vindication on that [the charges] and one cent would make her absolutely satisfied."[41] He compared her book to the Bible. The latter had been written to point out right from wrong. Her story had a similar intention.

A copy of Judge Mouser's remarks, which he had written out in advance of the occasion, found its way into the Harding Papers, and his remarks were almost as libelous, Judge Killits might have ruled, as had been those of Dr. De Barthe. Mouser told the jurors that during the adolescent period of the plaintiff's life, by testimony of Ms. Britton's mother herself, she had a wild imagination, a tendency to become moody, and a disposition to worship great men. At a tender age the plaintiff had gone to Chicago in poverty and there "drifted into the bright lights and became entangled in the web of things, that only tended to undermine and destroy her character." She exulted in the fact that "she surrendered the most precious jewel to any woman in the world—virginity! . . . And then think of it Ladies and Gentlemen of the jury! the shame of it!—the burning disgrace of it!—to broadcast this damnable fabrication to the ends of the earth." The Answer, the lawyer said, was true, revealing that she had become an adventuress, a designing and heartless woman, a victim of "sex madness." Her ambition was to be "crowned queen of all love-children born out of holy wedlock."[42]

Mouser did not fail to address the most basic of his adversary's purposes, albeit with the same hyperbole he employed for her other interests. He said she had tried to blackmail the Hardings. If she had gone to her relatives and friends in Marion, they would have helped her. "In fact, she proved wholly conscienceless; she had no respect for the holy marital relationship. She was distorted and deranged. She proved criminal to the point of blackmail!"[43]

In his instruction to the jury on Thursday, November 5, Killits backed up Mouser. In an instruction of thirty-nine double-spaced typescript pages he said its members should ask themselves:

> Was there the slightest reason, even to carry out a motive, why she should go into the most minute detail of the transactions which she baldly states were illicit, which she knew at the time were illicit and which she sought in cooperation with her alleged paramour to conceal from the public? . . . But was it necessary, or even expedient, aside from the question of debasing self-revelation, to tell us what she alleges a senator of the United States of America did in a sleeping car berth from Connersville, Indiana, to Chicago; or to intimate that there were effects upon the emotional system of that individual as the result of the non-satisfaction of his sexual desires that night?[44]

The judge went into some other details. "Disagreeable as it is, Ladies and Gentlemen," he advised the jury, "you have to go into these depths; you cannot help yourselves; you must do it."

Killits's instruction appears to have flabbergasted Marsteller, who at one point interrupted. "The court in his charge told the jury," he complained, "that there was no proof of any of the statements, no proof of the truth of any statements set forth in the plaintiff's book."

"Do you dispute that?" asked Killits.

"No, I do not," was the abject response.[45]

With such instruction the jury of ten men and two women went out on Thursday afternoon at 3:10, deliberated an hour, took three ballots, and returned a verdict of "no cause for action." The plaintiff was not in the courtroom when the verdict was returned, as she left for her hotel when the case went to the jury. Few spectators were present.

Two days later Marsteller asked for a retrial and gave fifteen reasons. In arguing against a retrial the defense said that "evidence or further evidence that Nan Britton had sexual relations with Mr. Harding would not prove or disprove any issue in this case, except in so far as it might further show the degeneracy of plaintiff." Killits ruled against a new trial on June 29, 1932, adjudging that "however exalted the motive, the manner of its promotion condemned the plaintiff to suffer . . . just such characterizations as were complained of."[46]

4 ——

Thirty years and more after De Barthe published his book and Nan Britton sued the Hotel Marion's owner who published the book and *Britton v. Klunk* came to trial in 1931, two altogether unpublicized testings of Ms. Britton's contentions took place. These were researches by the historians Randolph Downes and Dean Albertson. Neither of the historians published anything about their efforts to investigate Nan Britton's relationship with the late president of the United States. Downes did publish the first of what he planned to be a two-volume life of Harding. He ended this volume with the election of 1920 and died before finishing the second volume. Albertson too did not write the biography he had hoped to and similarly passed on. Both men left their papers to their respective academic institutions, the University of Toledo and the University of Massachusetts, making it possible for later writers to see what they had managed to find.[47]

Downes was a considerable scholar and writer about American history. Born in Connecticut in 1901, he graduated from Dartmouth College, acquired a master's degree at the University of Wisconsin and a doctorate at Ohio State University, taught for a while at the University of Pittsburgh, and became a member of the faculty at Toledo in 1946, teaching there until retirement in 1971. He died in 1975. A specialist in the history of northwest Ohio, he published thirteen books and several dozen articles. Thin, intense, hard of hearing (which may have made his scholarly tasks easier), pursuing with a vengeance whatever he was investigating, he began his study of Harding in the 1950s, well before the Harding Papers were opened, and sought to spread his net in every possible direction. Nothing pertaining to his subject escaped his attention. Zealous, fearless, honest in his opinions to a point where he related them to anyone who would listen, he was the sort of individual to find out whatever lay behind Nan Britton's story.

In the late 1950s Downes got in touch with Ms. Britton, who was at that time living in Evanston, in a comfortable apartment in a building on a pleasant, tree-shaded street, 488 Sheridan Road, a half block from Lake Michigan. She shared it with a friend, Gertrude G. Davis, with whom under an assumed name she conducted an employment agency in Chicago on the Loop: Davis Personnel. She had moved from New Rochelle to Chicago in 1933 and then later to Evanston. Elizabeth Ann, the pretty child of the Toledo trial who in her many photographs in her mother's books looked the very image of President Harding, had attended Kenwood School, a junior high on the south side of Chicago, Ms. Britton told Downes, and there completed the eighth grade at the time of the Chicago World's Fair. She took honors in her class and won a trophy "and $35 in cash!" She went to Sullivan High School on the far north side in Rogers Park, graduating in 1938. She received a partial scholarship to Lake Forest College, but she did not take it because her mother could not afford the extra expense and also because late in the summer she fell in love.[48] She married the assistant manager of a Chicago office building, Henry E. Blaesing, in September 1938, lived in the Midwest for several years, and thereafter in California. In 1964 when the Harding Papers were opened she identified herself to a Los Angeles reporter. At that time she was living in Glendale and the mother of three young boys. A photographer took her picture, a remarkably pretty woman, smiling pleasantly.

After Downes began corresponding he visited Ms. Britton, and afterward the two wrote back and forth desultorily, with an exchange of perhaps a dozen letters, until 1963, when the correspondence ended. At the outset, in 1959, Ms. Britton welcomed his interest and wrote that she trusted his biography would do Harding the justice too long denied the president, both as an individual and as a statesman. She said that financial assistance of a substantial character from the president, together with documentary and other proofs in her possession, including a written statement from her sister, who had spoken with Harding on behalf of Elizabeth Ann, established his paternity beyond question. Downes seems to have responded with a letter setting out seven points of proof that he would like to have: letters from Harding and carbons or other copies of letters to Harding, evidence that she did write *The President's Daughter*, correspondence, reviews and other commentaries on the book, the "little red book" she had mentioned in *The President's Daughter*, a Harding scrapbook and newspapers she had kept, and a diary she mentioned she had begun. The response to this request was on the stiff side, informing her academic correspondent that she respected his abilities but did not find it necessary for him to go beyond the investigations of people who thirty years earlier had looked into the statements in *The President's Daughter*. These people had had a direct interest in ascertaining whether she had told the truth. She believed he was quite young, perhaps in his twenties (Downes was fifty-eight). Had he been older she said he would not have overlooked the importance of the investigations into the book. She was sixty-three and understood the enthusiasms of young people, but the acknowledged misjudgments of which Downes himself had written (he had confessed that he made statements about her book he now knew were not true) convinced her he never had made himself familiar with her two books. Surely he could not be so naive as to ignore "these recountals."[49] Receiving this admonishment, Downes seems to have pulled back. The correspondence took a more diplomatic turn.

Downes told the *New York Times* reporter R. W. Apple in 1964 that the author of *The President's Daughter* was "charming, dignified and articulate." He said she had promised to provide him with what she described as "proofs" of her relationship with Harding. He was "not at all sure" what the proofs were. "A historian," he explained, "does not always accept as proof what other people do." He nonetheless was convinced, "and I think most authorities on the Harding period are convinced," that her story was true but told Apple he could not tell everything he knew because he was in the midst of his research. The reporter, incidentally, went to Evanston, found the Britton apartment, rang the bell, and was told by a tall woman who opened the door narrowly, and looked very much like the photographs of Nan Britton in her books, that Ms. Britton was not there.[50]

Nan Britton would not have been pleased if she had known that all the while Downes was confessing his error in not believing her books and—his letter has not survived—backtracking from his initial correspondence with her in which he asked for proof of her story, he was conducting an investigation of his own. He tried to identify the man whom Ms. Britton, using a pseudonym, had denominated Tim Slade, the Secret Service man who had been her contact with President Harding and who later, as a broker, she said, took her to luncheons at the Waldorf=Astoria and lent her several hundred dollars before his luck financially seems to have run out. Downes heard from the curator of manuscripts at the New-York Historical Society, Wilmer R. Leech, that the Secret Service detail at the White House included a Jack Slye—the name was close to the pseudonym of Tim Slade, and the other pseudonyms in Ms. Britton's books often bore similarity to real names.[51] The curator knew very little about him. "Perhaps we should have been more explicit. I was acquainted with Jack Slye socially until I left Washington in 1908. Since then had no personal contact with him. Although I knew that he was in the Secret Service of the Treasury Department and eventually assigned to the White House as constant attendant upon President Wilson, then to President Harding." Downes did his best to find records on Slye, for the books mentioned detailed meetings with Slade both in New York and in Chicago and offered dates. He pursued the head of the Secret Service in 1960, U. E. Baughman, with pointed letters. Baughman answered that Slye was deceased, and the service had "no indication that his assignment entailed a relationship with the president other than regular protective duties, and Mr. Slye could not be characterized as the principal agent attending President Harding. . . . Reports of agents in that period relate essentially to work schedules and would not have any historical significance." Downes wrote back that "There are other meetings claimed between Mr. 'Slade' and Miss Britton. These were at certain named times at Washington and Marion, Ohio. However, to know of Mr. Slye's presence in Washington and Marion on those dates would not be overly significant in respect to the veracity of Miss Britton's claims." She claimed to have seen Slade (Slye) at Eagle Bay, New York, in July 1920 and in Chicago late in August or early September 1922. Baughman responded, "We have obtained from National Archives the daily reports of agent John (Jack) Slye for the months of August and September 1922. The reports reveal that he was on duty in Washington during the entire period. It might be mentioned that these reports are very brief, one report listing expenses and travel, if any, for a full month. There was no report for Agent Slye for the month of July 1920."[52]

A sidelight on Downes's investigation of Slade, not necessarily contradictory, is a remark in the memoir of Colonel Starling that not long after Harding became president, one of the president's friends approached Starling and asked him to act "as a go-between for some correspondence with a certain young lady, unnamed, in New York." The colonel declined, saying it was not his job and a private matter the president would have to handle himself. Later he understood that one of the other members of the detail accepted the assignment and on one occasion brought the young woman to the White House for a brief meeting with the president. Starling assumed the woman was Nan Britton. But he was certain that Harding could not have had an affair while in the White House as he was constantly under surveillance. "His acts are things to which I can swear." He said Harding was the kindest man he ever knew, and intimated it was possible that the president was attempting only to hear her story.[53] That might have happened. After all, Ira Smith and George Christian Jr. between them had torn up three blackmail letters.

There was one other respect in regard to Nan Britton's story that the indefatigable Downes sought to check out. In *Honesty or Politics*, on pages 245–49, the author had written about a Mr. Kenyon and a Mr. Smith of the New York post office who, she said, interviewed her and her lawyer on December 8, 1927. She wrote that they took many notes and presumably made a report. Actually the investigation was not against Ms. Britton's book, as one might have suspected, but against the Elizabeth Ann League. Each copy of the book contained a pamphlet, slipped under the cover, soliciting funds for the league. The postal investigators, according to Ms. Britton, not merely took her testimony but also looked into letters she had deposited in the Irving-Bank Columbia Trust Company in New York. Downes wrote the New York postmaster, who responded on May 13, 1960, that records for 1927 had long since been discarded. He wrote the National Archives, and archivist Meyer H. Fishbein responded on May 31, 1960, that postal records at the archives did not contain correspondence and reports of the New York post office for 1927 and that he was referring Downes's letter to the Post Office Department. The department's librarian, Xenophon P. Smith, responded on June 14 that "No records concerning this matter have been located here after an exhaustive search" and recommended a letter to H. B. Montague, inspector, U.S. post office building, New York.[54] Hence Downes took this second testimony from one of Ms. Britton's books, an important piece of evidence if it existed, and tried to verify it.

In his contacts with Nan Britton, mostly quite friendly, the professor did discover one point that amounted to a marked weakening of her case. It is not certain he noticed it—his papers offer no evidence that he did. Years earlier, in 1928, Rep. John N. Tillman of Arkansas had introduced into Congress a bill to establish a national board of magazine and book censorship. He supported his bill with a speech in which he described what Ms. Britton had done. The book "has page after page of brazen description, sickening details, monstrous charges. The story is sordid, selfish, woven into the warp of shame and a woof of infamy, the grossest attack ever launched against the living or the sheeted dead." People rushed to the bookstalls to buy it and in some places paid seven dollars for a copy. He was careful not to insult Ms. Britton. "I make no war on women," he said. Then he came to a special point: "I do not believe a woman wrote the book. I believe that the volume was written by some 'fellow of the baser sort' for the money he saw in the enterprise." Ms. Britton had heard Tillman's other charges before, and they seem not to have bothered her, but the point about authorship did. She wrote him that "I, Nan Britton, author of *The President's Daughter,* hereby challenge Representative John N. Tillman of Arkansas to prove the correctness of his belief stated in his speech in Congress, that a man wrote my book. If he is successful, I will give Mr. Tillman my personal check for $1,000, and also another check for $4,000 for any worthy charity in which Mr. Tillman is personally interested." Downes told the *Toledo Blade* in 1971 that she had offered him, Downes, five thousand dollars "if in my research I could find documentary proof that the president was father of her child." She had changed her position, from offering to pay anyone who could disprove her story, to offering to pay Downes if he could *prove* her story.[55]

The other historian who investigated Ms. Britton's books and like Downes got in touch with her—and unlike Downes remained in touch until she moved from Evanston to Glendale in 1965, stayed in touch thereafter for a while, and received twenty-three letters from her—was Albertson. Like Downes, he too was a well-known scholar. Born in 1920, a veteran of World War II, he received a doctorate from Columbia University in 1955. There he worked closely with the nationally known historian Allan Nevins in a new program to interview distinguished people in various walks of life, thereby producing "oral histories." Taking advantage of the new availability of tape recorders, the program's historians sidestepped the painstaking business of having a stenographer take down conversation (the stenographer also was likely to inhibit interviewees). Afterward, at leisure, typists made transcripts. Among other individuals Albertson interviewed was President Roosevelt's secretary of agriculture from 1940 to 1945, Claude R. Wickard. He taught at New York University, George Washington University, Brooklyn College, and, beginning in 1965, the University of Massachusetts.

Like Downes, Albertson had questions for Ms. Britton. In an initial letter he related, "If you find yourself in a position to release photocopies of the originals of your correspondence with President Harding, I should be equally grateful to receive copies of these letters. I think such photocopies would serve your cause well." For this inquiry he received the same response as Downes. "You may readily understand," his correspondent replied, "and will not be offended when I point out, that I view as anachronistic the implication that it is to my advantage, or that it is expedient at the time to corroborate statements made in my book *The President's Daughter*." She pointed out that letters, mementos, personal background, and statements all had been released thirty-seven years earlier when she published the book. She had every reason to believe that everything had been investigated. She could not believe that he thought she did not have the letters and so on that were mentioned in the book. No matter what the issue, there would be believers and unbelievers, those who could envision high purpose and those who, without vision, detracted from it.[56]

Albertson persisted and asked for the correct name of every person mentioned in *The President's Daughter*. "If we could locate some person who saw you and President Harding together this would help to sustain the authenticity of our assertions. If you have any memorabilia (menus, snapshots, match books and the like) from places which you and Mr. Harding visited together, this would be interesting to see. But most important of all, of course, are letters."[57] From this second inquiry he discovered no more than had Downes.

Early in July 1964 Albertson made a side investigation. He wrote the manager of the Witherill Hotel in Plattsburgh, New York, to inquire if Harding had stayed there on August 17, 1918, and especially if, as related in *The President's Daughter*, Ms. Britton had registered there under the name of Christian. The investigation was only partly successful. The manager, W. H. Howell Jr., responded with alacrity. Harding's name did appear on the register as of the date Albertson mentioned. "However, I am in no position to give you the information as to whether the name Christian appears on the register. I appreciate the fact that you are writing a factual history, but it seems to me that some scandals of the past might better be left buried in obscurity."[58]

Shortly afterward the work of this second of Ms. Britton's scholarly investigators took a different turn because of national publicity given to the discovery of a cache of Harding letters to an undoubted mistress in Marion, Carrie Phillips (for which see Chapter 5). Either in correspondence not in Albertson's papers, or by telephone, or perhaps in a visit to Ms. Britton in Evanston, he learned from her that the Tim Slade of her books was the Secret Service operative James Sloan Jr. He wrote excitedly on August 27 that "At least one happy result of the sensational exposition of the Phillips Letters has been the stepping forward of men who have remained silent for 40 years. I have talked with four men who knew Jimmie Sloan Jr. and to whom Sloan confirmed your story essentially as you wrote it. And there will be more."[59]

The confirmation of which he wrote may have been premature. When he informed Ms. Britton of the four men, he was speaking of a single individual, the well-known reporter for the *Chicago Tribune* Walter Trohan, who turned out to be none too sure of what he was saying. In a telephone interview he had told Albertson that he had known Sloan in 1934 or so when Trohan was attempting to help Sloan write an autobiography, and when that enterprise did not work he had sent Sloan to a writer at the *Saturday Evening Post,* which again did not work. Trohan said Sloan did tell him that he had carried money to Ms. Britton. Trohan said Sloan told him all about Ms. Britton and he had notes of his discussions and promised to look for them and would call Albertson. Weeks later the reporter wrote that he had found the notes but they did not touch Harding, were sketchy, and might have something of interest "when I get a chance to decipher them." Albertson's papers contain no further correspondence with Trohan.[60]

Early in September 1964 Albertson telephoned Jay G. Hayden, who may have been the *Saturday Evening Post* writer Trohan mentioned. Like Trohan, he related that Sloan had taken money to Ms. Britton and said the president's emissary had visited her in the Adirondack Mountains.[61] Ms. Britton had vacationed there for six or eight weeks in 1920.

The references to Sloan by Trohan and Hayden were remarkably difficult to verify, and one might ask if Sloan, who was a White House figure as a member of the Secret Service, left any traces of his involvement with Ms. Britton. He had joined the service in 1902 and served on the White House detail from 1903 until 1916. He hiked through Rock Creek Park with President Theodore Roosevelt and remembered wrestling with "T.R." on the White House floor. He left the service in June 1920 and rejoined it in 1931. To thousands of White House callers he was known as "Jimmie of the Secret Service." His principal task at the White House seems to have been the screening of "psychopathic visitors," in which he interviewed as many as six callers a day and estimated that five hundred people had been committed to hospitals after being held for observation on his recommendation. During his absence from the service he had a close connection with Harding until the summer of 1921; he was employed by the Republican National Committee to guard the candidate and president-elect, and stayed over at the White House until June. He then went to the Shipping Board and private employment with the Cleveland brokerage firm of Samuel Ungerleider and Company, for which he was Washington representative. Harding was reported to have had an account with Ungerleider. But he does not seem to have recorded his autobiography, as Trohan hoped. If he had published a book it would have forced his retirement, and he remained with the service until he reached the age of sixty-eight in 1945. No time for writing remained, for he retired on July 31 and died that same year on December 26.[62]

When Ms. Britton identified Sloan to Albertson as Tim Slade, Sloan had long since passed on. If he had known her, he doubtless would have refused to acknowledge it until he retired. Stories of his retirement were published in newspapers, and she might have applied to him for assistance at that time. He moved to Danville, Ohio, not far from Marion, if she had wished to visit him; otherwise the mails were available, or the telephone. Instead she chose to pass up this opportunity to assist her cause, until nearly twenty years afterward, when it was too late.

In the letter mentioning the four confirmations of Ms. Britton's story Albertson enclosed an article in the national edition of the *New York Daily News* for August 23, 1964, by the longtime *Daily News* reporter Francis M. Stephenson, who offered two testimonies that President Harding had had an affair with Ms. Britton. Stephenson had been a White House reporter and said that in 1927 a member of the Secret Service, Walter Ferguson, told him how he once had spirited Ms. Britton out of the president's office when Florence Harding, sensing that the young woman was with her husband, was attempting to enter. Stephenson said "Fergy" had taken money to Ms. Britton in Chicago when Sloan was unable to go. Moreover, he wrote, former senator Charles Curtis of Kansas, vice president under President Hoover, had once vouched for Ms. Britton's reliability and told how she had gone to see President Coolidge's vice president, Charles G. Dawes, who had seemed friendly to her predicament but upon receiving her had lost his temper, harangued her, and said he would have nothing to do with her.

Albertson asked his correspondent what she thought of the Stephenson article, and again the result was inconclusive. "Regarding the news stories," she responded (he had sent another story that repeated the Stephenson account), "[t]hey are as mixed up as newspaper stories about my situation seem usually to be." She rested her case on *The President's Daughter*, that it was accurate and full. In fact *The President's Daughter* directly contradicted the principal revelation of the Ferguson testimony, the near confrontation with the president's wife. The "one and only time" Ms. Britton met Ferguson in Washington, she had written in her book published the same year Ferguson talked to Stephenson, was when he had taken her on a perfectly peaceful if private tour of the White House in which she did not mention being spirited out of the president's office—which, if it had happened, she surely would have announced. In her book she did write that Ferguson "did come on one occasion to Chicago with some money when the President was unable to secure Tim Slade's services," just as Ferguson had told Stephenson. Ferguson told the reporter he had gone to Ms. Britton's apartment, while the book related that she met him at the Congress Hotel.[63] It was a small contradiction. More important for the entire Ferguson testimony, however, was that Stephenson had nothing to back it up—no contemporary notes, nothing but his memory, which he indulged freely, as he quoted "Fergy" for several columns. Albertson at first had either seen or heard of an article by Stephenson in the New York edition of the *Daily News* and telephoned the reporter, who sent the historian a copy of the longer article in the national edition and a brusque commentary that "It contains a more complete account of my conversation with Walter Ferguson and all I know about the Nan Britton affair."[64]

The part of the Stephenson article concerning the conversation with Vice President Curtis was considerably less plausible than the Ferguson testimony. From all accounts Curtis was an agreeable, affable, and, on matters of public policy, trustworthy man. Prior to the vice presidency he was majority leader of the Senate. But that he believed Ms. Britton's story did not prove anything; Stephenson needed more than that, and Curtis did not offer it. So far as concerned his story about a conversation between his predecessor as vice president, Dawes, and Ms. Britton, the latter wrote Albertson that she "never had any conversation whatever with Mr. Dawes; in fact, I cannot recall ever having seen the man."[65]

Harding's birthplace near Blooming Grove. The house was destroyed long ago. (courtesy the Library of Congress)

The Hardings' house in Marion, with the front porch that was constructed for the campaign of 1920. (source: *Warren G. Harding—The Man*, by Joe Mitchell Chapple)

Harding's desk in the editorial office of the *Marion Star.* (source: *Warren G. Harding—The Man,* by Joe Mitchell Chapple)

Office building of the *Marion Star,* Center Street, Marion, Ohio. (source: *Warren G. Harding—The Man,* by Joe Mitchell Chapple)

THE SAWYER SANATORIUM

WHITE OAKS FARM   MARION, OHIO

Treats Nervous and Mental Diseases

Located on an 130 acre farm. Thoroughly equipped to treat Nervous and Mental Diseases by modern, scientific methods. Consists of sixteen bungalows of fireproof construction, erected for their present purpose and having all the refinements and accommodations of the best private homes. Presided over by a permanent skilled staff. Personal professional attention. Private rooms for all patients. Drug and liquor cases not accepted. Physicians having Nervous or Mental patients needing treatment away from home will find that the Sawyer Sanatorium's facilities are satisfactory and adequate.

THE PATIO

Send for Booklet, Address

Sawyer Sanatorium, White Oaks Farm, Marion, Ohio

The Sawyer Sanatorium, where Mrs. Harding died in 1924, was the hospital of President Harding's personal physician, Dr. Charles E. Sawyer.

In 1920 when a formal ceremony of notification was being prepared for the Republican presidential candidate in Marion, the arrangement was for a luncheon to be served to the national committee at White Oaks Farm. An assistant to the chairman of the national committee, Will H. Hays, wrote the chairman hastily that such would not do, because the hospital was for the mentally deficient. "Imagine what opposition newspapers could make, in the way of ridicule of the fact that the Harding notification committee proceeded from a 'nut factory' to inform the senator of his nomination for the highest office in the country. I was assured that the huge 'sanitarium' sign would be removed or covered up. This will but serve to attract further attention as all the newspaper men and press associations know these facts" (L. W. Henley to Hays, July 10, 1920, "July 7–11, 1920," box 6, Will H. Hays Papers). (source: *American Medical Directory*)

Florence and Warren Harding with the president's father, Dr. George T. Harding. (courtesy the Ohio Historical Society)

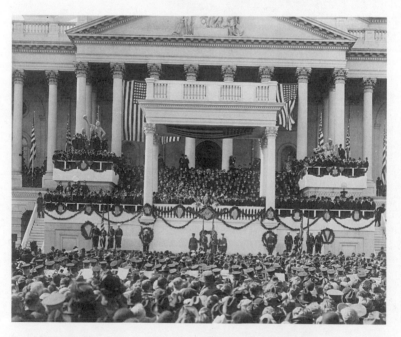

President Harding gives his inaugural address, March 4, 1921. (courtesy the Library of Congress)

The Hardings with Edward and Evalyn McLean and their son, the Hardings' hosts during the Florida vacation early in 1923. (courtesy the Library of Congress)

President and Mrs. Harding at the rear of the special train they used on the Alaska Railroad. (courtesy the National Archives, Washington, D.C.)

President Harding and "the little fellow," as he privately
described his vice president. (courtesy the Library of Congress)

Trying to look and act like a General.

Ce. E. Sawyer

Brig. Gen. M. Q. R. C.

To the Marion Club 4/16 - 21

Brig. Gen. Charles E. Sawyer. (courtesy the Ohio Historical Society)

Harry M. Daugherty and Jess Smith. (courtesy the Ohio Historical Society)

Senator Warren G. Harding. This photo appeared in *The President's Daughter,* by Nan Britton. Nan's caption was: "Snapshot received by the author in June, 1917, with a forty-page letter from Mr. Harding."

Harding's funeral car. (courtesy the Ohio Historical Society)

The cortege moves down Pennsylvania Avenue toward the Capitol. The *Washington Star* building is across the street at the right, the New Willard is at the far left. (courtesy the Library of Congress)

Harding Memorial in Marion, Ohio. (courtesy the Ohio Historical Society)

Richard Wightman, head of the Bible Corporation of America, business manager of the Elizabeth Ann Guild. (source: *Ashes and Sparks*, by Richard Wightman)

Nan Britton, 1917. (source: *The President's Daughter*, by Nan Britton)

Elizabeth Ann. This photo appeared in *The President's Daughter,* by Nan Britton. Nan's caption was: "This photograph of Elizabeth Ann was taken by the author to Mr. Harding at the White House."

Nan Britton at work on *The President's Daughter,* December–January 1926–1927, in Connecticut. (source: *Honesty or Politics,* by Nan Britton)

This picture of Gaston B. Means appeared in his book
*The Strange Death of President Harding: From the Diaries
of Gaston B. Means, a Department of Justice Investigator.*
Means's caption was: "Ex-Department of Justice Investigator.
Star witness for the United States Government in the Harry
M. Daugherty, Teapot Dome, and other sensational
investigations, as he appeared in the Committee Room,
in the United States Senate Chambers, with some of his
diaries."

Col. Charles R. Forbes and his inquisitors of the special Senate committee. Note the assistant in back, reading a newspaper. (courtesy the Library of Congress)

Senator Harding's handwriting, 1917. (source: Warren G. Harding Papers, Ohio Historical Society)

Register for the Hotel Imperial, New York, July 30, 1917. (source: *Britton v. Klunk* case file)

The presidential portrait, 1921. (courtesy the Harry S. Truman Library, Independence, Mo.)

4
Scandals

The connection of President Harding with the scandals that have borne his name was undoubted in the sense that he was in the presidency when they took place but very slight in terms of what he could have known of them. The principal scandal of the era took the name of the naval oil reserve near Salt Creek, Wyoming, and that name, Teapot Dome, became a phrase as familiar to Americans as anything they read about during their adult lives. Its shortness, two words, allowed Linotype operators to slug it across the top of a one-column story. It became shorthand for corruption and, as things turned out, it was connected not merely to the Harding administration but also to the reputation of the president. A cabinet member, Secretary of the Interior Albert B. Fall, went to jail. Another cabinet member, Secretary of the Navy Edwin L. Denby, was driven from office because he signed away his own supervision of the oil reserves, passing it to Fall's department. But Harding's place in this drama was altogether minor. He had allowed the transfer by executive act—to him it seemed a better administrative arrangement.

Teapot Dome appeared in the newspapers in October 1923 when Senate hearings began, and simultaneously a special Senate committee commenced hearings about a scandal in the Veterans' Bureau. In the talk about scandals, newspaper readers sometimes confused the oil scandal with the Veterans' Bureau scandal, and administration figures' and senators' testimonies that they had told the president about the scandals had some readers believing the depositions referred to Teapot Dome when they actually referred to the Veterans' Bureau and vice versa. It is not clear how much the president learned about the bureau's director, Colonel Forbes—the full story came out in the hearings beginning nearly three months after Harding's death. He nonetheless learned enough to take Forbes's resignation. He appears to have acted responsibly and quickly. After the hearings brought Forbes into further trouble, the wayward colonel was indicted, tried, convicted, and sent to jail.

A third scandal seemed to arise regarding the behavior of Attorney General Daugherty in regard to the above-mentioned scandals, during the prosecution of which the members of another special Senate committee believed he had shown insufficient diligence. This investigation turned in several directions, as opportunity offered, but at the outset focused on the activities of Daugherty's closest friend, Jess Smith, who lived with the attorney general at the Wardman Park Hotel. Smith's divorced wife was the Brookhart-Wheeler committee's first witness, and her testimony led an investigator to Smith's and Daugherty's bank accounts in the Midland National Bank in Washington Court House, Ohio, an institution controlled by Attorney General Daugherty's brother, Mally. The investigator spent an afternoon looking through the bank's books, after which Mally Daugherty refused further access. Another and later investigation and indictment by a New York grand jury perhaps revealed the reason. A German national had been attempting to receive reimbursement for sale of the American Metal Company, a firm taken over by the U.S. government during the world war. The former owner claimed it was wrongly confiscated because it was really Swiss-owned. His claim was fraudulent, but he won it by judicious bribery of Alien Property Custodian Col. Thomas W. Miller, together with an erstwhile Harding campaign official, and Smith. The latter obtained most of the money, presumably for sharing with Daugherty. Smith deposited forty thousand dollars in Daugherty's account in the Midland National Bank. To make the deposit he presented Mally Daugherty with Liberty bonds, which the attorney general's brother converted to certificates of deposit. He simultaneously cashed a twenty-two-thousand-dollar check, derived from the sale of Liberty bonds. When the investigation of the American Metal Company bribery began to heat up, Mally gave the ledgers for the accounts of his brother and of Smith to his brother, who handled the bank's legal business, and the by then former attorney general destroyed them. In two court trials, both of which resulted in hung juries (the second by vote of eleven to convict, with a single holdout), Harry Daugherty refused to testify about the ledgers. In his memoirs, published a decade later, he said that Smith had overdrawn an account and was putting back what he owed. In destroying records of the several accounts he said he burned the sheets "with a lot of other papers I had no use for."[1] He said he had used an account held jointly with Smith, "Jess Smith Extra No. 3," for the presidential campaign of 1920 and that it had no connection with the American Metal case. The popular presumption was that he was shielding Smith, his own personal acceptance of bribe money, and use of the political account for Harding, use in some unknown way.

1 ———

The present pages are not the place to set out in detail the Harding scandals, and it must suffice to relate their outlines and inquire precisely what Harding might have known of them. In the instance of Teapot Dome, several developments ensured that such a scandal would have much public attention. One was the notion of a naval oil reserve, stemming from conversion of ships of the U.S. Navy from coal to oil. Conversion had begun before the world war and continued apace thereafter. Coal was dirty, bulky, and required coal stations abroad if the U.S. fleet was to have any fighting range away from American shores. The securing of coal stations in such faraway places as Pearl Harbor, the Philippines, and the Samoas in the South Pacific had not been altogether supported by the public, and people wondered if conversion to oil might make the stations less necessary or even unnecessary. Moreover, coal gave off telltale smoke and announced the appearance of ships well before their masts rose over the horizon, and the navy wanted oil for that reason. It made sense, therefore, for the Taft and Wilson administrations to create oil reserves for the navy for use in some future emergency.

Involved in the Teapot Dome affair was the great popular interest in conservation, in the nation's physical inheritance, that arose at the turn of the century and became one of the principal concerns of the Progressive Era. During the Taft administration there was an outcry when the chief of the Forest Service in the Department of Agriculture, Gifford Pinchot, accused Taft's secretary of the interior, Richard A. Ballinger, of wanting to open withdrawn lands to private interests. Taft dismissed Pinchot. It was a murky affair in a series of confusions that resulted in Theodore Roosevelt's presidential candidacy under the Bull Moose Party in 1912.

The conservation issue arose in the summer of 1920 during the Republican National Convention, when President Butler of Columbia University raised it, albeit in the same murky way that Pinchot had spoken during the Taft administration. The issue was always good for an attention-getter. Butler on June 15, 1920, allowed that "A motley group of stock gamblers, oil and mining promoters, munition makers and other like persons seized upon so good a man as General Wood and with reckless audacity started out to buy for him the Presidential nomination." He was referring to Maj. Gen. Leonard Wood, one of the convention's two principal contestants for the nomination. Four years later, when Teapot Dome was at issue, Sen. Thomas J. Walsh of Montana wrote Butler and asked for names of the malefactors at Chicago. Butler responded pathetically, if with audacity. "None of these men were known to me personally," he wrote, "and I made no note of their names."[2]

Naval officers were of three minds about what to do with the reserves. Private operators were putting their wells close to some of the reserve lands, and there was danger of drawing off the oil. The question of the area drained by a single well varied with the terrain. Some wells three hundred feet apart could draw on each other, and two wells on Maricopa Flat—admittedly this was an extreme instance—influenced each other at a distance of more than twelve hundred feet. Strata were not uniform as to dip, thickness, gas pressure, porosity, gravity of oil, and surrounding water. One expert said he thought a reserve needed to be more than one mile from the nearest producing well. The same expert advised a consolidation of blocks of holdings in as great an area as possible, including the exchange of blocks between the government and private oilmen. Some naval officers believed in exchanges. Others took the position that there should be none, lest the oilmen get the better of them. Still others, mostly higher officers, did not care one way or the other.[3]

Former secretary of the navy Josephus Daniels in the Wilson administration had insisted that the reserves be under Department of the Navy jurisdiction, which he had so arranged. Beginning March 4, 1921, he was out of the government, back in North Carolina as editor of the Raleigh News and Observer. His was a voice that would be heard in case of any Republican monkey business concerning the reserves.

On the other side of the issue was increasing interest of oilmen in the reserves as automobiles multiplied after the world war, what with Henry Ford allowing that they were a part of the national inheritance and cutting the prices of his Model T to make them so. Counties and municipalities built roads or improved roads. Oilmen sought to lease the reserves, to exploit them.

The makings of a scandal hence were at hand, and Secretary Fall was the personage who brought them all together. He was a big, bluff westerner with a round face and sizable nose who was becoming bald, had a drooping mustache, and was typically dressed in a dark suit and bow tie, a figure who if a reporter or citizen glimpsed him striding down a street or, more likely, clambering into a limousine, would have impressed the observer with his importance. He had made his way up from penury, escaped its grasp. What was not so visible, however, was that he was deeply in debt at his New Mexico ranch known as Three Rivers, having accumulated more land than he could pay for. In the loose western way of handling pecuniary problems, he decided to accept loans from two of his friends who were oilmen. Fall resigned from the Department of the Interior early in 1923, but before he left he quietly arranged for Secretary of the Navy Denby to transfer the naval oil reserves to his own department and soon afterward leased them to his friends, one of the reserves without public bidding because, an assistant said, it involved national security and naval preparedness.

Fall had decided that his oilman friends offering money would be lending it rather than bribing him, but if he had looked closely at the lenders he would have known better. Especially he should have gazed at Edward L. Doheny who according to popular wisdom was worth $100 million. The writer George Creel, who knew Doheny, said that this elderly, grandfatherly man with the wispy white hair "had the clearest blue eyes I ever saw, and the most childlike candor, and he fascinated me to a point where I really wanted to write his life as a textbook, as an inspiration for young Americans." Getting to know him better, the same observer noticed that he was "utterly unable to view anything except in the light of his own desires."[4]

Doheny lent Fall $100,000 and in the hearings before the Senate committee on public lands and surveys said that it was not much money at all. It was a "bagatelle," no more than $25 or $50 to the ordinary individual. He lent the money because he had been "greatly affected" by the extreme pecuniary circumstances that had resulted from Fall's lifetime of futile efforts. He did it as a friend.

Senator Walsh observed, "I can appreciate that on your side, but looking at it from Senator Fall's side it was quite a loan."

Doheny admitted the truth of that.[5]

There was much less to be said about the other man who lent money to Fall, the oilman Harry F. Sinclair, who was younger than Doheny and whose stocky figure was offset by a hard face, especially the straight mouth, which presumably had been shaped by years of calculating oil deals. Sinclair gave various names to his companies, but for decades after Teapot Dome his name was known across the nation as the proprietor of a chain of gasoline stations that featured a dinosaur on its escutcheon. It is hardly necessary to add that in the business deals of twentieth-century America, Sinclair was no dinosaur.[6]

Fall's acceptance of $100,000 in cash from Doheny, carried to the secretary by Doheny's son in a small black bag, and acceptance of bonds and cash totaling $304,000 from Sinclair, shocked the secretary's friends.[7] Harding had sat with him in the Senate and doubtless appointed him in part for that reason. But the interesting aspect of Fall's years in the Senate was that no member of the upper house even suspected he was susceptible to bribery. "I had sat next to Fall in the Senate for two years," former New York senator William M. Calder wrote. "I believed he was a man of the highest integrity and am sure that was the judgment of every member of the Senate." Calder's colleague, Wadsworth, wrote similarly: "The Interior Department seemed a natural place for Fall, as he was a westerner and thoroughly familiar with all the problems of that region. Fall was finally persuaded to take the place and we were all very happy about it. I can't describe to you the dismay which overtook us later on."[8] After Harding's inauguration as president, the nation's new chief executive had unexpectedly appeared before the Senate and read off the proposed list of his cabinet officers. When he read Fall's name—with Fall seated at his Senate desk—it was greeted by tumultuous cheers and not even submitted formally to a committee for endorsement. Amid the cheering Fall rose and tendered his resignation as a senator, which was immediately accepted. For a moment he was in the anomalous position of a private citizen intruding on the floor of the chamber. His colleagues crowded around in mock anger, with cries of "Throw him out!" and "Get out!" Senator Lodge came up with a novel suggestion: "I move, Mr. President," he said to Vice President Coolidge, "that Senator A. B. Fall be immediately confirmed by the Senate as secretary of the interior without the usual formality of a reference to a committee." The motion was put and unanimously carried with another round of applause.[9]

Senator Walsh, who became Fall's nemesis during the Teapot Dome hearings, may have suspected his colleague while Fall was in the Senate, but his explanation of Fall late in 1923 when the hearings were in course but not yet conclusive was uncertain, and of course tinctured by Fall's evasions thus far. Mark Sullivan asked Walsh what his judgment was about Fall, and the senator responded that the evidence put Fall in a very disagreeable position. The reporter asked whether, from his recollection of Fall in the Senate, he thought Fall was a man who would do this sort of thing. "He said he always thought of Fall as having such an extraordinary vanity as to amount almost to a disease, and that when a man has vanity to this extent, this trait is frequently accompanied by lack of strict moral or intellectual integrity."[10] Thus from the principal Senate investigator there was at first uncertainty, a hunch rather than sureness.

The secretary's cabinet colleagues, with the exception of Daugherty, believed he had been a great success at the Department of the Interior. Secretary Hoover, who in 1920–1921 had hoped he himself would obtain interior rather than commerce, and one might have suspected would have been cautious in appraisal of the man who succeeded where he had failed, was fulsome to a fault. In a letter to Fall he allowed as to how the Department of the Interior "never had so constructive and legal a headship as you gave it." Daugherty disliked Fall because he had not been a regular Republican in 1912 and had followed the sheep into the desert with Roosevelt. He especially disliked him because when Harding was president-elect and choosing cabinet members he had delayed Fall's appointment, and Fall had sent a long telegram urging the appointment, signed Daugherty's name, and charged it to Daugherty's personal account.[11]

To people who should have known there thus was complete surprise, and the only question is what the president himself might have discovered. Here there has been a difference of opinion. What piqued the curiosity of journalists was that when Harding and his party were en route across the country to Tacoma and thence to Alaska, Fall's wife—matronly, tall, sad faced—visited the president at Kansas City. The visit seemed proof that Harding had known about Teapot Dome. Sen. Arthur Capper of Kansas and his wife were guests of the Hardings that day at Kansas City and present at the Muehlebach Hotel when Emma Fall arrived. Capper told the journalist William Allen White about the visit and said Mrs. Fall talked with the president for a long time, and White published what Capper said in his 1928 book *Masks in a Pageant*. A decade later, in 1939, the senator wrote Samuel Hopkins Adams, who was about to publish his nonfictional account of the Harding administration:

> She seemed to be greatly disturbed and talked quietly with the President
> for a few minutes then they both dropped into one of the private rooms
> in the suite occupied by the Hardings. They were there for nearly an hour.
> When they emerged from the room Mrs. Fall talked a few minutes with
> the rest of us and then we all had supper in the small dining room which

was a part of the suite. Immediately after supper the Hardings and the Cappers went to the Convention hall where the President made his Kansas City speech. Mrs. Fall bid them good-bye and that is the last I have ever seen of her.[12]

Once the Capper-White story was published it was impossible to contradict, although in fact there were two refutations, one more believable than the other. Emma Fall subsequently maintained that she never mentioned her husband's affairs to the president. She said as much to White before he published *Masks,* and he placed her denial in the book. "Never mentioned oil issues to Harding at any time," she wrote Dr. Boone in 1939. Mrs. Fall was a staunch champion of her husband until the end of her long life. She had reason to tell what happened in such a manner. But the president's private secretary, Christian, was present at the dinner in the Muehlebach and also related that at no time was she alone with the president. He never came to Emma Fall's defense publicly because, as he explained to a correspondent, rather oddly, the matter had become a public contention.[13]

The journalist White claimed that Mrs. Fall's talk with the president had visibly shaken Harding. Capper denied this in his letter to Adams. White wrote that he rode on the train with Harding the next day, when the train passed into Kansas, and the president asked him, in what became a famous phrase, repeated more about Harding than anything else attributed to him, what one did when betrayed by friends—that he, Harding, could take care of his enemies, but "my damn friends . . . my God-damn friends, White, they're the ones that keep me walking the floor nights!" It was the kind of commentary that went the rounds among politicians, doubtless not original with Harding. The president surely offered it to White, who repeated it several times, with and without the expletive.[14] Harding could have been referring to the problem with Colonel Forbes in the Veterans' Bureau rather than to Teapot Dome.

On the Alaska trip Secretary Hoover remembered that Harding was not at all worried about scandals:

> His whole outlook was forward-looking. During conversations on his Alaskan trip there was no indication of the supposed apprehension of his early end which has been circulated. . . . In fact conversations on many occasions on the general line as to what we should undertake and what should be done as to this, that, and the other. Many of the questions discussed stretched into actual action in the future over periods of years; he sometimes put in the reservation that "we will carry through this, that, or the other, if we are reelected."[15]

Fall's guilt seems fairly clear, for even a westerner of that time should have known better than to accept hundreds of thousands of dollars in loans from oilmen for whom he had done favors as a cabinet member. What needs to be added about the Teapot Dome affair is that Sinclair and Doheny had employed other prominent people to advance their interests, and these people, in turn, were not hesitant about accepting employment. Archibald Roosevelt, son of the former president, worked in Sinclair's office, earning a salary that in 1919 began at $5,000 a year and by 1922 was $15,000. He should never have been there, for his brother was assistant secretary of the navy. Nor was he very clever about analyzing his predicament. Once the Teapot Dome business came out, Archie had second thoughts about his employment, and on January 21, 1924, testified that he had heard from Sinclair's private secretary of a check to a foreman on Secretary Fall's ranch in the amount of $68,000. The oilman's secretary, nervous as a cat, disagreed, testifying that he had been talking about no check but a gift for Fall's ranch of "six or eight cows." Every newspaper reader in the country guffawed. Archie had been outwitted.[16] Not long afterward Doheny shed light about his own employees, and it was not a pleasant light. He had become ruffled over the pointed questions of Senator Walsh, who had virtually taken over the investigation from the chairman of the committee, Senator Smoot, and volunteered that he had employed Democrats (Walsh was a Democrat) as well as Republicans. He had employed four former cabinet members of the Wilson administration: Franklin K. Lane, former secretary of the interior, was paid $50,000; Lindley M. Garrison, who had been secretary of war, also took Doheny money; Thomas W. Gregory, once attorney general, was paid $2,000; and Wilson's secretary of the treasury, son-in-law, and a presidential aspirant in 1924, William G. McAdoo, was on a retainer of $50,000 a year, and he and his firm earlier had received $250,000. Doheny's statement caught McAdoo by surprise. He was about to come east from California to attend his father-in-law's funeral in Washington, and after arrival he irritated the late Democratic president's widow because, presumably on a mission of mourning, he was on the telephone all the time, attempting to repair his reputation. A story circulated in Washington that he was coming to attend Wilson's funeral on Wednesday and attend his own on Thursday, the latter being the day he was scheduled to testify before the Senate committee. Rather ineffectively he told the committee that his retainer for the past two years was $25,000 per annum, not $50,000, and that his firm had not received $250,000, but $100,000.[17] Doheny also had paid $5,000 to the journalist Creel, Wilson's wartime chairman of the committee on public information, known to the president's enemies as the chairman of his publicity committee. Secretary of the Navy Daniels had been one of Creel's sponsors during the war, and this was why Doheny chose Creel to try to persuade Daniels to release the naval oil reserves. When apprised of Doheny's testimony, the erstwhile chairman admitted taking money for this task, which of course was unsuccessful, but said he did not know the money came from Doheny. He said nothing about giving it back. Doheny's largesse not merely to Fall but also to notable Democrats raised questions. In his home state of California he was known as a leading

Democrat. He told the committee he made campaign contributions to both parties. Asked why he specially engaged the services of former public figures of both parties, he snapped, "I paid them for their influence."

Another attorney general in the Wilson administration, A. Mitchell Palmer, served during the hearings as attorney for a friend of Secretary Fall, the former Harding intimate Ned McLean, whom Fall at first said lent him the $100,000. (At that time McLean was recuperating in Palm Beach from what he described as a sinus infection and could not come to Washington to testify. Walsh went to Florida, and McLean testified that he had given some checks to Fall, but the latter had given them back uncashed. Doheny then said he himself had lent the money. For such confusions, McLean doubtless needed a good lawyer.)

As one newspaper put it, "The Senate investigation has become a 'gusher' and both Republicans and Democrats, in varying degrees no doubt, will carry the smell of petroleum, both crude and refined."[18]

Concerning payments to politically important people, it is now clear that the oil scandal touched even the chairman of the Teapot Dome committee, Senator Smoot. The Utah senator was a high official of the Mormon Church, the Washington Sunday services of which were held at his house. He was an individual apparently beyond reproach (Wadsworth in the early 1950s described him as "certainly an honorable man").[19] But it became evident many years later that he had borrowed money from Doheny. His diary reveals that he had a financially irresponsible son, Harold, who sold short on four hundred shares of Mexican oil stock. When the stock went up, Harold's broker called him for margin. Harold telegraphed his father, and on Saturday night, December 30, 1922, Senator Smoot took the train to New York. He arrived at 6:00 A.M., with an appointment to see E. L. Doheny at the Plaza Hotel at 11:00 A.M.. The appointment was postponed until 12:30 P.M. This was on a Sunday when Smoot ordinarily would have been attending services. At last, hat in hand, he met "Mr. Doheny" and the oilman's wife, both of whom were present during the interview with the senator. Doheny told him about the reasons for the rapid advance of the Mexican stock and "why the shorts were punched out." He thought that Harold's brokers, Dutton and Company, had induced Harold to sell short. "He agreed to loan Harold 35,000.00 payable on or before one year at 6% interest with my guarantee. I agreed to it and so wired Harold on my arrival at Washington at 7:25 P.M. Was tired and heavy hearted . . ."[20]

At the very least the senator should have disqualified himself from the subsequent hearings. Not merely did he not excuse himself, but on November 30, 1923, either before or after one of the hearings, he was forced to ask Doheny for an extension as well. "Mr. Doheny was present. I had a talk with him and he told me he would extend the time on Harold's loan of $35,000."[21]

In following years he saw Doheny in California at least three times and advised him on the best way to handle his defense against Teapot Dome (the hearings resumed for a while in 1928) and against the legal action that began in 1926 and resulted in acquittal in 1930. The diary ends in 1928 and perhaps for that reason does not show when Harold Smoot or his father paid back the thirty-five thousand dollars with 6 percent annual interest.

Senator Smoot was a close friend of President Harding, was often at the White House, and it would have been understandable if the senator had not told the president about the indebtedness. On his own part, Harding surely could not have imagined such an involvement.

2 ———

Unlike Teapot Dome, the Veterans' Bureau scandal was no subtle proposition involving bribery mistaken for indebtedness but a relatively simple, almost classical, piece of criminal behavior. The director of the bureau, Forbes, a bustling, energetic, clean-shaven executive, who seemed to deserve the description "dynamic," had begun his peculations by taking interest in sites for veterans' hospitals, paying exorbitant prices for them, and pocketing the difference. He acquired two partners in the construction business, John W. Thompson of the Thompson-Black Construction Company of St. Louis and that firm's associated companies and Charles F. Hurley of Tacoma who owned the Hurley-Mason Company. He then turned his attention to the sale of items—sheets, paraffin paper, moleskin, pajamas, gauze—stored in a huge depot in fifty buildings in Perryville, Maryland, that was under his supervision.

The initial bad judgment in regard to the bureau came when the then senator Harding and his wife visited Hawaii and there met Forbes, who immediately impressed them, especially Mrs. Harding, with his congeniality. They first encountered him at a social function at which the colonel was the honored guest. He was in charge of public utilities on the islands, and when he needed anything would get in touch if necessary with his friends on the mainland, perhaps the Hurley-Mason Company in Tacoma, of which he had been a vice president. He later said of his island experiences that "We fixed things so that no one lost any money."[22] But the Hardings did not know this part of the colonel's background, only that Forbes after meeting the Ohio couple had dropped everything to take them around the islands and show them the sights.

When Forbes learned that the senator he had met in Honolulu was a Republican hopeful for the presidency he returned to his home state of Washington and began pushing Harding's nomination. At this time Harding was only a dark horse, and it was necessary for the Ohio senator to be very careful not to offend anyone. Forbes's activities embarrassed Harding's manager, Daugherty, who did not want the senator to enter any contest in a state such as Washington where Sen. Miles Poindexter was a favorite son. Daugherty called Forbes off, which was the beginning of what proved a personal antagonism. When Harding was nominated, Forbes plunged into the campaign. After the victory he sought a place on the Shipping Board, but the vacancy had already been filled. He then obtained backing from the American Legion for the post of head of veterans' insurance, to which he was appointed, and afterward he became director of the Veterans' Bureau.

The president had plenty of advice against appointing Forbes, but as in the case of Senator Fall he chose to put his trust in the man he wanted. Neither Daugherty nor the GOP's national chairman, Will Hays, both of whom distributed patronage, endorsed him. Senator Wadsworth told Harding the appointment was ill-advised. "He's my friend," was the response. "He's been my friend for years. You can't talk to me like that, Jim Wadsworth." Dr. Sawyer disliked him and spoke to Daugherty about it. The latter, perhaps not ready to come out in the open about Forbes, joked with Sawyer and told him he was prejudiced against Forbes. Sawyer admitted it. "For that reason you can't be fair," Daugherty said to him. "Give him a chance. The President thinks he is capable of great things."[23]

The president's slowness was understandable, even if unwise. He was presiding over a huge bureaucracy, which he hoped to bend to the purposes of his administration. Having been in politics for years, he knew that he had to cajole and somehow influence his appointees, make them aware of his hopes for them, inspire them if possible. In many instances he, the president, had to trust people. The trust would receive its reward in good behavior. He could obtain far more for his decency than if he suspected everyone he appointed. By running against the advice of Daugherty, Hays, and Wadsworth he was taking a chance, for they too were politicians. Wadsworth, he may have felt, was more of an idealist than Daugherty and Hays and perhaps less capable of good advice. Sawyer was a clear-eyed idealist, and his advice, which the general communicated to the president, was less interesting. Party feeling, Harding probably believed, and the inspiration of a presidential appointment would hold Forbes in line.

Dr. Sawyer hoped that Harding's moral stature would preserve the president from trouble. He knew that the president would do nothing wrong. After Harding's death he wrote of his lifelong friend that "Mr. Harding's big, sympathetic heart and his generous disposition made him most forgiving but nonetheless relentless against facts indicating corruption or irregularities in individual operation of any Government matter. He was ever opposed to anything but the strictest of honest accounting for all of the affairs of state, and any course pursued contrary to that brought his condemnation." Having delivered himself, the doctor was not quite sure of the result but hoped for the best. Harding based every act, thought, and deed on honesty of purpose, generosity of disposition, and hope of accomplishment (Sawyer obviously thought in threes). "God endowed him as he was, and he could not have been different had he tried." He would not have changed if the entire world had disagreed with him. "Mr. Harding had a friendly feeling for all mankind, but those to whom he gave his confidence and those with whom he really associated intimately were always selected with the belief that they were honorable and upright."[24]

In the case of Forbes the honor of the appointment failed to compensate for the opportunity, and Harding's essential decency may only have stressed the opportunity, for Forbes's bailiwick was no small operation. The bureau spent $467 million in the fiscal year 1923 (which meant July 1, 1922, through June 30, 1923). This amounted to one-fifth of the entire expenditures of the federal government. Salaries annually were $42.5 million. The bureau employed thirty thousand people, and its eighty-eight hospitals held twenty-five thousand veterans, most of them from World War I—which war indeed had been the reason for bringing together all veterans' activities under a single bureau.

As the colonel surveyed his domain he was quick to realize the possibilities under the Sweet Act of 1921 that established the Veterans' Bureau and especially an appropriation of $17 million in 1922 to construct twelve hospitals (making a total of one hundred) throughout the country. Not long after he became director of the bureau he was at work to profit from choosing the sites. For this work he enlisted his friend Charles F. Cramer, general counsel of the bureau, whose cooperation naturally was important. He brought Cramer in on the site profits, which ensured his cooperation.

Meanwhile the $17 million under the Sweet Act—the name was prophetic— had caught the attention of contractors, and the Washington agent for Thompson-Black, Elias H. Mortimer, whom the reporter Will Irwin described in his memoirs as "a slight, youngish man, his face handsome almost to prettiness, yet hard," and his pretty young wife, Katherine, who lived in the Wardman Park Hotel, made the acquaintance of Forbes as quickly as they could.[25] The couple and the colonel liked each other, and in a short time Forbes was spending his evenings with the Mortimers, who proved so congenial that the director of the Veterans' Bureau himself moved to an apartment in the hotel.

It was not long thereafter that Mortimer and Forbes agreed on a formula for construction of the hospitals. Some difficulties were encountered, but Forbes was a man of experience and solved each one in turn. The object of immediate attention was the appropriation to construct the twelve hospitals. One of them, in Chicago, was to cost $5 million, but by averaging their cost a formula was worked out. With each hospital theoretically costing $1.5 million, and calculating that 10 percent could be taken off the top for division among interested parties, the arrangement was for Thompson-Black and Hurley-Mason to divide construction at the Mississippi River, with the St. Louis firm taking the East, the Tacoma firm the West. Because of the need for equity, perhaps that more hospitals might be in the East or in the West, the territorial arrangement was to be equal, and whatever the 10 percent fund the two firms were each to have one-third, with Forbes himself taking one-third. Hence on a $1.5 million hospital each constituent of the agreement would receive fifty thousand dollars. In the one-third arranged for Thompson-Black, 35 percent was to go to Mortimer and a friend because of their labors in making the arrangement.

The confusions in the arrangement were, first, that Forbes asked Mortimer for a five-thousand-dollar loan, because the colonel's wife, Kate, had gathered together his portable assets and departed for Europe. Forbes was quite open about this misfortune. He told Mortimer that he was hard up, and the agent asked, "What do you want, Forbes?" He said, "I need about $5,000." Mortimer answered, "Personally, I haven't got it, but I will see what I can do toward getting it for you." Not long afterward, in the Drake Hotel in Chicago, Mortimer handed Forbes ten five-hundred-dollar bills. He gave them to Forbes while the two men were in the bathroom of a suite, with a party going on outside, and the colonel hence was not able to give Mortimer the note the latter asked for—Mortimer needed it as a protection against his company, to which he would give his own note. This, incidentally, was the first of several unspecified borrowings by Forbes.[26]

Another problem was Forbes's initial remarks to the effect that he, himself, would award contracts on a cost-plus basis, a prospect dashed by President Harding who told the colonel that he wanted bidding. Forbes then gave his partners in construction two signal opportunities. For one, he quietly presented them with a list of the proposed hospital sites a month before other contractors received them, which allowed Thompson-Black and Hurley-Mason to send out their men and obtain local labor costs and other information necessary to make proper bids. Forbes's other assistance was to advise his friends to propose short-term construction dates, in knowledge that other bidders probably would set longer times for the work, and in the interests of the veterans of the nation the bureau would choose the contractor offering the least delay in construction.

As the arrangement was moving forward in the spring and summer of 1922 for the construction of the hospitals under the congressional act, Forbes became even closer with Mortimer and his wife during several trips around the East Coast looking at sites and then a transcontinental inspection trip to the West Coast. According to what Mortimer remembered, the trips were marked by continuous, wall-to-wall parties, in which everyone was drinking within an hour after arrival at a new hotel. At one place on the West Coast two dozen bottles of wine arrived from a grateful friend whose winery was being purchased as a site, but the attendant party-goers in the Fairmont Hotel in San Francisco were busily drinking scotch and decided to take the wine on the trip they were making to nearby Stockton. At that place in California, the hostess's wonderful home, as Mortimer described it, had a bar that was longer than the width of the room in which Mortimer, later, testified to the Senate committee, and the Forbes group spent the entire afternoon at this attractive place. Upon return to the East, Forbes sent an appreciative letter to his hostess that he claimed was written by his secretary but may not have been:

> From Stockton to Washington, some 3,000 miles intervene, but I believe I could astonish you, if I were to record in this letter the visualization of that never-to-be-forgotten room in your home, the name of which is a word obsolescent, if not obsolete. I think I remember not only the details of construction and the beauty of the whole effect, but the heat of Washington conjures up before me as in a mirage the innumerable things that greeted one's eyes and excited the palate of the thirsty.[27]

A luncheon was given by the president of the Alexander Steamship Company in honor of Forbes on board the *H. F. Alexander,* for which five hundred settings were made. At the luncheon Forbes said he had been sent out to Tacoma by President Harding to present H. F. Alexander with a medal showing President Harding's face on it, and he presented it on behalf of the president. Afterward he was sitting around with Mortimer and laughing, and Mortimer said, "Charlie, tell me, did the President ask you to present that?"

"No," was the answer, "I just wanted to make him feel good. He was pretty good to us and put us in his private suite on the boat. I knew him when he did not have any money. And he is going up in the world now, and he is a big man in Tacoma."[28]

Mortimer said that Forbes had half a dozen of these inauguration medals, struck for Harding's inauguration, and passed them out as if they were special. "The kind of thing that is struck on the inauguration of every President?" asked Senator David A. Reed of Pennsylvania, the committee chairman. "Yes, sir; that was it," replied the witness.

Mortimer paid for everything on the eastern and western trips, save for Forbes's transportation (which the government paid for). The cost to Thompson-Black was $5,400.

In the hearings Forbes found himself in trouble concerning his inclusion of Mortimer and the latter's wife on the trips, and especially the picking up of the trips' cost, and answered as best he could. He was up against the committee's counsel, John F. O'Ryan, an able New York lawyer who had been a National Guard major general in the war. General O'Ryan asked the colonel if "you expect this committee, who have seen Mr. Mortimer and heard his testimony and observed his intimate knowledge of the details of so many of the various contracts, to believe that Mortimer was spending his time running around the country with you and spending his money on you month after month and making these inspection trips in connection with these contractors without any business purpose connected with you?"

"Absolutely," was the answer. "If he was not with me he would have been with somebody else."

O'Ryan asked his question again: "That might be; but do you believe now, as you look back at it, that he did not have some ulterior purpose in accompanying you on these trips?"

"I do not know," snapped the colonel, "what he had in his mind."[29]

Mortimer's testimony alone was enough to bring Forbes's indictment. And it is interesting that O'Ryan secured it only because Forbes took liberties of an undefined nature with Mortimer's wife. On Labor Day 1922, after several arguments with the colonel, Mortimer broke with him, and when the Senate investigation began early the next year O'Ryan had no difficulty obtaining the former agent's cooperation. Mortimer hated Forbes for this reason and would never have turned against him, he said, had it not been for this reason. Sen. David I. Walsh of Massachusetts pressed the point, leading Mortimer to say that his purpose was to keep Katherine Mortimer "away from that fellow Forbes," and "if that could have been accomplished I would have never been hostile against Forbes at all."[30]

It is important to point out, in defining the Harding scandals, that there is no evidence that the president knew anything about Forbes's hospital site and construction schemes. Harding died early in August, and Mortimer's testimony began on October 24, nearly three months later. If General O'Ryan and the Senate committee members knew Mortimer was going to testify as he did, they surely would have alerted Harding. They might have informed the president during the Alaska trip that began in June, but again there is no evidence to that effect.

Instead the president found out about Forbes through another scam that the director of the Veterans' Bureau put in motion almost as soon as he had finished with his hospital arrangements. In September 1922 Forbes decided to hold a clearance sale at the vast Perryville depot for medical supplies that were under his direction. The sale got underway within weeks and came to the attention of the president in November. Harding took immediate action, and Forbes lost his job shortly thereafter.

What Forbes did at Perryville was as elementary, and classical one might say, as he did with the hospital sites and construction. This time he did not have competitive bidding but gave a contract to a Boston surplus firm, Thomson and Kelly. Meanwhile he placed a reliable man in charge of Perryville, a former navy lieutenant commander, C. R. O'Leary, so there would be no complaints when material started going out at prices that were ridiculously low, averaging 20 percent of the original purchase price. The alleged reasons for selling the items at Perryville were that they were bought at wartime prices and had deteriorated in storage.

In the ensuing hearings Forbes's clearance sale became clear in all its particulars. Take the instance of sheets, which the depot's reliable men made available to Thomson and Kelly. A list established the presence of "2,622 sheets, bed, assorted," but the delivery to the Bostonians was of 84,920 bedsheets. Almost all of them were new, in unbroken bundles as they had come from their manufacturers. The same thing happened with paraffin paper, though Thomson and Kelly obtained a better price on it, five cents a pound for what cost the government sixty cents. So-called moleskin, useful for making heavy coats and linings, a substitute also for upholstering, went out, 21,047 yards of it in a single delivery. Pajamas went to Thomson and Kelly, contributed by the Red Cross and actually made during the war by American women as a patriotic duty; the Boston firm took them without sentiment. Similarly 47,175 packages of gauze, each roll containing twenty-five yards, received in Perryville in January 1922, left the depot en route to Boston and the firm's other routings late that year, as new as when they had come from the manufacturer, Johnson and Johnson. Colonel Forbes related to Mortimer, with whom he had broken, and for whose hostility he doubtless was becoming concerned, that he had sixty-seven thousand quarts of liquor at Perryville. "Now, here, Mort. . . . If you can find a market for it, while I will have to make some return to the Government, we can fix that part of it all right." He had $5 million worth of narcotic drugs at the depot and offered them to Mort as well.[31]

What proved Forbes's undoing, and showed the president of the United States to be as honest as Sawyer afterward said he was, was information that came to the Public Health Service about the sales to Thomson and Kelly. Dr. Hugh S. Cumming, in charge of the service, and an assistant, Dr. Frederick C. Smith, called on General Sawyer and told him of an executive order stipulating that the service was entitled to one-fifth of all the supplies at Perryville. The three went to the Veterans' Bureau and spoke with Forbes in a heated conference. Sawyer then talked with the president, who asked Sawyer to go to Perryville and investigate, which the three dissidents did. Sawyer saw "great activity" in the depot, with one large truck that was full of towels about to be moved out. The general directed the officer in charge to unload and await further orders. Returning to Washington, he talked with the president, who ordered a stoppage of all loading until compliance with the requirements of the Public Health Service.[32]

Forbes made a written agreement to honor the executive order of the health service and then reneged on it. About three weeks later Sawyer learned from a service employee at Perryville that material was still being shipped, that nearly 125 carloads had been forwarded to Thomson and Kelly. "I then took the subject up again with the President, and he immediately called Colonel Forbes and said to him that nothing further must go. Regardless, however, of this order, directly from the President, other carloads within the next two or three days were shipped out, and as a result of this insubordination Colonel Forbes was asked to resign."

In the course of the above developments a group of agents of other surplus companies complained to the president, and Senator Calder of New York called upon him on behalf of constituents, but these representations only reinforced the action of Sawyer, Cumming, and Smith.

President Harding later was criticized for allowing Forbes, the recreant director, to go off on an inspection trip to Europe, during which Harding accepted his resignation. The contention was that this constituted only a slap on the wrist and that it was the Senate investigation that brought indictment and conviction of Forbes and John W. Thompson of the St. Louis construction firm Thompson-Black and their sentencing to ten-thousand-dollar fines and two years in prison. Harding's action perhaps was light-handed, though Forbes's eventual conviction appears to have come not from the Perryville derelictions (where proof of malfeasance was only circumstantial as there was no evidence of a bribe from the Boston surplus firm of Thomson and Kelly) but from the much later testimony of Mortimer, of which Harding had no knowledge. At the time, January 1923, the president had no clear evidence against Forbes that would have put him in jail. On February 9, Theodore Roosevelt Jr. had a conference with the president in which Harding discussed in general the Veterans' Bureau, telling young Roosevelt about his troubles with Forbes. The assistant secretary of the navy wrote afterward in his diary that "Matters have gone so far that he is not even sure that he has not been financially crooked."[33]

Rumor had it that prior to the trip the president summoned Forbes to the White House and shook him "as a dog would a rat," shouting "You double-crossing bastard!"[34] The shaking was true, the words approximate. As mentioned in Chapter 2, a reporter for the *New York Times* had come upon Harding shaking Forbes.

Not long after Forbes's fall the general counsel of the Veterans' Bureau, Cramer, who had purchased Harding's house at 2134 Wyoming Avenue after the senator was elected president, stood before a bathroom mirror and put a .45-caliber bullet through his right temple. It was said that he was depressed by rumor of troubles at the bureau and by recent financial reverses. A clipping on the forthcoming Senate investigation lay on the desk in his bedroom.

3 ———

Early in 1924 Sen. Burton K. Wheeler of Montana, then a freshman member of the upper house, teamed up with another freshman member, Smith W. Brookhart of Iowa, ignored the unspoken Senate rule that freshmen are to be seen and not heard, and launched an investigation into the activities of Attorney General Daugherty. The purpose appeared to be clear enough: "to investigate circumstances and facts, and report the same to the Senate, concerning the alleged failure of Harry M. Daugherty, Attorney General of the United States, to arrest and prosecute Albert B. Fall, Harry F. Sinclair, E. L. Doheny, C. R. Forbes, and their coconspirators." But the investigation was, to use a later word, freewheeling, as befitted the middle name of the Republican committee chairman, which was Wildman. For Brookhart, a member of the rebellious, nonpartisan, mostly Republican farm bloc in the Senate, the investigation would discomfit his party's regulars who had shown little feeling for Brookhart's constituents. It would also add cubits to his stature. For Wheeler, whose mail from the wide-open spaces of Montana, he confessed in his memoirs, was running a dozen letters a day, the committee offered something to do and a chance to match the investigative achievements of his Montana colleague, Sen. Thomas Walsh.

The Brookhart-Wheeler committee's hearings were necessarily complicated, since the senators did not know what they might find and were fishing around. Suffice to say that by looking into the accounts in the Midland National Bank in Washington Court House, Ohio, they pointed the way to the eventual discovery of Colonel Miller's activities. Unlike Forbes, whom Harding had met casually, Miller possessed an impeccable background. He was a Yale graduate. He had managed a Nevada ranch and worked for the Bethlehem Steel Corporation. Hence he was a westerner and an easterner. He served for two years as secretary of state of Delaware. He was elected to a term in Congress in 1914. When war began for the United States he enlisted in the infantry, received citations for gallantry in action, and rose to the rank of lieutenant colonel. He was one of the original incorporators of the American Legion and a member of its executive committee. In 1920 he was an eastern director of the Republican national committee. He was a member of the Episcopal Church and of the Union League Club of Philadelphia. The committee helped expose this paragon as a thoroughly venal appointee. He had taken $50,000 out of the bribe of $391,000 to give the American Metal Company back to its former German owner. He was indicted, tried, fined $5,000, and jailed for eighteen months.

The accusation against Daugherty of being inactive in the Teapot Dome prosecution and in the investigation of the Veterans' Bureau made no sense on the face of it, since few individuals had suspected Fall, or if (like Sen. Thomas Walsh) they were uncertain about him had the slightest proof against him until after Harding's death. In the case of the bureau there was no real proof against Forbes until Mortimer's testimony beginning in October 1923. The hope of the Brookhart-Wheeler committee, therefore, despite its bluster, was to link Daugherty with his friend Smith.

Daugherty in popular imagination, and in the conversation if not the minds of Brookhart and Wheeler, was the mastermind of the Harding administration. But Harry Micajah Daugherty was not a principal figure in whatever it was that the Brookhart-Wheeler committee was searching for. The committee never managed to link him to anything illegal or for that matter immoral. Born in Washington Court House, thirty-five miles southwest of Columbus, he had migrated to the state capital where he pursued a minor law practice. Many years before Harding became president the two had met, when the editor of the

Marion Star was traveling around the countryside attending political meetings. Reportedly they were staying at the same private house, and Harding sauntered out to the privy, galluses hanging down, and encountered Daugherty in the little building decorated with the half-moon. Actually they met in 1899 in Richwood, Ohio (in Union County, south of Marion), at a cast-iron pump where Harding was washing his boots, behind the Globe Hotel. Daugherty earlier had sought political office on his own but had not gotten far, perhaps because he was not a good orator, a requirement of politics during the post–Civil War golden age of oratory. He sensed that the editor from Marion could have a much more promising political career and undertook to help him. As Col. Edward M. House in similar circumstances attached himself to Woodrow Wilson, so Daugherty became the assistant of Harding.

The presumption was that Daugherty and Harding were very close. This was not altogether true. Once in a while Daugherty misestimated what Harding desired. During the Florida trip Daugherty, after talking over with Harding the president's decision to run for reelection in 1924, had taken it upon himself to announce that Harding would run again, and the president was irritated with his attorney general. Daugherty's announcement made it seem as if the western trip and the Alaska voyage were just campaigning, which was perhaps somewhat true, but the president probably had counted on its seeming a trip to make himself visible in the West on a nonpolitical basis, after which he would reveal his plans for the next year.

In other ways Daugherty was not the deus ex machina that he was thought to be. Over the years he had incurred the wrath of Ohio leaders. Some of it came because he did not hide his light and took credit for being a master politician in a state full of master politicians. Before the 1920 Republican National Convention in Chicago, he announced that his man, Harding, would win, which he did. A story circulated about a smoke-filled room: Daugherty had made a bantering remark to a reporter that his man would be chosen in a smoke-filled room "about eleven minutes after two, Friday morning of the convention," when everything was at a standstill regarding the other candidates. There was a smoke-filled room at the Blackstone Hotel, but Daugherty's alleged wizardry at the convention or in the room was otherwise false. Prior to the convention he had found himself handicapped by a divided Ohio delegation, with the Cincinnati leader, Rudolph Hynicka, a weak Harding supporter. The soap magnate of Cincinnati, William C. Procter, was supporting General Wood.[35] The only thing that saved Daugherty's prediction was luck, for Harding won because the two principal candidates, Wood and Gov. Frank O. Lowden of Illinois, fought each other to exhaustion and Harding was the best choice thereafter.

The Ohio leaders detested Daugherty and were quite open about it. No man of great power would have had to endure such criticism. Nor would Harding have tolerated it. When a Department of State official spoke with the former

Ohio governor Myron T. Herrick just after Harding's death and reminded him that his "dearest friend," the attorney general, might be less safe than he had been before, he obtained a quick response. "I never said anything to Harding against the man," Herrick replied. "I merely told him that Daugherty was a damn scoundrel."[36] Herrick was ambassador to France and had enjoyed the post. He would not have ventured such advice to Harding (if indeed he ventured it) unless he knew Daugherty was not completely in the confidence of the president. Daugherty had opposed the appointments of both Fall and Forbes, but Harding paid no attention to him.

For the Brookhart-Wheeler committee the question became how to get at Daugherty, once his mentor passed on, and by chance a way opened in the person of Jess Smith's divorced wife, Roxie Stinson, then living in Columbus. The two had been married for a year or so but remained close friends.

The availability of Ms. Stinson became known to the committee by accident. It happened that a Buffalo lawyer, Henry Stern, went to the U.S. attorney there, William J. Donovan, and said he had come on some odd information. A client of his, a resident in Cleveland, A. L. Fink, had met Ms. Stinson at the Hotel Hollenden where Fink hoped to discuss an investment deal, for he had heard that after Jess Smith's death his former wife had come into money. Ms. Stinson had journeyed from Columbus to talk with him. Instead of talking about investments, however, she desired to talk about the business deals of Smith with Daugherty and other individuals. Donovan had Stern dictate a statement about what he had heard and telephoned Senator Wadsworth, who advised Stern to go to Washington, where the senator sent him to Brookhart.[37]

Brookhart shared his knowledge of Ms. Stinson's knowledge with Wheeler, and the latter together with Stern went to Columbus to serve a subpoena. "And Senator Wheeler came to my door," Ms. Stinson testified, "and I didn't know what a subpoena was." As Wheeler told the story in his autobiography, he may well have grazed propriety if not the law when he gave his paper to the buxom, redheaded Ms. Stinson. She asked if she could make a telephone call, and he refused her request. He took her back to Washington, placed her in the custody of his sister who was his secretary, and she became his star witness, fascinating newspaper readers as she related what "Jess told me."[38]

The divorcée's exaggerations, which she carefully protected by relating that Jess had told them to her, were always interesting, but it became clear that her stories about Daugherty and Smith were prosaic to a fault. Daugherty's association with him had gone back to the Washington Court House days, when the older man virtually adopted the younger, who was at that time still a youth. Smith did well financially in the small town, in which he owned a general store. As Daugherty's political activities increased, Smith participated in some of them, and during the Chicago convention in 1920 he kept Daugherty's accounts. When the Harding administration opened in 1921, Smith received visitors attempting to see Daugherty and either passed them along or fended them off. When Daugherty moved to the Wardman Park Hotel because his wife was an invalid and spent much time in the Johns Hopkins University Hospital in Baltimore, and wintered in Florida, Smith became a sort of companion to the attorney general. Daugherty considered him extremely helpful. "He had become in many ways indispensable to my personal comfort and I relied absolutely on his honesty and loyalty."[39] In the years 1921–1923 his principal task was to maintain the apartment. As a courtesy the attorney general allowed him a desk in the Department of Justice, but he was not employed there.

Smith was no attractive personage. Dr. Boone, who was Daugherty's physician and saw much of him, disliked Smith with a passion. The fat, loud-talking small-town merchant was difficult to put up with. During the trip to Florida by President and Mrs. Harding in the spring of 1923, Daugherty and Smith accompanied the presidential party until it boarded the houseboat of the McLeans, after which Daugherty and Smith stayed in hotels and returned to Washington. Boone was with them and was at the outset assigned to room with Smith and could hardly stand him, as Smith was on the telephone all the time. The doctor was pleased when after adjourning from the Flamingo Hotel in Miami Beach to the Ponce de Leon in St. Augustine, he found himself in a single room, so Smith "could telephone to his heart's content and talk as loud as he wished without disturbing me."[40]

Smith's suicide on Memorial Day 1923 was rumored to be a murder but was really a plain, garden-variety suicide according to Boone who was on the scene. The assistant White House physician had noticed how eager Smith had been to perform chores for the attorney general, that a word of praise or expression of appreciation from Daugherty would cause Jess to "purr" happily. But Daugherty, Boone wrote in his autobiography, became convinced that Smith had overstepped the bounds of propriety, and it was necessary to lay down the law to him. One evening in Boone's presence Daugherty said, "Jess, if you do not discontinue your seeming assumptiveness and do not change your ways down at the Department of Justice, and in and outside of Washington, you will have to cease to live with me and move out of this apartment." Smith was stunned and was thereafter more subdued, less hyperactive and voluble, and appeared to withdraw into his shell. Boone traced Smith's suicide to Daugherty's displeasure, as he heard it expressed.[41]

Daugherty had another story that was not really contradictory and also had the ring of truth. The attorney general wrote in his book of a decade afterward that Smith in 1922 had gone into the hospital in Columbus where it was discovered that he had not merely diabetes but also appendicitis. After several days he was operated on, and the result was an abscess that refused to heal (Boone corroborated this in his autobiography). Daugherty believed that it virtually changed Smith's personality—thereafter his friend was unsettled, irritable, strange. And in the spring of 1923 had come the final blow when

Harding told Daugherty that Smith had not been conducting himself properly and would be well advised to go back to his hometown in Ohio.

"What is he doing?" Daugherty asked.

"I am informed he is running with a gay crowd, attending all sorts of parties," said the president. "And you should know too that he is using the Attorney-General's car until all hours of the night."

"I'm amazed," was the response. "I will look into the matter at once."

The president hesitated a moment and then spoke regretfully: "I suggest that you tell him it will be impossible for him to go with us on the trip to Alaska. The party is already filled."[42]

Daugherty knew what that meant and faced Jess as quickly as he could find him.

Early that summer of 1923, Daugherty and Smith had been in Ohio, and upon return Daugherty went to stay in the White House, knowing that Smith was to clear out his belongings. He arranged to have one of his assistants at the Department of Justice, Warren F. Martin, stay in the apartment with Jess for the few days he expected him to be there.

Boone played golf with Smith on the morning of May 29 and noticed that Jess showed no interest in the game. According to Secretary of Commerce Hoover, Harding called Smith to the White House that evening, told him about his malfeasance, and informed him he would be arrested the next morning. Where Hoover learned this is impossible to say; his memoirs are its only proof.[43]

On Memorial Day, Boone was awakened by a persistent ringing of the telephone (he later thought it must have been shortly after half past six in the morning). It was Martin, who told him to get over to the Wardman Park Hotel as fast as he could. Boone knew Daugherty was at the White House and could not understand what was happening. When he met Martin it was to hear him say, "There has been a terrible tragedy here! Jess Smith has shot himself!" Entering Smith's room, Boone saw Smith's doubled-up form on the floor, feet and lower legs under the bed, his large head stuffed into a metal wastepaper basket. Investigating, he saw a hole in the temple region with the skin and hair blackened for a sizable area, probably from powder burns. There was a great deal of blood from his nose and mouth and on the floor and on the pajamas in which he was dressed. Boone had no doubt it was a suicide, and the District of Columbia's coroner, whom he summoned, agreed immediately.

Boone "got down to the White House just as fast as I could," and upon entering rushed up the steps to the second floor, not using the elevator, knocked on the president's door, and entered. He found Harding almost completely dressed, shaved, and about to go to breakfast. "I told him what had occurred."

The president was stunned. "Have you told Harry Daugherty?" he asked.

"No," Boone said, "you are the first person I ever told."

"Do not go to his room," Harding said. "We'll let him have his breakfast. You come along with me and we'll go downstairs to the private dining room on the main floor, have our breakfast, and then you and I together will go and inform the Attorney General."

After breakfast the two went to Daugherty's room. "Harry," the president said, "Boone has some news for you and it's very bad news, so get hold of yourself."

"General," Boone said as quietly and calmly as possible, "Jess Smith has shot himself."

All the color left the attorney general's face, he stared at Boone and at President Harding, dropped his head into his hands, and there was a terrible silence in the room. The president and Boone did not utter a word.

"Why did he do it?" asked Daugherty. "My God, why did he do it? Why did he do it?"

"None of us has the slightest idea," Boone said.[44]

The Brookhart-Wheeler committee made a disgraceful contribution to the question (there should have been none) about Smith's suicide. Roxie Stinson intimated that it was a case of murder. Typically, she made the point by indirection and in such a haze of words that no one could have accused her of saying what she did. Daugherty claimed in his book that Wheeler coached her every night, which may well have been true. Her testimony was too coy and too careful to have been without instruction. Jess Smith's body had been brought back to Ohio for burial, and together with a companion she looked at the corpse and saw where the bullet entered the temple—there was a neat hole. She did not see where it exited, which was the back of the head and would have involved turning the body. She allowed for facial bruises because the head had tumbled into a wastebasket. "I am perfectly convinced in my mind," she concluded, "—of course, as I stated before, I don't know the circumstances of Jess Smith's death, not being present, and it is only through being told of the circumstances that I know anything about it." At that juncture any responsible committee chairman would have cut her off. But she went on.

> The Daughertys engineered the proceeding entirely, which was satisfactory,
> I should think, no one else being in a better position to do so, as they have
> been as brothers. But so far as I am concerned it may not even be true
> that he committed suicide or passed away in that manner. . . . I am sure
> that he did take his own life. However, I also consider Harry Daugherty
> as morally responsible for the death of Jess Smith.[45]

Ms. Stinson was no neutral witness where the Daughertys were concerned. She was unhappy about them because Jess Smith did not leave everything to her but to several heirs including the Daughertys as well as herself. Moreover, Mally Daugherty had placed in the estate an account she claimed belonged to her because Jess had told her so. She said he had opened it with the Cleveland firm of Samuel Ungerleider and Company under an assumed name, "William R. Á. Hays No. 3," because the brokerage house would not open accounts for single women.

In the years 1923–1924 Daugherty proved he could be impulsive, flighty, and melodramatic, and to some observers it seemed that such behavior showed he was trying to cover up something, doubtless something dark and devious. Two explanations denied that such was the case. Early in 1923 his son, Draper, a near-hopeless alcoholic, had to be put in an institution, and the experience was horrifying to the father, who required the ministrations of both his brother, Mally, and Boone to contain his distraught state of mind. The other problem at this time was more intrusive and easily could have affected his judgment for a while, his defensiveness and assertiveness that often passed the bounds of good sense and made his enemies think he was guilty of something. In January 1923 Boone was summoned to the Wardman Park Hotel and found the attorney general with high blood pressure and a threatened cerebral hemorrhage, "if one had not actually occurred." An ensuing illness, reported as the result of influenza, lasted for months and was "very, very serious." During the Florida trip Daugherty was in bed most of the time. Gradually his speech improved and he walked better; sometimes there was a thickening of speech, and he had a tendency to drag his affected foot. When Boone saw him on this trip and in Washington, which was many times, the physician never saw any awkward visitors or unseemly behavior.[46]

Harding's successor, Coolidge, had much trouble regarding Daugherty and some trouble directly from Daugherty. The presumed stroke could have been the reason, not a frantic effort to protect himself from connection with the American Metal Company bribery. Coolidge, who was an excellent judge of character, never thought Daugherty was dangerous and considered him only erratic, unpredictable, and of course politically inconvenient. He told Dr. Boone that Daugherty was a strong man, courageous, won people to him, the department was in fine condition, his accomplishments were remarkable, and people looked upon Daugherty as a politician and not a lawyer, whereas "he is a good lawyer." But he, the president, needed an attorney general free from attack, disinterested in the investigation of himself and his office. The Senate committee, he believed, would continue its work well into November— which meant that Daugherty would become an issue, and not a very helpful one, in the presidential election. During the investigations of the Brookhart-Wheeler committee Daugherty on one occasion went to the White House and spoke roughly with the president. Afterward Coolidge went to his friend William M. Butler, who was a White House guest, and told him, "He should not have talked to me like this."[47]

Late in March 1924 Daugherty refused to allow the Brookhart-Wheeler committee to see Department of Justice records. The president on March 27 asked for his resignation. Daugherty sent it, with an admonition that he had not had opportunity either to testify or to present witnesses in his behalf. The president's action concerned Grace Coolidge, who told Boone she regretted Daugherty's resignation.[48]

In a letter to Boone, after the attorney general had resigned at the request of President Coolidge, Daugherty flatly denied he knew Smith had taken money in collusion with Miller. "Of course, he never said anything to me about the matter in which his name is involved. It was the understanding that he was not to become connected in any way with any government matter, and he never did that I knew of, unless it was in this and I learned of his connection with this matter long after I left the attorney general's office." Earlier in the same letter he wrote that he had no doubt Smith's nervousness and general condition during the last two years of his life had made him "practically crazy part of the time."[49]

But the big question raised by the Brookhart-Wheeler hearings was what a special joint account for Daugherty and Smith in the Midland National Bank, "Jess Smith Extra No. 3," was for. In the course of the hearings Senator Wheeler, who if anything was more flamboyant than his Iowa colleague, journeyed to Washington Court House and during the local proceedings informed the record that he was in a room five hundred feet from the building (and vault) of the Midland National Bank. Mally Daugherty had refused to let the Senate committee investigator continue his researches in the bank's records. Later, after taking out the ledgers of any accounts pertaining to himself and Smith, including the joint account, Harry Daugherty burned them. In his book he said the political account, "Jess Smith Extra No. 3," related to individuals, Democrats as well as Republicans, who contributed to Harding's 1920 presidential campaign. "I did not propose to be dragged before the public on a fishing excursion by those who sought to pry into what had been done in a political campaign." He refused to testify during his court trials because, he said, he might have to speak in embarrassing ways about people whose reputations he desired to protect.[50] At the end of his first trial his lawyer explained his behavior by relating that

> The destruction of these ledger sheets did not conceal anything that had the slightest bearing on this case. . . . If the jury knew the real reason for destroying the ledger sheets, they would commend rather than condemn Mr. Daugherty, but he insisted on silence. . . . It was not anything connected with this case that impelled him to refrain from so doing [taking the stand]. . . . He feared, however—and perhaps absolutely without reason— . . . matters political that would not involve Mr. Daugherty concerning which he knew and as to which he would never make disclosure. . . .[51]

One speculation was that the political account was to protect the president against financial claims. Nan Britton wrote of Harding's receiving stock that he had not paid for, just before his death, and a payment of a forty-thousand-dollar claim by a brokerage house. President Butler of Columbia University said the president was up to his ears in speculation. Jess Smith might have been in charge of losses, though it seems extremely unlikely. Losses were entirely manageable by the Hardings in view of the fact that just before the Alaska trip the president sold the *Marion Star* for a sum that placed his estate's worth close to half a million dollars.

The other possible use for the political account was that it covered "woman trouble." In the instance of Nan Britton this does not seem possible. Before Harding went on the Alaska trip he made his will, and Daugherty drew it up. "If Nan Britton or any other woman had ever borne a child to my friend he could not have passed through this solemn hour with me without the frankest discussion of all the facts. He was never a secretive man. He couldn't have concealed such a thing from me if he tried; it would have inevitably come out." As Daugherty related, it would have taken only a few minutes for the attorney general to draft in his own hand a deed of trust that would have provided for Ms. Britton and her child, outside the terms of the regular will.

> I resent the imprint of callous cruelty which this slander puts on my friend even more than the slander itself. Any strong man might fall for a woman if tempted, but no man of Harding's character could have found it in his heart to treat her afterwards with studied, beastly neglect. He had a small fortune. Mrs. Harding had an estate of her own also. He had no children. His people were all well-to-do and capable of taking care of themselves. And he loved children. He was never known to pass a child without a smile or a touch of his big, gentle hand. My experience with Harding in this tender, solemn hour writes the word "Fake," "Fake," over every page of the book that bears the name of Nan Britton.[52]

In the case of Carrie Phillips there might have been some substance to the allegation that the fund was for woman trouble. Ms. Phillips sought to blackmail Harding in 1920 (as we will discuss later). She and her husband were reported to have gone that year on an extended trip to the Orient.

4 ———

All in all the Harding scandals did not touch Harding in any serious way, apart from his general responsibility for them. Nothing ever appeared, least of all from his connection with Daugherty, to indicate any complicity with them. That he knew about Fall is almost unbelievable, since no one else did. He knew about Forbes and acted at once on the basis of what he then knew. When he learned that Smith was misbehaving, he spoke to Daugherty about it, advising Smith's immediate departure from Washington. As to whatever it was specifically that Harding heard about Smith, apart from what he told Daugherty, and where he heard it, there is no evidence, save the memoir account of Secretary Hoover. This melodramatic story of a White House warning of imminent arrest, followed by a suicide, differs markedly from the more prosaic and hence more believable accounts in Boone's autobiography and Daugherty's memoirs.

The talk about an Ohio Gang surely was misplaced. Senator Wheeler believed he was the first individual to use the phrase, in a statement on April 23, 1924. In his memoirs he could not remember quite what he was referring to, except that he had brought into his hearings a parade of bootleggers, promoters, and influence peddlers.[53] There certainly was no organized effort to loot the federal treasury. The Ohio Gang, the historian Murray has written, "had very few of the characteristics of a gang because it had no concrete form, no cohesion, and no plan. If it had any leadership, it was provided by Jess Smith."[54] To be sure, Smith was not much of a leader.

Much of the testimony and other evidence presented to the Senate committees—Smoot's standing committee, together with the two special committees—was half-baked, tendentious, and in any event secondhand, thirdhand, indeed so far removed that no one could remember. During one Senate session Senator Lodge read some doggerel that aptly showed what was going on:

> Absolute knowledge have I none,
> But my aunt's washerwoman's sister's son
> Heard a policeman on his beat
> Say to a laborer on the street
> That he had a letter just last week—
> A letter which he did not seek—
> From a Chinese merchant in Timbuctoo,
> Who said that his brother in Cuba knew
> Of an Indian chief in a Texas town,
> Who got the dope from a circus clown,
> That a man in Klondike had it straight
> From a guy in a South American state,
> That a wild man over in Borneo
> Was told by a woman who claimed to know,
> Of a well-known society rake,
> Whose mother-in-law will undertake
> To prove that her husband's sister's niece
> Has stated plain in a printed piece
> That she has a son who never comes home
> Who knows all about the Teapot Dome.[55]

The committees seemed to want to subpoena anyone, always with a reason. A senator supposedly was heard to say, "Serve a subpoena on Thomas A. Edison. We want more light on the subject."

The investigations of Teapot Dome, the Veterans' Bureau, and Attorney General Daugherty were in one special respect political. During the Wilson and Harding administrations the Senate was inordinately proud of its powers and importance. The members of the upper house deeply resented the subordinate status to which President Wilson had consigned them during passage of the progressive legislation of 1913 through 1916 and then their subordination during the world war in 1917 and 1918, a time when everyone looked to the president for leadership. When the Senate rejected the League of Nations and the Treaty of Versailles, it was demonstrating its desire to reassert itself, as well as reacting to Wilson's imperiousness in negotiating the peace without really consulting the upper house. The senators present at the Republican National Convention in Chicago in 1920 nominated one of their own, Harding, and thereafter expected him to behave himself, show suitable attention to the Senate's prerogatives. At the beginning of his administration Harding tried, but the senators were ungrateful, and gradually he came around to believing that he would have to manage them as Wilson did—that is, he would have to marshal public opinion in support of his own legislation and force them to toe the line. By 1923 Harding was beginning to push Congress, particularly the Senate, and his western tour was part of the pushing, an effort to bring public opinion behind his own measures. The several investigations were the Senate's way of rebuffing the Harding presidency. Because the results became apparent during the Coolidge administration, they served a dual purpose of warning the new president.

As the investigations stretched into the spring of 1924 they looked ever more closely toward the presidential election, in which several of the senators were personally involved—hoping to displace Coolidge who had come to prominence so unexpectedly and was himself maneuvering, as best he could, for the Republican nomination.

In some ways Coolidge gave in to the Senate, as in his unwillingness to make any large move to keep Secretary Denby in the cabinet. He waffled on Daugherty, giving the latter the impression he would support him down to the end, and seizing upon a technicality—Daugherty's refusal to hand over Department of Justice records to the Brookhart-Wheeler committee—to demand his resignation.

By this temporizing, for a while giving in, Harding's successor allowed the investigating committees to overplay their hands and eventually show their work as ineffective. The Teapot Dome committee hearings petered out in May 1924, and at the last hearing there was not a single spectator present. The Veterans' Bureau committee had almost finished its serious work after it heard the testimony of Mortimer, who had determined to get Forbes and did so. The Brookhart-Wheeler inquiry into the attorney general's failure, it said, to pursue the other two investigations, and its efforts to discover anything else, such as the joint account, could not really touch Daugherty.

The Harding scandals lacked large historical importance. The participants displayed no remarkable skills. "Compared with the great bosses and professional grafters in American politics," Murray concluded, "these men were amateurs and their actual take was relatively small." Eugene Meyer lived through Teapot Dome and later scandals and told an interviewer, "There are a hundred Teapot Domes in the record of the last twenty years."[56]

The story of the scandals persisted long after the reality was forgotten. Sen. Alben W. Barkley of Kentucky, the beloved "Veep" of the Truman administration, wrote in his memoirs in a humorous vein that Secretary Fall, he was ashamed to say, had been a Kentuckian who had gone west, as so many had, and that after the New Mexico senator became a cabinet member, with his picture in the papers, the attorney for a former Fall landlady wrote Barkley that Fall owed his client a large board bill. Barkley forwarded the letter to Fall, without comment, and Fall paid the bill with interest and elaborate apologies. This was the only time, Barkley wrote, when he had collected a board bill. He then took a de rigueur shot at the Harding administration by recalling one of his 1928 speeches in which he had said that "we have witnessed in the United States of America a series of political crimes so nauseating and revolting as to make grand larceny sound like an announcement of a hymn or golden text at a Sunday school."[57] The exaggeration was impossible to put down. In a telephone interview in 1964, Dr. Boone related that he had seen part of a play titled *The Gang's All Here* on *The Ed Sullivan Show* and had read a review of it in *Time*. He was enraged by the play's handling of Harding and could hardly speak articulately. He shouted over the phone, "To have the President of the United States up on a table, dancing with a harlot!" He said that Sullivan had told his audience, after the skit, that it was a good thing to bring the facts to the American people.[58]

5
Aftermath

In the years before and especially after Harding's death and all the speculation that attended it, and publication of *The President's Daughter* and the titillation that attended it, and the exposing of scandals during the Harding administration, a virtual wave of cynicism rolled across the country, known as *debunking*. There was nothing new in American history about debunking, for Americans from the beginning of the Republic had poked fun at their betters, such as political leaders whom they described, not altogether respectfully, as politicians. But in the 1920s debunking turned away from humor and became almost savage—inspired by the end of the Progressive Era, of which so much had been expected during the administrations of Theodore Roosevelt and Wilson, and by the revulsion against the world war that came suddenly with the war's end and then the defeat of the League of Nations and the Treaty of Versailles by the largely Republican members of the Senate and by, for he was himself the coarchitect of his creation's defeat, President Wilson.

Another factor that reduced respect for the nation's twenty-ninth president was the writings of a talented group of journalists who for several reasons, personal as well as political, took up the cudgels against Harding. One was the leading journalist of the time, the Emporia, Kansas, newspaperman William Allen White. Another was his virtual peer in political writing, Mark Sullivan. A third was the talented author of *Revelry*, Samuel Hopkins Adams. And there were others who assisted them. These writers wrote from memory (White and Sullivan had known Harding in their journalistic capacities) and from what little information lay at hand, such as the Teapot Dome hearings and the other investigations, and they spoke with former members of the Harding administration who for one reason or another, not all of them estimable, wished to be quoted. Theirs clearly were preliminary analyses. But for years after 1923 they were the only analyses.

Still another factor in reducing Harding's reputation was the awkward manner in which his personal papers were handled. It was almost a nightmare of errors, in which his widow openly avowed that she had burned the papers, and the papers themselves then disappeared, secreted in the basement of the Harding house in Marion, although few people knew that. It all seemed an enterprise by Marion insiders to keep terrible things, presumably in the papers, from becoming known. In 1963 and 1964 the papers were transferred from Marion to the Ohio Historical Society in Columbus and opened. But along with their opening—it was typical Harding ill luck—came the revelation in the summer of 1964 of a bona fide Harding mistress and that Harding's letters to her had been found in Marion in a locked closet in her house. The Harding heirs, unnerved, secured the letters and sealed them for fifty years, until the year 2014.

Lastly, and as if these body blows to the reputation of the president of 1921–1923 were not enough, came publication of biographies that followed upon the opening of the papers (and closing of the Phillips letters). As luck had it, two of the three and one-half biographies (Randolph Downes published only his first volume) were hostile, the more readable of them mockingly so. Downes's half-biography was mostly about Ohio politics and not fascinating. The other biography, by Robert K. Murray, was an admirable book but published by a university press and perhaps for that reason failed to obtain the notice it deserved.

1 ———

Debunking—the word itself was amusing and believable—had long been an attractive part of American political life and filled a useful role, for when American politicians were inclined to stand upon their soapboxes and like the White Queen in *Through the Looking Glass* believe (in their cases relate) as many as six impossible things before breakfast every morning, unbelievers invariably called attention to the silly remarks. What distinguished the debunkers of the 1920s was the savagery behind the debunking—there was something venomous about it, a dislike that went beyond the horizons of humor, that was no simple taking of funny occasions. The debunkers had what a later generation would describe as a hidden agenda. They did not like any American president of their generation and did not mind if they tore reputations to shreds, in gentlemanly prose if possible, in humor if that suited them, but with no real effort to search out the truth. Behind these tactics it might be said that they did not much like, not to mention admire, the American people, and considered democracy an impossible form of government.

One of the principal debunkers of the early 1920s was Clinton W. Gilbert, author of two books published in 1921 and 1922 by Putnam's in New York.

They were titled *The Mirrors of Washington* and *Behind the Mirrors: The Psychology of Disintegration at Washington.* The initial volume sold nearly one hundred thousand copies, so the second testified. The successor may not have done so well, perhaps evidenced by the fact that no more such books appeared. The purpose of the books, apart from the theme revealed in the second volume's subtitle, was that a book, far more so than a newspaper article, would "scare a politician."[1] A book, Gilbert decided, or so his publisher wrote (on their title pages both books were anonymous), would bring not a smile nor a shrug but angry protest.

The style of the Gilbert books was careful, as the publisher's preface to the second related. The reason was not altogether convincing, but whoever wrote the preface (probably Gilbert) advanced it. A book should be "far less bitter, far more balanced," than a newspaper story. This said little for the prose of newspapers and was belied in the columns of many newspapers even of that perhaps less balanced journalistic era. The *Mirrors* books nonetheless so announced their appearance, and a reader of several generations later must allow that the prose of the books was careful and did not go to extremes.

The message was anything but careful, middle-of-the-road. The author had a point of view that was jaundiced and sour and seemed to say that American politics of the preceding generation and assuredly of the moment, the first years after the world war, had been a tissue of errors. Each of the presidents of the past twenty years—Theodore Roosevelt, Wilson (Gilbert considered Taft unworthy of mention), and Harding—had been unworthy of the country. When Roosevelt was in the White House he gave a cachet to his time. He made himself the image of his fellow Americans, or they of him—this point did not seem clear to Gilbert. The Typical American (the capitals were the author's) was "gay, robustious, full of the joy of living, an expansive spirit from the frontier, a picaresque twentieth century middle class Cavalier." This American hit the line hard, and without flinching. His laugh "shook the skies." Then came Wilson, and the Typical American had trouble with his soul. With roots in his churchgoing past, he carried the banner of the Lord, democracy, and idealism. He voted for Prohibition and suffrage for women. He was a Round Head in a Ford. Then, after eight years of this nonsense, the Typical American brought in "Warren Gamaliel Harding of the modern type, the Square Head." Harding's artistic taste was the movies. The postwar president found mental satisfaction in the "vague inanities" of the small-town newspaper. He put his faith in America, liberty, virtue, happiness, prosperity, and law and order, distrusting anything new except mechanical inventions.[2]

Before 1914 there was belief in Progress, and two beliefs followed. In the Progressive Era the Typical American had paid five cents to ride the streetcar and hoped it might be three. Hope lay in the ideas of people of that time, which exposed businessmen and other unethical individuals for the trifling people they were; it was an era in which Americans could hope for new things; President Roosevelt was sure that during his administration, and for a short while that of his friend Taft, they would arrive, not in due time but in Republican time. Then the Democrats took over, and President Wilson instructed his fellowmen not to believe in Progress but in Man. The cost of streetcars did not go down but up, to (in 1922) seven or eight cents. The Great War was society's effort to compensate for the idea of evolution, of Progress. Man "wanted to show what he could do, in spite of his slimy origin." During the war, governments performed the impossible, even taking in hand the industrial mechanism that ordinarily was left to the control of "the forces," those inanimate objects that moved society. With the successful end of the war, Americans half suspected that they might be able to do the impossible in peace. Instead, although they did not know it, the war had broken the picture in their heads. In their uncertainty they did not know whether to put their money on Man or on Progress, "so we put it on Mr. Harding."[3]

Harding, in the mind of the author of the *Mirrors* books, was a sure example of confusion, for like the Typical American he did not know what to believe. He had come to manhood in the 1880s (Harding was born in 1865), when God was in heaven and the United States was surpassing Great Britain and Germany in steel production. From this perception of order Harding, like the Typical American, shifted to Progress under President Roosevelt. He echoed the phrases of belief in Man announced by President Wilson—the Brotherhood of Man, War to End War, and "We must be just even to those to whom we do not wish to be just." Then "some monstrous hand had turned the page and there was Harding," who knew no more than his countrymen.[4]

In Gilbert's opinion, Harding was no individual to change anything. His mental atmosphere, comfortable as it was, was naught but that of a small town. His public experience before coming to Washington was brief service in the Ohio legislature and a term as lieutenant governor. His service in the Senate was short, beginner's work. He left no mark on legislation, and if he had retired at the end of his term his name would have existed only in the congressional directories, like that of a thousand others. As a public speaker he said nothing anyone could remember. He passed through the Great War and left no mark on it. He shared in the fierce debate about the League of Nations and the Treaty of Versailles, and it was possible to recall small personages such as Senators Porter J. McCumber of North Dakota, Frank B. Kellogg of Minnesota, George H. Moses of New Hampshire, and Medill McCormick of Illinois, all of whom said some things in the Senate's discussions, but no one recalled Harding. He said he had made a great speech, but no newspaper thought fit to publish it.

If during his presidential administration, which had just begun when Gilbert's books were published, Harding was in doubt about anything, which was unlikely, he still would do nothing. He would consult the "best minds" endlessly (he had used this phrase to characterize the members of his cabinet).

He would consult business minds outside of the cabinet. He would consult party opinion, though nothing could come from that: "His party has no opinion, it exists by virtue of its capacity to think nothing about everything and thus avoid dissensions." He would use his tact, of which he possessed a great deal, for it was his primary quality to find a solution, but the task would be essentially hopeless. A friend had said that "Warren is the best fellow in the world. He has wonderful tact. He knows how to make men work with him and how to get the best out of them. He is politically adroit. He is conscientious. He has a keen sense of his responsibilities. He has unusual common sense." The friend named other similar virtues. "Well, I asked him, 'What is his defect?' 'Oh,' he replied, 'the only trouble with Warren is that he lacks mentality.' "[5]

The author of *Mirrors* was saying that the country, the Typical American, had voted for nothing in government in Washington save "an immense inertia." And having defined total inactivity, Gilbert gave some advice to his readers. "The only thing to do is to laugh. You have trouble laughing? Look about you and you will find plenty to laugh at. Look at your President and laugh. Look at your Supreme Court and laugh. Not one of them knows whether he is coming or going."[6]

Gilbert, one might conclude, was a gentlemanly debunker, who wrote in measured periods, and even if he drew caricatures they did not puncture balloons and assault political reputations in the manner that his contemporary in debunking, Henry L. Mencken, did. There was a large difference in method. Withal the purpose was the same.

Mencken had the same disdain for American politics as did the author of the *Mirrors* books. To him, politics was hopeless. He avowed that the presidents of the United States in the past thirty or forty years—he was more expansive than Gilbert—had done nothing for the sum of human knowledge. Their ideas had not enriched that sum. "On the contrary, most of these great men have discharged little save piffle . . ."[7]

Like Gilbert, the Sage of Baltimore made the same appraisals of Presidents Roosevelt and Wilson, and the readers of his columns in the *Baltimore Sun*, and the many readers across the country whose newspapers reprinted the columns, did not have to use much imagination to sense what he was going to say about Harding. Roosevelt he liked in an inverted, roundabout way. He admired his "daily mountebankery," if only because it kept the ball in the air.[8] In T.R.'s day it was a pleasure to read the newspapers. Roosevelt, to be sure, was a bogus progressive. He was a maker of white protestations and black acts. His were bold stratagems and duplicities, sacrifice of faith and principle to the main chance, displaying "magnificent disdain of fairness and honor." But all this was better than what followed, which were weekly appendices to the Revelation of St. John the Divine. Wilson was a bogus liberal. He was "the Anglomaniacal Woodrow." "Dr. Wilson's so-called ideals" were sickening, from the initial time he "loosed his first evangelical dithyrambs upon the world." Woodrow came home from Paris in 1919 ranking with the masterminds of the ages. Writing on October 4, 1920, about the then president of the United States, Mencken observed that "he is now regarded by everyone save a despairing band of last-ditch fanatics as a devious and foolish fellow, of whom the nation will be well rid on March 4."[9]

Mencken did not look forward with pleasure to what was going to happen on the first Tuesday in November 1920. On July 28 he related his reasoning, that the presidency tended, year by year, as democracy was perfected, to represent, more and more closely, the inner soul of the people. "We move toward a lofty ideal. On some great and glorious day the plain folks of the land will reach their heart's desire at last, and the White House will be adorned by a downright moron."[10] After Roosevelt and Wilson, the American people naturally were ready for a change. No sane American believed in any official statement of policy, foreign or domestic, having been fooled too often, callously and impudently. Whenever an idea roused him to enthusiasm and passion, its propounder dragged him into the mud and made it evil and disgusting. The average American in 1920 hence wanted a change. "He wants a renaissance of honesty—even of ordinary, celluloid politician's honesty. Tired to death of intellectual charlatanry, he turns despairingly to honest imbecility."[11]

In sorting out what was about to happen, the Sage did not think it mattered if the average American voted for a Democrat or a Republican. This had been proved in the recent war. Every time a Democratic patriot, capitalist or toiler, obtained an easy dollar at Hog Island, which was the huge wartime shipyard near Philadelphia, a Republican patriot would receive another dollar. Every time a German factory was sold for ten cents on the dollar to a deserving Democrat, a German mill went for eleven cents on the dollar to a Republican "full of exalted rage against the Hun."[12]

As for Senator Harding, who became the Republicans' choice for the presidency at Chicago that summer, there was little that Harding could have done, if he was reading Mencken's columns, other than anticipate the worst from the Baltimore critic of American politics, which soon came; thereafter as a candidate he had to grit his teeth and bear it. Mencken had predicted as early as February 9, 1920, that Harding was a second-rate provincial. Gleaming through this preliminary analysis was a belief that Ohio was run by the Anti-Saloon League, and this if nothing else turned the critic against the man he soon was describing as "Gamaliel." By July 26, with Harding in place to win—his nomination meant his election, as Mencken well knew, given the extraordinary anti-Wilson feeling after the defeat of the league and the treaty—the analysis had hardened. Harding "is simply a third-rate political wheel-horse, with the face of a moving-picture actor, the intelligence of a respectable agricultural implement dealer, and the imagination of a lodge joiner."[13]

Mencken voted for Harding. That, to be sure, as he described it to his readers, was an ordeal, upon which he loosed his choicest invective. It was

Mencken at his best, and smiles and laughter must have reverberated around the living rooms of Baltimore and wherever Mencken's columns were read:

> After meditation and prayer of excessive virulence for many days and consultation with all the chief political dowsers of the Republic, I conclude with melancholy that God lays upon me the revolting duty of voting for the numskull, Gamaliel, on the first Tuesday in November. It is surely no job to lift the blood pressure and fill the liver with hosannahs. Since I acquired the precious boon of the suffrage, in the year 1901, I have never had to cast my vote for a worse dub. The hon. gentleman is an almost perfect specimen of a 100% American right-thinker. The operations of his medulla oblongata (the organ, apparently, of his ratiocination) resemble the rattlings of a colossal linotype charged with rubber stamps.[14]

He did not let well enough alone. On November 1 he opened his column with "Tomorrow the dirty job. I shall be on my knees all night . . ."[15]

The columnist may have voted for Harding because he anticipated four years of throwing brickbats at Harding the orator and surely was disappointed when he received the opportunity for only two and one-half. He had published *The American Language* in 1919 and would follow that classic with two supplements. Anyone who has read around in the books—they sometimes read like telephone books, enormous compilations of words and meanings, note cards beyond belief—can see how Harding's oratory, however short the opportunity, was in for a bath. A century earlier, Mencken had written, the nation had experienced the Jacksonians, who came to power after the Republic's founders believed they, the fathers, had expressed the nation's soul in precise, intelligent eighteenth-century words, dedicated to an age when a word meant what it said. He obviously anticipated that history would repeat itself. The Jacksonians, he wrote in *The American Language,* lived in an era when newspapers suddenly multiplied and people everywhere were hungry for news, and unfortunately in Congress there was almost no business, nothing to talk about so it would fill up the newspapers. So the country's "corn-fed etymologists" filled out the language by placing adjectives and adverbs before every noun and verb and by pulling out nouns with suffixes such as "ation" and turning good nouns into verbs by adding "ize." The result was a horror that people for the rest of the century had to endure and try, if it were possible, to sweep back the waters. Some progress had been made. But then with the advent of Roosevelt, Wilson, and then, horror of horrors, Harding, the nation's prose was bound to be ruined for another century. It would be Mencken's self-appointed task this time to sweep back the waters.

The writer hoped that the sheer exercise of Harding's style in his speeches, some of which he believed had shown clarity and vigor, would help the Ohioan pick up facility in writing. After all, writing was easy, "a trivial art, and well within the capacities of any normal adult with sufficient patience." He believed writing to be a literary gift valuable to a politician, "particularly if it take the form of a talent for mere words, as opposed to ideas."

But then came the inaugural speech. On "the question of the logical content of Dr. Harding's harangue of last Friday" he confessed to confusion. The president had said that the United States entered the late war because of a "concern for preserved civilization." He presumed that Harding should be "holding down the chair of history in some American university." When the orator remarked that "ours is a constitutional freedom where the popular will is supreme, and minorities are sacredly protected," he remembered the "red scare" after the war, abandoned himself to mirth, and sent picture postcards of Wilson's last attorney general, Mitchell Palmer, and of the Atlanta penitentiary, at that time still the home of Eugene Debs, to all of his enemies who happened to be socialists. As for the words in which Harding clothed his ideas, "When Dr. Harding prepares a speech he does not think it out in terms of an educated reader locked up in jail, but in terms of a great horde of stoneheads gathered around a stand."

> . . . I rise to pay my small tribute to Dr. Harding. Setting aside a college professor or two and half a dozen dipsomaniacal newspaper reporters, he takes the first place in my Valhalla of literati. That is to say, he writes the worst English that I have ever encountered. It reminds me of a string of wet sponges; it reminds me of tattered washing on the line; it reminds me of stale bean-soup, of college yells, of dogs barking idiotically through endless nights. It is so bad that a sort of grandeur creeps into it.[16]

The amusing thing about Harding's inaugural address was that Harding did not write it. It was written by one of his advisers, a professor of political economy at Johns Hopkins University—in Mencken's home city.

The speech moved Mencken to yearn for "the sweeter song, the rubber-stamps of more familiar design, the gentler and more seemly bosh of the late Woodrow."[17]

According to Mencken, Harding had no purpose in life other than to be reelected. When Daugherty in the spring of 1923 announced that Harding was a candidate for reelection, Mencken announced that it was certainly not news, that the plain fact was that Harding became an active candidate for a second term at 12:01 P.M., on March 4, 1921. When Harding died, and newspapers said he had passed on because of the intolerable cares and burdens of the presidential office, the columnist observed that at the time Harding collapsed he was not engaged in presidential duties but in a canvass for renomination and reelection.

In observing the president of 1921–1923, Mencken touched every field of Harding's endeavor, including foreign policy. He declared himself in favor of the League of Nations because, although he regarded it as "thumpingly dishonest," like democracy it deserved to be tried.[18] Within a few years its principal members would be trying to slaughter one another. When Harding came out for American membership in the World Court, the critic declared it would edge the United States into the league, for the court was only the league in a new false face, with the Union Jack concealed beneath the undershirt.

In January 1924 the columnist together with George Jean Nathan and the publisher Alfred Knopf founded the *American Mercury,* with the duty "to track down some of the worst nonsense prevailing and to do execution upon it."[19] In its first year the *Mercury*'s every issue contained at least one disparaging remark about Harding. First it was Mencken's description of the "funeral orgies," which spared nothing. "No man ever passed into the Eternal Vacuum to the tune of more delirious rhetoric." The account related the "ghastly progress" of the funeral train as it passed "that double file of village mayors, newspaper photographers, scared school children and anonymous morons," who gurgled, sniffed, choked, and moaned. As the Teapot Dome hearings filled the newspapers, the *Mercury* collected and quoted such obituary remarks as that of the *Bookman,* that Harding was "the most thoroughly trusted by the people at large of any President of our time." Bishop William F. Anderson of Cincinnati had quoted Harding as saying, "My prime motive in going to the White House is to bring America back to God." The Kiwanis Club magazine's tribute caught the eye of the *Mercury:*

> Oh, Son of God—to God returned—
> Peace to thee with a rest well earned,
> Thy gentle face and quiet calm
> Remains to us a golden balm.

For the *Mercury* the problem thereafter became how to memorialize President Harding, and a two-page editorial noted the work of the Harding Memorial Association. What, specifically, could it do? Erect an equestrian statue of the Martyr in Marion? Place hand-painted oil paintings of him in all the far-flung halls of the Benevolent and Protective Order of Elks? Endow a Brig. Gen. Charles E. Sawyer chair of homeopathy in the Johns Hopkins Medical School?

Mencken's political judgment, let it be added, was as poor as his prose was bright. Indeed it was not merely poor; it was terrible. Consider his judgment in the presidential year of 1924, when the Democratic Party nearly committed suicide in nominating the Wall Street lawyer John W. Davis on the 103d ballot, all this in Madison Square Garden, which of course in those days was not air-conditioned. When this absurdity of politics and physical endurance took place, Mencken had no idea what was going on. Somewhere near the end of the casting of ballots he sat down before his Corona portable typewriter and wrote the following lead for a story in the *Baltimore Sun:* "Everything is uncertain in this convention but one thing: John W. Davis will never be nominated." Told that Davis was nominated shortly after he filed his story, the reporter was stunned for a moment and said, "Why that's incredible! I've already sent off a story that it's impossible." Then as an afterthought: "I wonder if those idiots in Baltimore will know enough to strike out the negative."[20] That year Mencken pronounced Davis a liar, Coolidge a prospect worse than Harding, and voted for the hopeless Robert M. LaFollette.

2 ———

Late in the 1920s books by journalists began to appear, each representing Harding's presidency as a time of great presidential weakness, and no one was more dedicated to that interpretation than William Allen White, who was first in the field, in 1928, with *Masks in a Pageant,* a survey or run-through of the presidents he had known beginning with Benjamin Harrison and ending with Coolidge. He included an utterly malicious interpretation of Harding.

Any explanation of why White took such a stance must of course include his incurable, inoperable worship of the late President Roosevelt, who had passed on in 1919 and who if he had lived would undoubtedly have taken the Republican nomination in 1920. White once wrote that "Roosevelt bit me, and I went mad." He never forgot that day in December 1918 when he saw Roosevelt for the last time, ill in Roosevelt Hospital in New York. It is easily understandable therefore that when Harding received the nomination in 1920, White remembered sadly his old friend who had died. He especially would have remembered that the Ohio politician in 1912 turned his back on the great T.R. by helping renominate President Taft that year, instead of giving the nomination to Roosevelt who had broken with Taft and wanted another presidential term for himself. Harding was a party regular and refused to have anything to do with a party split. The same was not true of Roosevelt, who defied the regulars and took his followers to another hall in Chicago, let them march around singing "Onward, Christian Soldiers," and allowed them to create the Progressive Party that became better known from his own wondrous remark, "I feel like a bull moose." To White it did not matter that Roosevelt's candidacy in 1912 divided the Republican Party and gave the election to the Democratic candidate, Wilson. The only thing that mattered was that the regulars including Harding had thwarted Roosevelt.

In White's view Harding's first error was that he was not Roosevelt and had acted against Roosevelt, and there may well have been a second—namely, that Harding like White had been a small-town newspaper editor. Years later the historian Downes received a letter from a correspondent containing a shrewd appraisal. "I always felt," Ben H. Mason opined, "that W. A. White never reconciled himself to the fact that a fellow editor made the White House and he didn't." He thought there was a vein of jealousy all through White's writings on Harding. White thought of himself as the spokesman for small-town editors, and "when the man from Marion came into sight, White was pushed into the background." White, he wrote, in memory of White's having backed Roosevelt and the Bull Moose candidacy in 1912, was a poor politician and a jealous editor.[21]

Curiously, in the campaign of 1920 (and by chance in opposition to another upstart small-town editor, James M. Cox, of Dayton, Ohio, who was the Democratic nominee), White backed Harding. It is true that White later wrote of himself at the Chicago convention as a "sad fat figure" toddling around the hall during the traditional uproar for Harding's nomination, while bands played, trumpets brayed, and the crowd howled.[22] But White did more to support Harding than get out on the floor. After the nomination he complimented the candidate in words that readers of *Masks in a Pageant* might have remembered, had they known of them. "You are making a great impression on the American people," he wrote. "You have grown every moment since the day of the nomination. It seems to me that your sincerity, your sense of dignity and your steady thoughts have made themselves felt in the American heart."[23]

Then, not long after Harding died, White turned around and soon was thundering about Harding's iniquities. Apparently the reason was Teapot Dome, which to White was a terrible affair as he wrote about it in his book of 1928. Words could hardly describe his contempt. He mustered up his most choice phrases to describe how awful the scandal was. "Then slowly all the scandal which had been hidden came out, and with the truth, which was bad enough, came lies and innuendoes. Before scandal had reached him, men started to raise a memorial to him. A myth was born that he was a beloved president, a sweet and kindly man, like Lincoln. But—alas!—the myth was abortive. His friends, cronies, allies, and the Ohio gang were haled into court." The scandal reminded White of the Greek tragedy that all the youths of his era read about (Greek tragedy is no longer the stuff of modern education, no longer has any place in American political measurements). Without hesitation he scurried to ancient Athens to draw the scene:

> Always there must have been, in the dark periphery of his consciousness, cackling, ribald voices: Daugherty's voice, Fall's voice, drunken voices, raucous in debauch, the high-tensioned giggle of women pursued, the voices of men whispering in the greedy lechery of political intrigue; cynical voices cackling like the flames of the pit in scurrilous derision at the booming presidential rhetoric, Harding's high faluting yearnings. This was his hell; the hell which he could only escape by sinking further into it, and forgetting his lofty emprise. So fools rattled their heels in the White House and on the decks of the *Mayflower* while Harding relaxed.[24]

In *Masks*, White exhibited proof of Harding's knowledge of Teapot Dome. Just after the *Henderson* left Alaskan waters for Vancouver, he wrote, Harding received from Washington a long message in code, brought by seaplane. "This message clearly upset him. For a day or so he was near collapse. He recovered somewhat, but remained distraught and worried."[25] It was a good story, agreeable to imaginations of the time when seaplanes were on the pages of every Sunday newspaper in the glossy, sepia-colored rotogravure section. The story, however, never has had the slightest proof, the seaplane delivery never verified, the contents of a message, if delivered, never revealed.

The truth was that White's allegations reached a great deal further than his evidence. Teapot Dome seemed to have mesmerized him. "Rumor said," he wrote, "probably apocryphally" (which was hardly enough warning to a reader about the rumor he was spreading), that Harding signed over the oil reserves from Secretary of the Navy Denby to Fall when the president was drunk. He grasped for anything to criticize Harding: Jess Smith, "in the midst of his activities, under a threat, probably from the White House, of prosecution, killed himself—or was murdered by those whom his confessions might have involved."[26]

Reading the yellowing pages of *Masks in a Pageant*, library copies of which are torn and fragmented, corners bent where some student of old wished to remember a torrid passage, pages underlined in pencil and the fountain-pen ink of that time, one has the impression that White chose to pillory Harding for several reasons—devotion to Roosevelt, possibly the small-town-editor problem, perhaps Teapot Dome. And then there was something else, which could be described as a literary opportunity. White wrote privately to the Wilsonian reformer Brand Whitlock, the erstwhile mayor of Toledo, on July 15, 1926, that he was thinking of writing a biography of Harding. "If ever there was a man who was a he-harlot, it was . . . Warren G. Harding," he advised Whitlock. "But I suppose it ought not to be written now. It would hurt too many hearts. I don't know. I could write it, but it would be a bitter and awful thing."[27] Then late that year came publication of *Revelry*, during the next year *The President's Daughter* was published, the time was right, and so White wrote it.[28]

Frederick Lewis Allen was not a journalist but editor of *Harper's* and in *Only Yesterday*, published in 1931, wrote not so much about Harding as about "the golden twenties." But his distortion of what happened during that decade was highly important for what people remembered, including college and university students of the 1930s and thereafter who read the book as collateral reading in their courses. That his book was a New Yorker's view of the United States passed completely over their heads; they did not recognize that across the length and breadth of what was a very large country most Americans not merely never saw but never even heard of much of what Allen passed off as American history. Moreover, when the editor of *Harper's* described the Harding era he treated it as a journalist might have, stressing sensational events. As Murray has cataloged his treatment, he devoted four pages to the Harding administration's constructive activities—including two lines to the peace treaty with Germany in 1921, seven to creation of the Bureau of the Budget giving the country a careful budget for the first time in its national existence, one line to the tariff that was a serious issue after World War I, six lines to tax policy that was even more important, four lines on war debts and reparations, and four on labor problems. He gave twenty-two pages to the Harding scandals.[29]

Four years after White's book, a year after Allen's, there appeared a far different production, a scholarly article on Harding by Allan Nevins in the *Dictionary of American Biography,* half a dozen double-column pages, and it deserves inclusion in the works of Harding journalism because its origin was as political and personal as were the Harding pages in *Masks in a Pageant,* the result almost as irresponsibly trivial as the pages of *Only Yesterday.*[30] As White was a Rooseveltian Republican, so Nevins worshipped at the shrine of the late President Wilson. Nevins had been a graduate student at the University of Illinois when Wilson became president and could not forget his hero, the gallant fighter for a new world order who went down to defeat before the malevolent senators who mainly for reasons of regular Republican politics defeated the League of Nations Covenant. How could he forget the leather-lunged Republican, William E. Borah of remote Idaho, who had never been out of the United States and never would go out of the United States and who claimed to be a Progressive but always wandered back to regularity? Or the elegant Boston Brahmin, Lodge, a Harvard graduate who once said of a Wilson speech that it might get by at Princeton but not at Harvard?

Nevins had another reason for hating Harding. The present writer remembers vividly seeing Nevins give his presidential address to the American Historical Association and hearing him tell his auditors how in his early years as a newspaperman, before he became a historian in the 1920s and taught first at Cornell University and then for the rest of his long life at Columbia University, he had worked for the Dayton editor Cox, whom Harding defeated. He idolized Cox, almost as much as Wilson. Harding defeated Cox by an enormous majority of 14 million votes to 8 million. Cox had gone down the line for Wilson's league and met ignominious defeat.

From these two points of view of Wilson and Cox, which were likely to produce a distorted result, not much different, one reinforcing the other, Nevins came at his presidential sketch of Harding. But another factor entered the equation that ensured error, guaranteeing that the sketch would lack any distinction at all: it was too soon to make a considered judgment because of unavailability of source material—such as the Harding Papers, then languishing in Marion. Here probably was an error of the *Dictionary* for which he wrote. The *Dictionary* was a grand project to do definitive short biographies of American subjects and was sponsored by an impeccable group of learned societies, its editorial board filled by the finest historians of the time, but a cap should have been put on the subjects considered in the twenty large initial volumes, probably the year 1900, instead of the cap placed on them, which was the requirement that subjects must be dead. And so from Wilsonian principles and totally inadequate sources Nevins produced an apparently evenhanded biographical sketch that grossly misestimated Harding yet passed for the accepted outlook for many years thereafter. He wrote, most unfairly (for what were his proofs?), that Harding as a youth possessed "some dissipated habits" and led the neighborhood blades in their amusements. As a senator he was "drinking a good deal and playing poker," and the source was none other than "White, *post*," the Latin reference lending éclat to the point and indicating citation of *Masks* in the accompanying bibliography. Harding had a "limited range of ideas." Because Daugherty was "the head of the Ohio machine or 'gang'" and was on Harding's side, the die was cast, Harding nominated and elected. Nevins repeated White's allegation that Jess Smith died because of "his sudden suicide or murder." He said Harding found out about Teapot Dome from Mrs. Fall, his source being Capper, quoted by "White, *post*, p. 432; partially denied by Mrs. Fall." On return from Alaska the president received the long Washington message in cipher, duly brought by seaplane, and was so disturbed that "for a day or so he was near collapse," and the source was "Ibid.," again meaning White. The historian concluded that Harding by cruel misfortune "was lifted"—the passive voice raised a question of who or what lifted him—to a post beyond his powers. Among Nevins's titles in the bibliography was *The President's Daughter*.

Next year Alice Roosevelt Longworth, daughter of the president of 1901–1909, published her reminiscences in *Crowded Hours*. Although her purpose was to relate up to the time of writing (she lived many more years) the life of the once beautiful young woman who was married in the White House to Rep. Nicholas Longworth of Ohio, in the latter 1920s Speaker of the House, and for whom was named the color of "Alice blue" and a song that endured for generations, this narrative of a prominent life was as journalistic as its less personal predecessors. She was ever the champion of her father, whom Harding opposed in 1912. She told how the Hardings celebrated the defeat of the league and the treaty in the Senate, for after the votes (there were three, one in November and the other two on the same day the following March) a merry group went out to the McLean estate and enjoyed an impromptu supper of scrambled eggs, with Mrs. Harding cooking the eggs. The purpose was to show that the Hardings took the league and treaty lightly. So did her father, and Alice and Nick, but the idea was to make fun of the Hardings. In her vignette of the celebrations she also showed the future first lady cooking eggs, a mundane scene. Later came the appraisal of Harding the president, during which assessment Longworth compared Harding's study on the White House second floor to a speakeasy: "the air heavy with tobacco smoke, trays with bottles containing every imaginable brand of whisky stood about, cards and poker chips ready at hand—a general atmosphere of waistcoat unbuttoned, feet on the desk, and the spittoon alongside." As for judgment of Harding: "I think every one must feel that the brevity of his tenure of office was a mercy to him and to the country. Harding was not a bad man. He was just a slob."[31]

It was all caricature. Apart from the bad manners of criticizing one's host, Alice forgot that Nick had been at Harding's poker sessions, whatever their proportions, and Alice, too, had been known to take a hand. If they were so bad, why did the Longworths go in the first place? Indeed, if there was all that much liquor around, why did Dr. Boone who was on the second floor on far more occasions than Alice (whose familiarity ended in 1909) never observe such spectacles? Boone never saw a bottle in the White House. The daughter of Theodore Roosevelt, one suspects, may have inveighed against the liquor in knowledge that her own husband had been a hard drinker for years.[32] And Downes's correspondent, Mason, had another explanation about her opposition to Harding, namely that Alice Longworth "never got used to the fact that her husband never made the White House, but that a small-town editor made it and to rub salt into the wound, an Ohio small-town editor." If Ohio was to have another president—it was known as "the mother of presidents" (Grant, Hayes, Garfield, McKinley, Taft)—in her mind it should have been Nick.[33]

Another piece of journalism was Mark Sullivan's sixth and last volume of *Our Times*, published in 1935, and it again advanced an evaluation of Harding that was as critical as White, Allen, Nevins, and Longworth. Like White and Longworth, Sullivan was a Rooseveltian. In Sullivan's case dislike came also from what he picked up from Washington gossip in his role as a journalist. He scouted the capital and heard the stories, and on August 2, 1923, while Harding lay dying in San Francisco, he was informing his diary of an alleged Harding girlfriend, a Washington woman.[34] But another wellspring of his dissatisfaction was his close friend Hoover, who before Harding's death had been fond of the president but afterward disliked him. In San Francisco, Hoover conferred several times daily with the medical team and was treated like one of them and told the doctors they had to save Harding because he was the only man who could hold the Republican Party together. After Harding died and Hoover saw his body lying there in the sickroom, he came out of the presidential suite in tears. Shortly after the president's death Hoover told a group of engineers:

> When he came into responsibility as President he faced unprecedented problems of domestic rehabilitation. It was a time when war-stirred emotions had created bitter prejudices and conflict in thought. Kindly and genial, but inflexible in his devotion to duty, he was strong in his determination to restore confidence and secure progress. All this he accomplished through patient conciliation and friendly good will for he felt deeply that hard driving might open unhealable breaches among our people. We have all benefitted by the success of his efforts.

Within weeks Teapot Dome changed Hoover's mind, and Sullivan recorded him saying at the same dinner party in which Wilbur offered the doctors' reasoning for Harding's death that "Harding got all his recreation . . . sitting around playing poker and telling shady stories night after night. He said it was a strain for him to talk to me or Hughes and he only did it when business required it but the others rested and amused him." It was a scurrilous appraisal, and Sullivan shared it.[35]

For Sullivan to find a principle about which to organize his Harding narrative was not difficult, and it was Nan Britton's book. In setting out Ms. Britton's points he said they were not his. Setting them out nonetheless brought them to the attention of readers, just as White passed on the rumor that Jess Smith was murdered. Suitably, in a footnote, the device of scholarship, he remembered what White artfully described as the primrose path—primroses were nearly required parts of gardens of small-town America in the 1920s, and along their paths ardent young men took their ardent girlfriends. Sullivan talked at length with Daugherty and asked whether there was any "woman scrape" in Harding's life, and Daugherty said, "if there had been one Harding would have told me." The former attorney general, known for his quickness, subtracted from this utterance by adding, "I know there was never any woman scrape in my life." Sullivan pressed the issue, and the response was an epigram, "I never talk about dead men or living women." A long account of Teapot Dome gave Sullivan opportunity to relate that Jess Smith kept the account labeled "Jess Smith Extra No. 3." The conclusion Sullivan came to was that it was to pay off individuals involved in the late president's "woman trouble." He might have been right, had he ascribed the account's utility to the case of Carrie Phillips. Not knowing about her, he obviously was referring to Nan Britton.

He did not neglect Ms. Britton's fellow vilifier, Means. In another footnote he remembered crudely, in the racial metaphor of the time, a remark made to him by "a colored bootblack at the old Shoreham Hotel, the compromise he made between his native delicacy and his curiosity," as to whether Harding had been "bumped off."[36]

Sullivan like Mencken tagged Harding with making bad speeches and did it in his usual indirect way rather than Mencken's procedure, which was an auto-da-fé. Harding one day, doubtless with a grin, had told the members of the White House press corps, which might have numbered six or eight reporters, that he liked to get out on the speech circuit and, as he put it, "bloviate." He thereby invented a word. ("Normalcy" was not his invention.) The other reporters had the decency not to push the point, save Sullivan, who saw an opportunity. Sullivan put the word in *Our Times*.[37]

Lastly among the journalists was Adams, and his contribution to the mis-representation of Harding's personality and administration was to embody White's criticisms, as testified to by Allen, Nevins, Longworth, and Sullivan, in a single readable volume that became the accepted account of the Harding era.

Adams was a master at making an unfair point, as in the following, about Harding's reading:

> The fact is that Warren G. Harding was and remained an unread man. Books did not enter his scheme of life in any important sense. The magic and the music were alien to him. He cannot fairly be called illiterate, although some of his verbiage, when he strives to attain the impressive, furnishes a sad example of the grandiloquently inept. We shall find it later in his speeches. He was aware of it and sensitive to criticism on the point. No; he was not illiterate. But he was unliterate. Or perhaps pseudo-literate would be the juster characterization.[38]

The author did not stop to let the reader sense that most political leaders, for that matter leaders of any sort, were outward-turning people who had little time for books. If they surrounded themselves with books, as did Franklin Roosevelt and Adlai E. Stevenson, the books were unread, for their owners did not have the time. A man who knew Roosevelt well wrote of him that he did not think Roosevelt ever read a book; he once asked him about the well-known best-seller by Kathleen Winsor, *Forever Amber*, and the president said, with a grin, that he only had read the dirty parts. A friend of Stevenson was in the latter's house and looking at the book-filled library and instinctively knew that the governor had not read those books. Harry Truman, known as a man of books, sometimes went for years without reading very much. A Truman biographer, Jonathan Daniels, observed that Truman knew history of a sort that David S. Muzzey might have written. When Truman talked about Andrew Jackson it was from Marquis James and for Thomas Jefferson he turned to Claude Bowers.

To relate Adams's points is to repeat those of his predecessors, to whose books he often cited, as "On the same page Mr. Sullivan refers to a 'woman scandal.'" Adams cited a pamphlet by Professor William Estabrook Chancellor of the College of Wooster, which claimed that Harding possessed Negro blood, as one of the factors during the convention of 1920 that might have defeated Harding's nomination. He did not say he believed it, nor did he refuse to believe it; it was a piece of evidence of some sort. Another piece of evidence in which he believed in all its detail was *The President's Daughter;* he related its explanations as fact. He employed stories and aphorisms if critical of his subject. George Washington—he recited the gibe—could not tell a lie, but Harding could not tell a liar. This mot he credited to one of Harding's friends. The three needs of the Republican Party were positions on the three Ts that spelled trouble: tariff, taxation, and treaties. In Adams's narrative the man who talked himself out of the three Ts was Harding. Robert Murray has aptly dismissed Adams's book as "the primary transmission belt by which all the various slanted accounts and oft-repeated myths were carried to later generations."[39]

The inventiveness of the journalists of the 1920s and 1930s was, one must say, surprising. When the able writers of those years ran out of information they took what lay at hand.

Their books were brought out by the leading publishing houses of New York and Boston. White's publisher was Macmillan, Allen's of course was Harper, Nevins's and Alice Longworth's and Sullivan's was Scribner's, Adams's was Houghton Mifflin. Their editors assisted with the books. When former attorney general Daugherty wrote irately to Adams's publisher, protesting the book's errors, Ferris Greenslet informed him that "The forthcoming work is entirely historical in purpose and method. In writing it, Mr. Adams has had the advantage, in addition to his own very thorough investigations, of the discoveries made during more than five years of research by the leading authority on the period, Professor Alderfer of Penna. State College." (Harold F. Alderfer was the author of an unpublished doctoral dissertation on Harding.) "The greatest pains have been taken," Greenslet explained, "to document and substantiate all factual statements and there is hardly a page that does not carry at the bottom footnote references to the sources and authorities used."[40]

Once published, the books displayed a staying power that was as surprising as their uncertain provenance. They passed into the canon of respectability. In 1963 Dr. Boone, who when it came to plays and whatever appeared on television and in *Time* did not believe in leaving sleeping dogs lie, wrote to *CBS News* about a portrayal of Mrs. Harding that he had seen and considered a marked perversion of the truth, to put the case mildly. The producer, Perry Wolff, wrote back that four sources had been consulted. One was *White House Profile: A Social History of the White House, Its Occupants and Its Festivities,* published by the newspaperwoman Bess Furman in 1951. The other three were the books of Allen, Longworth, and Adams. The producer had the nerve to offer the page numbers.[41]

3 ⸺

The issue of Harding's papers took its beginnings from the decision of the president's widow to cull her husband's papers, to do "what Warren would do," and thereby and with the best of intentions she inaugurated the confusion that was to continue for many years.[42] After Harding's funeral she returned to Washington to pack her White House belongings and in the course of the packing undertook to destroy anything that might bring criticism to his memory or that of his administration.

The story of destruction of papers was nothing if not complicated. The widow undoubtedly destroyed papers but not nearly as much as was thought. She really got hold of only one group of Harding papers, perhaps the most important group but a fairly small body of papers—and, to be sure, in the way of complex bodies of material it was not possible to obliterate traces or marks of issues on subjects, and if handled by amateurs the impossibility was simply underlined. The group of papers that Florence Harding culled was on the second floor of the White House in the president's study; ever since construction of the executive offices by Theodore Roosevelt at the time of the refurbishing that was arranged for the White House in 1902, presidents have had two offices and kept papers in both. The president's widow was assisted by her social secretary, Laura Harlan, and her husband's military aide, Maj. Ora M. Baldinger, the latter a protégé of the first lady because years earlier he had been one of her *Marion Star* newsboys. The group worked in the second-floor office from August 11 to August 17, and then the widow left the White House to stay for a short time, prior to return to Marion, with her friends the McLeans and took some papers to their estate, Friendship, to read and perhaps destroy. Meanwhile Baldinger sent to Marion several— the number was between five and eight—large wooden crates of second-floor papers, crates measuring one foot wide and one foot high and ten feet in length. The papers were packed tightly into the boxes. Upon her arrival in Marion, Mrs. Harding and Baldinger spent more time, Baldinger thought it was six weeks, going through the remaining papers and destroying individual papers or files that she felt should be eliminated, with the result that the boxes shipped from Washington were reduced from between five and eight down to two. Destruction hence was at least as high as 60 percent.

Not long after she finished with the second-floor papers the widow returned to Washington on what was to be her last trip, and while there she made another large error in regard to her husband's papers. She talked with Charles Moore, an official of the Library of Congress, and told him forthrightly she had burned all of the papers. She must have known she burned only part of them. Moreover, she did not know that other important groups of papers remained. She was an ill woman, which may have accounted for her remark. She said the same thing to the publisher Frank N. Doubleday, whom she also saw in Washington.

The result of her saying she had burned the papers was that a year after her death Moore made her remark public, doubtless with the intention of putting pressure on the Harding Memorial Association to give up the papers it had. He may have realized that other groups of papers were not yet in the hands of the association. In any event all he accomplished was to give the impression that the Harding Papers, for good and sufficient reasons, had been destroyed, an impression that did no good to the memory of the late president. For years thereafter journalists and even some historians asserted that the papers were burned. Adams so wrote in 1939 and followed in the same paragraph by relating that government agents in 1922 destroyed a biography of Harding by Chancellor (the author of the 1920 pamphlet on Negro blood), as if the Harding Papers and the Chancellor biography were of the same importance, doubtless realizing that his account gave the impression that everything pertaining to Harding needed destruction.

In fact, as mentioned, there were other groups of Harding papers, notably the papers of the executive offices, found in the basement of the White House in 1929, where Christian perhaps inadvertently had left them. By that time Florence Harding was dead, and these papers went to Marion intact, into the custody of the Harding Memorial Association in accord with the widow's will concerning the Harding Papers generally.

Meanwhile officers of the association had possession of papers from the period when Harding was editor of the *Marion Star,* papers from his early days including two terms in the Ohio senate and one term as lieutenant governor. Florence Harding would have had opportunity to go through those papers, but there was no evidence she looked at them during her culling sessions with the papers from the White House's second-floor office—no evidence appeared when years later the *Star* papers opened with the other Harding papers.

The fourth and last group of papers came from Christian, who had kept them in his house in Washington before giving them to the Library of Congress, which in turn gave them to the Harding Memorial Association in 1953. These were papers on Harding's term in the U.S. Senate, together with papers for the presidential campaign of 1920.

On October 10, 1963, the transfer of papers from Marion to Columbus to the Ohio Historical Society began, and the papers—350,000 pages of them, in eight hundred archival boxes—were opened on April 25, 1964.

Compared to the odyssey of the papers, the biographer Francis Russell's discovery of the Carrie Phillips letters and their final disposition (which was closure under an arrangement with the Harding heirs) was of far less importance, though it offered a good deal more drama, and as before, any drama connected with Harding's memory was likely to do more harm than good.

The existence of letters to the wife of James E. Phillips, owner of the Uhler-Phillips dry-goods store on East Center Street in Marion, had not been generally known prior to Russell's trip to Marion in the autumn of 1963, though the possibility of a liaison had been discussed in several books since Chancellor had written in his 1922 biography that Harding and Carrie Phillips had met on occasion at Upper Sandusky, twenty miles north of Marion. References to her in subsequent books were veiled because to have named her in a book published by a traceable publisher (Chancellor's was credited to "The Sentinal Press," a name with a gross misspelling and no place of publication) could have opened the author and publisher to court action as libelous. Nan Britton mentioned Carrie Phillips in *The President's Daughter,* albeit with a pseudonym, "a certain Mrs. Arnold." She repeated Chancellor's assertion that Republican leaders in 1920 gave "Mrs. Arnold" money to go to Japan; she did not mention precise payments, relating only that the beautiful Mrs. Arnold had taken a trip to the Orient. The source that inspired Russell's trip to Marion was *Masks in a Pageant,* which referred to "a primrose detour from Main Street which Florence Kling, the Duchess, had chosen to ignore." Means wrote cautiously of "a milliner in Marion" whom he described as Mrs. Milliner. Jess Smith, he claimed, told him about her, and spoke of her as a presidential ex-flame, using one of his, Smith's, favorite words, a "lollapalooza." Mrs. Milliner claimed to have letters, which Means obtained for fifteen thousand dollars. Adams repeated White's primrose path description, with an embellishment, a couplet about the late president:

> His right eye was a good little eye,
> But his left eye loved to roam.[43]

Russell's course should have been taken earlier by some Harding scholar, and the fact that it was not says something about scholarly reading, that the scholars were not reading all of the literature they believed to be journalistic, even though they cited it.

Russell had only to ask in Marion if anyone remembered the name of the store about which White wrote and learned it was the Uhler-Phillips establishment. Several people told him that a Marion attorney had letters from Harding to Mrs. James Phillips, and upon calling on the attorney, Donald Williamson, Russell received an invitation to look at the letters. Williamson had found them in 1956 when Mrs. Phillips, a recluse who lived in a house with six dogs, was so deteriorated in health that she had to have a guardian and went to a nursing home. He had cleaned out her house preparatory to selling it, discovered a locked closet, and upon opening it found a cardboard box with ninety-eight Harding letters written between 1910 and 1920, some short, several running twenty pages, one to forty. Mrs. Phillips died in 1960.

The enterprising Russell could not have found the Phillips letters at a worse time. At that precise moment the historical society was shipping the Harding Papers from Marion to Columbus. The first shipment had gone to Columbus on October 10, 1963, the second and what would prove the largest went on October 15, and Russell by chance had gone to Marion on October 19. The Phillips letters contained no secrets of state and were almost worthless in their few testimonies about public matters but did show the later president's momentary love for a woman other than his wife and for that reason would be embarrassing to the Harding family. If the family and the officers of the Harding Memorial Association learned of what Russell had found, they could stop the transfer of the remaining Harding papers to the Ohio Historical Society and perhaps tie up any use of the papers that had arrived.

What happened thereafter, like the handling of the papers by Mrs. Harding and the association, could hardly have been worse. Anything connected with President Harding seemed to make everyone act irrationally. After Williamson showed Russell the letters, the biographer confided his discovery to the manuscript curator of the historical society, Kenneth W. Duckett. Russell and Duckett obtained the Phillips letters from the dead woman's guardian, Williamson, who had no legal right either to have kept the letters from 1956 until 1963 or to have given them away, and took them to the society in Columbus. Duckett said no more about them for several months, until April 15, 1964, when he told the society's president, Fred J. Milligan, of their existence. The latter told his board, and they advised him to talk to the Marion County probate judge, Edward J. Ruzzo, for Carrie Phillips in her last years had been penniless; the state had paid her old-age insurance, which provided the money for her to live in the nursing home. If the letters had monetary value, which they obviously did, they would have to be used to extinguish the debt of the estate.

At that juncture, the possibility of destruction of the letters arose. The Harding family, represented by the president's nephew, Dr. George T. Harding III, wanted the more lurid letters, which contained open sexual references, destroyed, or at least desired some sort of protection of the president's memory from "printing lurid details," so their lawyer said in an interview. "My clients," he explained, "would like to destroy the letters, but I don't think that will happen. They want to suppress them."[44]

The possibility of destruction was unlikely but seemed quite real. Duckett was told "that one of the board members . . . became quite violent when he learned about these things and said something to the effect that they should be destroyed." This was not a member of the Harding family but of the historical society board, Judge Lehr Fess, son of the former Ohio senator Simeon D. Fess. Duckett said that when he, Duckett, and the president of the board, Milligan, went to Marion and conferred with Judge Ruzzo, the judge had said, "You want a solution to your problem, send the things back up here and we will get rid of them." At that remark the former guardian of Mrs. Phillips, Williamson, added, "Yes, we will burn them," to which Milligan twice responded, "Fine." During the day in which the letters were discussed in Marion, Williamson said to Milligan, "I bet you wish, Fred, I burned those damned things when I got my hands on them the first time." Milligan did not answer. Duckett became so anxious about the Phillips letters that he told a *New York Times* reporter, "I have heard the words 'burn, destroy and suppress' so many times since I acquired the papers that I have determined that extraordinary precautions must be taken to ensure their preservation and their use by historians."[45] Before the letters passed into the hands of Judge Ruzzo he arranged for Oliver Jensen, the editor of *American Heritage,* to receive photographic copies, which Jensen deposited in the vault of a New York bank.

Meanwhile, or perhaps it was later, two Harding biographers managed, through no fault of Duckett, to see the letters. In 1998 the owner of a Columbus copy shop remembered how one evening two lawyers brought the letters to his store and made a copy. Dr. Harding was understandably up in arms, both because of the family's embarrassment from discovery of the letters and because allowing anyone to see them was likely to mean publication, which would violate the well-known rule of common law that literary rights reside in the writer or his or her heirs, not in whoever has physical possession. If it did not mean publication, that is, quotation, it could mean paraphrasing, which would be as bad and maybe worse because it would be inexact. The Harding heirs enjoined quotation of the letters. Judge Ruzzo ordered the letters sealed and turned over to an administrator for sale.

Gradually, and the process took seven years, from 1964 until 1971, during which time any development in the case was public because of its being a matter of court record, the strange, almost weird business of protecting the Phillips letters wound down to an arrangement satisfactory to all parties. The suit by Dr. Harding, which asked for the impounding of the letters and $1 million in damages, was against Duckett, Russell, the McGraw-Hill Publishing Company (Russell's publisher), and the American Heritage Publishing Company. When the *New York Times* published quotations from two or three of the letters, Dr. Harding added the *Times* to the list of defendants. He said the printing of material by the newspaper resulted in embarrassment, extreme humiliation, and mental suffering to the Harding heirs; it was all legal boilerplate but read well in the newspapers. At the time he added the *New York Times*'s name to his suit Dr. Harding added the name of one of the Ohio Historical Society trustees and editor of the *Dayton Journal Herald*, Glenn Thompson, because Thompson had suggested the microfilming of the letters to Duckett. The *Times*'s lawyer sought to have the case tried in federal court, because ownership of both the *New York Times* and *American Heritage* was outside the State of Ohio and probably thought a federal judge would be more sympathetic than a state judge, but a federal judge in Columbus through a technicality remanded the case to a common pleas judge. All the while Judge Ruzzo in Marion was arranging to have the letters appraised by experts selected from a list provided by the chief of the manuscript division of the Library of Congress, David C. Mearns. Guesses as to the value of the letters ranged as high as $100,000, exclusive of literary rights. The appraisers set their value at $15,000. Ruzzo stipulated payment of $3,900 to the appraisers, the administrator of the Phillips estate, the administrator's lawyer, and $3,854.11 to the State of Ohio, the latter being the amount Mrs. Phillips cost the state for old-age insurance. The question became whether Mrs. Phillips's daughter, Isabelle Mathee, of Genoa City, Wisconsin, desired to accept responsibility for the debts of the estate and take the letters in return or let the letters go up for sale at auction. She paid the debts, took the letters, and in January 1965 Dr. Harding bought them from her. In 1971 Dr. Harding's lawyer concluded an agreement with the defendants to send the microfilm copy of the letters to the Ohio Historical Society and for *American Heritage* to pay the physician ten thousand dollars, in exchange for which the Harding family would donate the letters to the Library of Congress with the proviso that they not be opened until July 29, 2014. The case against the *New York Times* was dismissed, and Dr. Harding dropped his demand for $1 million in damages.

Considerably more than the mishandling of the Harding Papers by Mrs. Harding and by the Harding Memorial Association, the affair of the Phillips letters kept the light of publicity on the memory of Warren G. Harding. During Harding's lifetime there had been much talk of his extraordinary good luck, that everything turned out so well for him, including the way in which he rose to the presidency after a single Senate term. When the president died all this good fortune came to an end.

The letters were trivial compositions; Harding never should have written them. They were not worthy of a high school student, overstated and anxious, silly, maudlin, with bad poetry to back them up. So said the people who saw them before Dr. Harding locked them up. Carrie was a schemer, not very interesting intellectually, a grade school teacher in Bucyrus who to escape her unmanageable pupils (Russell assumed) at the age of twenty-one married the thirty-year-old "Jim" Phillips. A head shorter than Carrie, Phillips was the owner of a thriving store and could get her away from Bucyrus to a larger town with more cultural advantages, among them associating with neighbors such as the Hardings. Carrie Phillips was physically attractive. If her face, as Russell appraised it, was cold and almost hard, "the lines of her body were warmly female." Duckett described her as "pleasantly chubby, a sort of Gibson girl." Her face, he agreed, was not sensual. "She certainly was no Mata Hari. But she had something that attracted men."[46]

The affair began in 1905 when Jim Phillips was ill in the Battle Creek Sanitarium (which Harding had recommended to him) and Mrs. Harding, suffering an intense episode of her kidney malady, was in a Columbus hospital. The romance passed through phases when Harding met her in New York while allegedly on a hunting trip to Texas. He seems to have met her in Europe before the world war when she was living in Germany. Duckett said in 1972, when the court decision on the letters allowed him to speak of their contents in general terms, that Florence Harding knew of her husband's relationship with Carrie Phillips almost from its start, probably as early as 1909 when the Hardings and Phillipses toured Europe together. The letters, he said, showed that Carrie Phillips lived in the hope that Harding would divorce his wife and marry her and that once she tried to precipitate a divorce by sending letters to Harding from another of her lovers.[47]

The *New York Times* published parts of a letter from Harding to Mrs. Phillips in 1920 that showed she was blackmailing him, as Chancellor claimed two years after the blackmail took place—raising a question of whether part of the blackmail consisted of her telling the story to her Marion neighbors. Indeed Chancellor wrote almost as much, although claiming that it happened afterward: "The Phillips [sic] went to Japan early in October, but not until Mrs. Phillips, who is a very talkative woman, had told all her friends just what she was to receive." The letter quoted by the *New York Times* showed that she desired a considerable sum, more than Harding could afford, and that he offered to return to Marion if she desired. If he were to remain in public service, if she thought he could be more helpful to the American people that way, he promised to pay her five thousand dollars annually as long as he was in office. The letters seem to have said nothing about twenty-five thousand dollars and two thousand dollars a month, the terms Chancellor described.[48]

Discovery of the Phillips letters raised obvious questions. One was in regard to the account of Jess Smith in Daugherty's brother's bank in Washington Court House, known as "Jess Smith Extra No. 3." Another question was whether the undoubted Phillips affair made more likely the truth of the charges by Nan Britton. Both Russell and the *New York Times* reporter Apple answered the latter question by saying that the letters made Ms. Britton's claims more likely. But one could argue the other way. When the letters became public knowledge in the summer of 1964, Ms. Britton told a reporter for the *Chicago American,* "I did not know about Mrs. Phillips or about the letters President Harding wrote to her."[49] She may well have said more than she intended. For the first time the glass of publicity was focusing on another woman, and that might have galled her. The remark also sounded as if she were nonplussed and gave out a statement without calculating it, unlike her various press remarks of the more distant past. In that unrehearsed remark she may have been revealing what the *New York Daily News* reporter O'Donnell had published in 1927, from the assertions of the former guild staff member Earl Smith who said that Wightman had written *The President's Daughter.* The next year Patricia Wightman in her separation suit said the same thing. Wightman could have learned about Carrie Phillips from reading Chancellor's book. Despite the stories of its destruction (Means claimed he had accomplished that task), copies survived, and even though the book was a rare item there was a copy in the New York Public Library (the Library of Congress and Ohio Historical Society also possess copies). If Wightman wrote *The President's Daughter,* he would have used the copy of the Chancellor book in the New York Public Library. He would have employed the pseudonym "Mrs. Arnold." Given the haste with which Ms. Britton's book, a long book, was being written, its supposed author could have forgotten some of the things Wightman put in it, including the references to Carrie Phillips as "Mrs. Arnold." When she said in 1964 that she had not known of Mrs. Phillips, she would have been admitting that her own case was insecure, because Wightman had created it for her.[50]

One might observe in conclusion about the Phillips affair and the letters that supported it, and apart from the point made earlier about what appalling ill luck it represented in the series of misfortunes that dogged Harding's memory, that like the Teapot Dome scandal so the Phillips liaison was blown far out of proportion. It did not add to Harding's stature. By the end of the affair in 1920 he must have known that his judgment in involving himself, quite apart from the impropriety, had been terrible: he laid himself open to blackmail and for a while must have been in real danger of having to withdraw from the nomination—from what the *New York Times* printed of the blackmail letter of 1920. One senses that Florence Harding stood behind him in this near-tragic blunder, for if (as Duckett claimed) she knew about the affair she must also have known—Harding would have told her, for it involved a large amount of money—what he was up against. If indeed she supported him, which one can guess was the case, her standing up for him gives her memory an almost noble quality, as compared to the calumnies it suffered in the years after her death. And, finally, measuring the episode, historians need to place it against other such happenings to American public figures throughout the country's history, large figures such as Benjamin Franklin, Alexander Hamilton, and within Harding's time Grover Cleveland. The president of 1885–1889 and 1893–1897 admitted a connection with a Buffalo woman, Maria Halpin, who like Carrie Phillips had connections with other men. He took responsibility for her son even though he was not certain he was the father. This scrape came out just before Cleveland's election to the presidency in 1884 and thereafter was never held against him personally nor against his administration.

4

At last, in 1964, the papers became available, and Harding enthusiasts (what few there were of them) and Harding haters alike had opportunity to hold up their hero or villain against his own papers and a dozen and more collections of Harding's associates, also available at the Ohio Historical Society, and see what the truth was about the man from Marion. The resultant biographies were, by and large, disappointing.

First to publish was a scholar from Cambridge University, Andrew Sinclair, whose biography *The Available Man: The Life behind the Masks of Warren Gamaliel Harding* appeared a year after the papers opened. Considering the size of the papers and the usual lead time for publication of books—at least half a year between turning in manuscript and receiving finished, bound volumes—a reader might have wondered whether Sinclair was quick with his book, and the answer has to be that he was. The book did not show enough of the new material; it used the papers lightly.[51]

Sinclair chose as his theme not the idea of Harding's availability, which in American politics means that a man or woman has not antagonized any major group of possible supporters, but a notion of there having been various "myths" in the American mind around the year 1920, myths that Harding perpetuated at a time when there should have been a large moment of truth. The notion of myths was a contrivance, perhaps designed to take the author across the thin ice of his research in the Harding Papers. The author's principal myth was that Harding represented the generality of Americans when in the census of 1920 it became apparent for the first time that rural—that is, small-town and country—America had given way to urban America. Sinclair said Harding thereby was behind the times, which may have been true in the sense that he had been brought up in the country and in small towns, which was hardly his fault, but he might have been able (Sinclair obviously did not think so) to understand cities despite his residential handicap. Having pointed out Harding's unfortunate accident of birth and upbringing, the author evoked other myths that mostly seem unmythical: he wrote of the myth of the Country Boy (which was true), of the Self-made Man (no man or woman is self-made), of the Presidential State (by which he meant that the president constituted the government, another theory seldom believed), of the Political Innocent (here was no myth, for no one saw Harding as politically innocent), of the Guardian Senate (this myth had its believers), of America First (which also had some believers). He wrote of the myths of the Reluctant Candidate, Dark Horse, Smoke-filled Room, Solemn Referendum (that was Wilson's myth), and Best Minds. In his biography of Harding the citation of myths became, after a while, annoying.

The book's principal fault was the author's refusal to believe that ability at politics is a mark of intelligence. The author was sure Harding "remained the small-town gentleman playing a part too large for him." The president had a "fuzzy mentality." He was "a man of mediocre intellect." His predecessor Wilson described people like Harding as possessing bungalow minds. Harding, Sinclair wrote, "knew nothing of the science of government." Withal he admitted Harding was no "political innocent" and fought with "the craftiest politicians of his day." Harding was a "hardworking and shrewd Ohio politician. He was always his own master. He used compromise and humility as political tactics . . . he was a formidable opponent in an election."[52] Shades of H. S. Truman! The latter political leader, now much appreciated, always considered political judgment as much a part of intellect as the thoughts of anyone in any other walk of life, such as a physician, clergyman, or scholar.

The book had a few problems with understanding the American scene, doubtless because of Sinclair's British background. For instance, Sinclair placed the Battle Creek Sanitarium where Harding and Jim Phillips went on occasion in Ohio (this lapse also said something about Sinclair's editors at Macmillan). As for American colleges and universities, the author misunderstood the nature of Ohio Central College in Iberia, from which Harding graduated. He said the college's curriculum was insufficient. Of course it was insufficient. Ohio Central was naught but a high school or what in the nineteenth century was known as an academy; Harding attended it for two years and graduated at the age of seventeen. American colleges and universities of size and quality were hardly visible until the 1890s, when a baby boom after the Civil War and training of faculty members in German universities at last brought the twin requisites of enrollment and scholarship.

Other details were out of order. On the train moving cross-country to Tacoma in 1923 the author placed Secretary Hoover, who joined the Harding party on the West Coast. He exaggerated the casualties in the Veterans' Bureau scandal, two suicides he wrote, when there was one suicide. He put Doheny in jail, though the oilman never went to jail. He placed the death of Florence Harding "within six months" of that of Dr. Sawyer, which was technically true but disconcertingly general, as she died two months later. He discovered 250 Harding letters to Carrie Phillips, which number he discovered in the *New York Times* rather than reading the ninety-eight letters in Columbus, and he also declared that *American Heritage* bought the letters from Mrs. Phillips's estate.[53]

It is perhaps unfair to relate these smaller errors, but in regard to the fight between President Wilson and the Senate concerning the League of Nations and the Treaty of Versailles at the end of Wilson's administration—which was the prelude to Harding's electoral victory in 1920, a matter Sinclair might have studied in detail—Sinclair remarked flatly that President Wilson "lay in a coma in the White House from the fall of 1919 to the spring of 1920," which was a new interpretation of the Wilson era, since the ill president was never in a coma. In relating a prime event in foreign affairs of the Harding administration, Harding's endorsement of United States membership in the World Court during the transcontinental train trip to Tacoma, he confused the World Court, composed of League of Nations–appointed jurists, with what he described as "The Hague Court," which was a panel of judges chosen by signatories of a protocol produced by the First Hague Peace Conference of 1899, from which governments of nations might, if they wished, draw for arbitration of their differences.[54]

Sinclair accepted every word in *The President's Daughter,* with a sniff to anyone who disagreed: "In this work, Miss Britton proved to all except the most charitable that she was the mother of Harding's daughter."[55]

In 1968, three years after Sinclair's publication, Russell's book came out and was a best-seller, offering misinformation of a different sort than its predecessor. Earlier, in an *American Heritage* article, Russell had discerned four "mysteries" about Harding, and he set them out in his biography. One of them was the color of Harding's skin; the president's face was dark-hued, and Russell bolstered Chancellor's accusation that Harding possessed Negro blood. From this contemporary canard (people in the race-ridden 1920s considered it an accusation) came the title *The Shadow of Blooming Grove: Warren G. Harding and His Times.* The second mystery, "no less disturbing," was the "woman question." The third was the manner of the president's death; the fourth was the fate of his private papers.[56]

Of Russell's mysteries, none was enigmatic. They were no more worth reading about than Sinclair's myths, as Russell in his 663 pages—twice as many as Sinclair's book—gradually revealed. The mystery of the woman question he handled in part by leaving cryptic gaps on his pages when he long since had known—the issue had arisen four years before—he could not safely quote from the Phillips letters. For the rest of it he entertained readers with descriptions from Nan Britton's book. Like Sinclair, although with far more elaboration, he accepted anything Ms. Britton wrote. There was no question about it. He allowed that if this affair "could not be documented to the satisfaction of Dr. George Harding," the "gushing, redundant" pages of her book rang true. It was impossible, he said, rather queerly, to counterfeit such artlessness.[57]

In addition to retailing sex, Russell wrote in an attractive way, as when he described Harding on the Chautauqua circuit. To read the account was to believe it:

> After the applause, the stir, and the clatter of wooden seats, the audience filed out into the cool air of the summer evening. No one was very sure of just what the speaker had said, but everyone going home under the stars remembered how well he had said it! Harding enjoyed such folksy audiences, enjoyed them even more when the Duchess's health kept her in Marion. Doggedly she traveled with him whenever she could manage it, perched by his side in the daycoach from one Chautauqua center to the next, her edged voice rasping at him all the way, querulous, persistent, while he sulked in his plush seat, a cigar wedged into his mouth, his frown growing deeper under her nagging until finally he would turn on her with "Goddammit, shut up!" and she would lapse into brief, offended silence.[58]

Francis Russell was a talented essayist and writer who, when dealing with what he knew, was impressive. Born in Boston in 1910, he had grown up with memories of the Boston police strike; one of his school friends was the son of a striking policeman who had been dismissed by the police commissioner, under direction of Governor Coolidge, in 1919. He remembered how proud Officer Fitzgibbons had been of his uniform and how after the strike one of the policeman's children was playing with his father's helmet and a spoon, sitting on the curb in front of the Fitzgibbons's house. He wrote an interesting if large-D Democratic account of the police strike, flamboyantly titled *A City in Terror*. He wrote about Sacco and Vanzetti and arranged to have the bullets that were fired at the paymaster, who was killed, analyzed ballistically with the murder weapon, which had never been done; he discovered, and published, the fact that at least one of the two men electrocuted in 1927 was guilty. But when he turned to the biography of Harding, for which task he was awarded two Guggenheim Fellowships, the result was not a scholarly success. Robert Murray counted the lines Russell devoted to important subjects, such as the tariff or the Washington Naval Conference of 1921–1922, and found the counts ridiculously short compared to the dozens of pages on sex and storytelling.

The Downes biography published in 1970, *The Rise of Warren Gamaliel Harding: 1865–1920*, neither subtracted from nor added to Harding's stature and received little attention in the group of biographies published after the opening of the papers. It amounted to a close, detailed, and—because of the nature of Ohio politics at the turn of the present century, which were filled with byzantine maneuvers—almost impossible-to-remember narrative of Harding's political career prior to the presidency. Downes knew a great deal about Harding. For years he devoted his life to Harding. A friend and colleague at the University of Toledo, Robert Freeman Smith, reported to the present writer that when the Harding Papers were opened at the Ohio Historical Society, Downes worked so hard he could not finish his labors during the hours allotted to researchers and was accustomed to elude the society's building guards and secrete himself in the stacks at night, where he could read the documents in the small hours. Kenneth Duckett disputes this possibility but admits that one morning the guards did find Downes asleep in a society office.

In one respect other than its details, and its ending in 1920, Downes's book may have disappointed readers, considering the juicy descriptions Sinclair and especially Russell presented of Nan Britton and Carrie Phillips. The book contained nothing on either of these individuals, which was perhaps a relief, but nonetheless curious. The reason must have been that when he submitted his manuscript to the Ohio State University Press the director, Weldon A. Kefauver, sent it to Dr. Harding. The Harding descendant had heard Downes speak at a meeting of the Harding Memorial Association and had listened to the historian air his feelings about his inability to see the Phillips letters. Furious that Downes chose a celebration in Marion to make this complaint, Dr. Harding was ready to look over the manuscript with care and did so, and informed Director Kefauver, who informed Downes, that certain references should come out.

There is not much point in going into the issue that arose between Downes, on the one side, and Dr. Harding on the other, and the advice that Kefauver gave Downes, which the author eventually took, which was to remove all references to which the Harding heir objected. Kefauver received a considerable criticism for offering his own judgment, which was that Downes should go along. It certainly could be argued that scholarship does not need censorship. Still, it was not necessary for Harding biographers to make as much of the woman question as Sinclair and Russell did. Downes, too, had put himself in a corner on the Britton matter. It was wrong of him to support Ms. Britton's allegations— he should have supported President Harding's reputation until he discovered reason not to. When Dr. Harding asked Kefauver to remove the offending passages in Downes's manuscript, he was only making a request and could not have forced the issue. Kefauver on his part felt that there had been too many arguments about Harding and may be excused for tiring of them. Downes had another volume to go and could make his points there, when tempestuous issues had settled down. The biographer went along with Kefauver, but irritably so, and told a Dayton newspaper reporter of his anger with the director of the Ohio State University Press.[59]

Turning backward, chronologically speaking, to Murray's book, published in 1969, the sole biography of quality to emerge after the opening of the papers, it is necessary to look only (for the present book has considered the Murray book earlier) at this remarkable author's explanation of why American historians failed to understand Harding. Here Murray offered advice beyond his description of the journalists, which was quite true, as Rooseveltians or Wilsonians. In his final pages he turned to the historians, and not merely drew the Sinclair book more charitably than he might have and made a merciless dissection of the Russell book but also indulged very interesting speculations about the training of historians after World Wars I and II. He wrote that as the politics of the journalists affected their conclusions, so the training of the historians explained their willingness to accept errors in estimating Harding's place in history.

American historians, young or old, are by no means a fascinating group, and hence no large subject for speculation, except that they write the books and make the historical speculations, and now that the Harding era is too far back for the journalists to distort it is of interest why the historians picked up the journalists' ideas. The reason may well be, as the biographer related, that the historians who taught the biographers and other historical writers of the 1960s themselves grew up with not merely such descriptions of presidential administrations as those offered by Gilbert in the *Mirrors* books, and enjoyed the pungent essays of Mencken and either welcomed his political views or accepted them because of the éclat of his writings, but to this they added the journalism of White, Allen, Nevins, Longworth, Sullivan, and Adams. In coming to manhood in the 1920s and 1930s (hardly any historians of that time were women) they remembered the domestic political failures, or what seemed domestic failures, of the 1920s, in particular the economic policies of the 1920s that, they believed, brought the Great Depression of the 1930s. They of course could have accepted the belief of President Hoover that the depression did not come from the policies of the 1920s but from abroad—from "those Europeans" (Hoover privately referred to the citizens of France as "frogs") who would not pay their war debts and instead enjoyed a saturnalia of economic largesse during the 1920s, courtesy of American loans, and then threw the world into depression in the next decade. But most historians who were adults in the interwar era believed the trouble lay with Harding and Coolidge (some included Hoover) who passed their delinquencies to the Democratic Roosevelt. Domestically speaking, therefore, the 1920s were at fault, and it was only to be expected that the generation of historical scholars trained after World War II believed what their teachers told them.

As economically the 1920s seemed a wasteland, so did the decade appear in foreign policy. Murray has justly remarked the overestimation of President Wilson that marked a good deal of pre- and post-1945 historical writing. Sinclair in his biography of Harding was clear on this point: "Wilson's scheme of the League of Nations was the first practical step toward controlling the national state, which was becoming dangerous and obsolete in the new age of quick communication. If Wilson lost and Harding won . . ."[60] The omissions and insensitivities of the nation's leaders in the 1920s led to the worldwide aggressions of the 1930s. The errors of U.S. foreign policy in the 1920s were so deeply ingrained that even a great leader such as Franklin Roosevelt could only correct them gradually, in part by subterfuge, as in the destroyers-bases agreement of 1940 and lend-lease in 1941, and the nation had to pay the penalty with Pearl Harbor and involvement in World War II.

But something more was at fault in the writing of historians about the Harding era. One must ask why, despite the passage now of half a century since 1945, historians continue to place Harding at the bottom of the lists they make of presidents? Arthur M. Schlesinger Sr. polled experts on the presidency, mostly historians, in 1948 and 1962, and Harding came in last. Those ratings, to be sure, were before the Harding Papers opened. In 1981 David L. Porter, a historian at William Penn College, asked forty-one colleagues to rate the presidents; the next year Steve Neal of the *Chicago Tribune* conducted a poll; and that same year Murray, the Harding biographer, together with Tim H. Blessing, did an extensive and unlike the others statistically sophisticated poll. The sixth and seventh polls in 1995 were by William J. Ridings and Stuart B. McIver in *Presidential Studies Quarterly* and again by Neal, this time in the *Chicago Sun-Times*.[61] In every poll Harding came in last.

It is true that the historians who rated the presidents in the two Schlesinger polls would not have read Murray's biography. But all the later historians could have read it, and would that not have raised Harding at least above Ulysses S. Grant, Richard M. Nixon, James Buchanan, and Andrew Johnson?

The answer may be that because of pressure to publish so as to receive stature in their profession—publish or perish—and if not that then pressure to produce lectures that engage students, the historians saved themselves the trouble of reading more than they simply had to. They went to the books of the journalists rather than their fellow historians. Or, if the latter, then they went to Russell where they could learn what Harding said to his wife while riding the day coach on the Chautauqua circuit, take notes on Nan Britton and Carrie Phillips, and review such mysteries as the president's death.

6

Conclusion

As the pages of this book opened with a personal observation of half a century ago, so let them close with another of half a year ago. It was summer, and the no-longer-young historian, who was born when Harding was president, was driving through Marion looking for the Marion County Historical Society. The city's downtown, let it be said, is not what it once was. The huge courthouse built in 1884 still towers above the surrounding buildings. But like so many cities across the United States, Marion's Center Street and Main Street are no longer centers of commerce, places to which residents and visitors throng for shopping or dining. Businesses have moved to the outskirts, to the malls with their acres of asphalt. Traffic patterns downtown also have changed. They were designed for an age before automobiles. Streets going south in the direction of Columbus, north to Findlay and Toledo, west to Lima, and east to Cleveland are now one-way.

The historical society, eventually found, bore the name of Heritage Hall, and upon a welcome by the director and a tour, upstairs and down, displayed the remarkable enterprise and pride of Marion's citizens. It is a building to be proud of. The original post office structure was built in 1910 and was enlarged to its present size a dozen or more years after President Harding's death. When purchased by the society, it required many changes. Six hundred thousand dollars have gone into it, and the exhibit areas show marked attention to Marion's past. The downstairs Harding rooms are, in a word, splendid. In Marion the nation's twenty-ninth president is no distant figure; there is much local pride in his having spent his adult years in the city. The former post office building is a museum that honors the city's past in large part through him. Heritage Hall should be the envy of all the historical societies in the state, save those of the larger cities. It is comparable to the historical society of Canton, home of President McKinley.

In the Marion County Historical Society the former post office safe downstairs has been converted into a resource center, with boxes of manuscript material carefully arranged on shelves on one side and bound copies of the *Marion Star* and the city's early newspapers on the other. To the left and the right of the entrance to the resource center are respectively a document preparation room, complete with a computer, and a research room, the latter housing an admirable collection of Harding books.

Driving south toward Columbus, the visitor notices the churches for the first block or two, large churches considering the size of the city, and can imagine that Warren G. Harding once saw them, perhaps attended them, singing the hymns of the time from the books of the gospel duo of Dwight Moody and his trombonist, Ira Sankey. After the services Harding would have shaken hands with his friends and neighbors.

A mile or so to the south, next to a large cemetery where the markers change from Victorian shapes and colors to the tombstones of Harding's era and later, stands the Harding Memorial. With its circle of white marble pillars it is an awesome sight. There appears to have been only a single change since I saw it fifty years ago. Something is different about its prospect, its approaches. The city cemetery has reached into the area behind the memorial. The highway to Columbus has been widened. These subtractions from the long grassy expanse surrounding the memorial may not have made much difference and might be largely in memory, now filled with longer expanses seen or imagined. The memorial still stands as beautiful today as when it was finished in 1927, when the president and his wife were entombed within.

The people of Marion are proud of their past, as evidenced in Heritage Hall and in maintenance of the memorial. President Harding is one of their own.

For them it is impossible to believe that elsewhere the memory of the past has been different. They cannot understand why Harding's reputation, so high during his lifetime, plunged so low after he died. Or how a great public career that reached the highest office the nation could bestow—Harding received the greatest majority given any presidential candidate since the Civil War, save Franklin Roosevelt in 1936—could have encountered so many, and such successful, assailants within a few years after Harding passed on.

History, they might conclude, is sometimes thoughtless about the people who make it.

Notes

Chapter 1

1. Sawyer to Ray Lyman Wilbur, August 21, 1923, "President Harding's Death," box 19, Ray Lyman Wilbur Papers; Warren Harding to Sawyer, March 15, 1916, frame number unreadable, roll 262, Charles E. Sawyer Papers.

2. Randolph C. Downes, *The Rise of Warren Gamaliel Harding: 1865–1920*, 7–8.

3. Battle Creek Sanitarium to Ray Baker Harris, June 9, 1939, copy in "Harding 1939–1967," box 21, Dean Albertson Papers.

4. Joel T. Boone oral history, 1967, by Raymond Henle, 81–82.

5. Boone autobiography, ch. 20, pp. 186–87, box 45, Joel T. Boone Papers.

6. Harding to Christian Sr., June 19, 1922, frame 29, roll 249, George B. Christian Sr. Papers; Harding to Fletcher, July 31, "Special Corres.—Warren G. Harding 1922–1923," box 1, Henry P. Fletcher Papers.

7. Ross in *St. Louis Post-Dispatch*, October 5, 1923, in Ronald T. Farrar, *Reluctant Servant: The Story of Charles G. Ross*, 79; Votaw to Dean Albertson, October 8, 1961, "Heber H. Votaw," box 24, Albertson Papers.

8. Edgar E. Robinson and Paul C. Edwards, eds., *The Memoirs of Ray Lyman Wilbur: 1875–1949*, 374. The dictation of March 7, 1944, was slightly different from what appeared in the memoirs. It has an annotation in Wilbur's hand that the individual with whom he was speaking was Myron T. Herrick, the former Ohio governor and ambassador to Paris ("President Harding's Death," box 19, Wilbur Papers). See also a letter from Wilbur to Libman, January 13, 1940, which relates the above in abbreviated form. Libman's remark appeared, duly garbled, in Samuel Nathaniel Behrman, "Hyper or Hypo?" According to Behrman, Libman observed Harding at a dinner in 1922 and said the president would not live six months. The writer obtained the story from a daughter of Mr. and Mrs. Meyer. Libman learned what Behrman was going to say and tried to correct it, but Behrman refused to make any change (Libman to Wilbur, January 9, 1940, "President Harding's Death," box 19, Wilbur Papers).

9. Fraser to Cyril Clemens, September 26, 1939, copy in "Harding Aug./1923," box 21, Albertson Papers.

10. Sawyer to Harding, June 20, 1922, frame number unreadable, roll 262, Sawyer Papers.

11. Frame 7, roll 248, Sawyer Papers. See also Sawyer to Florence Harding, February 10, 1922: "If you had my job as a Liaison Office between yesterday and tomorrow you would certainly say 'It beats H—'. How many birds fly this way! If you and I have never earned a seat in the Kingdom before, certainly after the expiration of our sentence here Peter will say 'Come in and Stay in. The water's fine.' 'Smile and the

world smiles with you; weep and you weep alone.' Moral—keep smiling" (frame 512, roll 262, Sawyer Papers).

12. Ira R. T. Smith, *"Dear Mr. President . . ."*: *The Story of Fifty Years in the White House Mail Room,* 115.

13. Roll 4, Irwin H. (Ike) Hoover Papers; Boone autobiography, ch. 17, p. 113, box 45, Boone Papers.

14. Boone autobiography, ch. 18, p. 17, box 45, Boone Papers.

15. Florence Harding to Elsie Harding (Mrs. G. T. Harding II), January 20, 1923, frame 1030, roll 242, Florence Kling Harding Papers; to Evalyn McLean, January 22, frame 1033, roll 242, F. K. Harding Papers; to Mrs. Tod, January 25, frame 325, roll 242, F. K. Harding Papers; to "Dear Hazel," February 5, frame 1065, roll 242, F. K. Harding Papers; Boone autobiography, ch. 17, pp. 121–22, box 45, Boone Papers.

16. Edward B. MacMahon and Leonard Curry, *Medical Cover-ups in the White House,* 81–82.

17. Edmund W. Starling and Thomas Sugrue, *Starling of the White House,* 189.

18. George B. Christian Sr., "Biography of Warren G. Harding," frame 248, roll 249, Christian Sr. Papers.

19. Letter of April 16, 1923, "Sawyer," box 29, Boone Papers.

20. Boone oral history, 30–31.

21. Starling and Sugrue, *Starling,* 195–96.

22. Florence Harding to "Aunt Nellie," February 13, 1923, frame 804, roll 243, F. K. Harding Papers; Robert K. Murray, *The Harding Era: Warren G. Harding and His Administration,* 443–45. In January 1923 Harding certainly was looking forward to reelection. He wrote George B. Christian Sr. that "There are about thirty or forty men in public life, many of them in the Senate, who are thinking of their own aspirations to be president and it is inevitable that they shape their course in public life accordingly, and that they impede the progress of the executive branch of the government in every way possible. I have very little concern about those who belong to the Borah, La Follette or Norris type. I do not think Johnson is to be included among them, though he admittedly has aspirations, provided that I am not able to swing the nomination" (letter of January 29, 1923, frame 34, roll 249, Christian Sr. Papers). Hoover remembered the president sometimes saying on the trip that "we will carry through this, that, or the other, if we are reelected" ("President Harding's Last Days," commerce papers, p. 15, box 481, Herbert Hoover Papers).

23. Clarke to Jennings, June 7, 1923, frame 281, roll 261, Malcolm Jennings Papers; Harding to Jennings, June 11, 1923, frame 279, roll 261, Jennings Papers.

24. Horace Albright oral history, 1960, by William Ingersoll, 157, copy in "Harding July/1923," box 21, Albertson Papers.

25. Letter of May 5, 1923, frame 272, roll 261, Jennings Papers. A month later Harding was concerned about the proportions the trip was assuming. "It is a pretty big job to get things ready," he wrote Jennings, "and we have a tremendous task in bringing about a limit to the journalistic, photographic and publicity caravan" (letter of June 4, frame 275, roll 261, Jennings Papers).

26. Boone autobiography, ch. 19, p. 38, box 45, Boone Papers; there is a similar remark in Starling and Sugrue, *Starling,* 195.

27. "Observations of Ernest Chapman, Captain Police, Baltimore and Ohio Railroad, on Tour to Alaska with the President of the United States, Warren G. Harding," September 11, 1923, frame 10, roll 237, Warren G. Harding Papers.

28. Boone autobiography, ch. 19, p. 40c, box 45, Boone Papers; Mark Sullivan, diary, October 20, 1923.

29. Boone autobiography, ch. 19, p. 108, box 45, Boone Papers.

30. Ibid., p. 113 and ch. 20, p. 3. The president similarly explained himself to Sawyer: "Doctor, I went to Alaska to get the truth of the situation of that great northern possession. I want to give that message to the American people. All of this Northwest has congregated here to hear me, and if I were to fail to deliver this message, or fill my engagement here, they would feel I have not done my part as their president" ("Reminiscences of Warren G. Harding," frame 345, roll 248, Sawyer Papers).

31. Boone autobiography, ch. 20, pp. 7, 21–22, box 45, Boone Papers.

32. Grants Pass, Ore., July 28, 1923, in *New York Times*, July 29.

33. Boone autobiography, ch. 20, pp. 23–25, box 45, Boone Papers. Dr. Sawyer later remembered that he, himself, had discovered the cardiovascular problem when Harding reached his train that night in Seattle. "I discovered that his physical engine, his heart, which had been operating his human machine for more than a half century, was faltering. His big heart had gone beyond its endurance and this comparative physical giant had joined the invalid list" ("Personal Characteristics of Warren G. Harding," frame 326, roll 248, Sawyer Papers). Boone remembered that "Before we left Alaska, we had electrocardiograph tracings made upon him. The only abnormality reported and indicated that I saw was some left-side deviation. His heart measurements were all within normal limits. He did not evidence false abnormality. He was good about reporting to us physicians when things did not seem right with him, he didn't feel just right, or, for instance he got an infection like he did in the finger while we were aboard the *Henderson*, at which time he sent for me to come to his cabin" (Boone autobiography, ch. 20, pp. 163–64, box 45, Boone Papers).

34. Ibid., p. 26.

35. San Francisco, July 29, 1923, in *New York Times*, July 30.

36. Cooper, "the great cardiologist of San Francisco, had been specially selected by Doctor Ray Lyman Wilbur to be the consultant in Mr. Harding's case on cardiology and akin subjects" (Boone autobiography, ch. 20, p. 67, box 45, Boone Papers).

37. San Francisco, Monday, July 30, 1923, in *New York Times*, July 31.

38. Charles E. Sawyer et al., "President Harding's Last Illness: Official Bulletins of Attending Physicians."

39. Bulletin, Monday, July 30, 1923, 9:00 P.M., in ibid.

40. Sawyer et al., "President Harding's Last Illness"; caption and Sawyer quotation in *New York Times*, August 1, 1923.

41. Sawyer et al., "President Harding's Last Illness"; Ray Lyman Wilbur, "The Last Illness of a Calm Man."

42. San Francisco, August 1, 1923, in *New York Times*, August 2.

43. Herbert Hoover, "President Harding's Last Illness and Death," August 25, 1923, commerce papers, pp. 12, 15, box 481, H. Hoover Papers; Robinson and Edwards, *Memoirs*, 381. Hoover drew up two accounts of the Alaska trip and Harding's death, of which the above-mentioned is perhaps closer to the event. It contains handwritten emendations by Hoover. Very probably it resulted from a visit to the secretary by Mark Sullivan, who wrote in his diary, September 20, 1923: "I called on Hoover at his office. I asked him some questions about Harding's last trip and the replies were taken down by his secretary with a view to getting this story on record." A second account, undated, titled "President Harding's Last Days," opens with the departure from Tacoma

and Harding's efforts during the Alaska trip to compose several addresses; it begins to repeat the dated and almost contemporary narrative and telescopes it to the president's death, the last two pages relating Hoover's first encounters with Harding, together with an appraisal. This second account with some changes was included in Herbert Hoover, *The Cabinet and the Presidency,* 48–52.

44. Plymouth, Vt., August 1, 1923, in *New York Times,* August 2. An early Coolidge biography asserted that the vice president had heard prophecies of Harding's ill health. Only a few weeks before the president's death a Boston friend said, "I've heard bad reports of Mr. Harding's condition. You'll be President before the year is up." At that moment the vice president's wife was playing solitaire on the back of the piano in the Coolidge suite in the New Willard Hotel. Addressing the friend by name, Grace Coolidge asked, "How can you say such an awful thing!" There is no record of what the friend replied nor of what Coolidge said (Horace Green, *The Life of Calvin Coolidge,* 177–78).

45. Charity M. Remsberg to Cyril Clemens, January 13, 1937 (?), copy in "Harding Aug./1923," box 21, Albertson Papers.

46. It was said afterward that Mrs. Harding was reading an article by Samuel G. Blythe, "A Calm Review of a Calm Man." Blythe wrote genial articles celebrating such subjects as life in rural places or happy marriages or presidents who loved their fellow citizens. This is possible, but Boone thought the article was the above-mentioned, about Ford. If the latter was true, this is of interest in itself, for it shows Harding interested in the 1924 presidential election in which, presumably, he would run, but for which a remarkable boom had developed for the Detroit automaker. The San Francisco publisher and friend of the president Alfred Holman, who visited the sickroom shortly before Harding's death, asserted afterward that the ill man's last words were, upon hearing Florence Harding's reading of part of the Blythe article, "That's good! Go on, read some more" (San Francisco, August 2, 1923, in *New York Times,* August 3).

47. The above account is from Boone autobiography, ch. 20, pp. 53–55, 69, box 45, Boone Papers.

48. Early to William L. Pitts, May 10, 1945, "Harding's Death," box 29, Stephen T. Early Papers. Press secretary for Roosevelt, Early gave up that post early in 1945 and was acting appointments secretary when F.D.R. died. Because his successor as press secretary, Jonathan Daniels, was new to the post, Early gave out the news of Roosevelt's death. He left the Truman administration to become an officer in the Pullman Company, but he rejoined the administration as deputy secretary of defense, in which post he died. Bartley became president of the White House correspondents association in the opening months of the Coolidge administration and resigned from the A.P. to become secretary for Vice President Charles G. Dawes. Afterward he was head of the news bureau at Indiana University, where the present writer met him and once advised him to write an account of his life, which unhappily he never did.

The papers of Harding's press secretary on the Alaska trip, Welliver, disappeared. A historian learned from Welliver's son that "I know at one time my mother did have quite a number of letters and papers that had to do with the Harding administration; but after my father's death, she moved a number of times. We have not been able to find any of the material which I do know did exist. . . . I do know that there was a remarkably close relationship between President Harding and my father, and I hope that these papers can be uncovered. In some respects I think they might uncover some information that might alter the image of the President" (Allan J. Welliver to Randolph C. Downes, November 17, 1966, folder 10, box 6, Randolph C. Downes Papers).

49. *New York Times,* August 3, 1923.

50. Ibid.

51. Ibid.

52. Sawyer et al., "President Harding's Last Illness."

53. Will J. Thorpe, "The President's Funeral," *The Mortician* 3 (August 1923), cited in Francis W. Schruben, "An Even Stranger Death of President Harding."

54. *New York Times,* August 4, 5, 1923.

55. Unless otherwise specified, the following account is from the *New York Times* and "Observations of Ernest Chapman," for which see above, n. 27.

56. The Ohio description is in Murray, *Harding Era,* 452.

57. Theodore Roosevelt Jr., diary, August 7, 1923, box 1, Theodore Roosevelt Jr. Papers.

58. "Biography of Warren G. Harding," frames 257–58, roll 249, Christian Sr. Papers.

59. James G. Herrick, "Clinical Features of Sudden Obstruction of the Coronary Arteries."

60. Kenneth R. Walker and Randolph C. Downes, "The Death of Warren G. Harding," 11.

61. "Dr. George Dock, who was in Pasadena, California, when President Harding took sick," Levine wrote, "was the only physician on the Pacific Coast as far as I know, who was familiar with this condition and might have recognized it correctly" (Levine to Downes, October 23, 1961, in ibid.). When Harding took ill, the cardiologist Libman telephoned Eugene and Agnes Meyer to say that from the newspaper description he thought the president was suffering a coronary thrombosis. To Agnes Meyer— her husband was in Milwaukee—he said, "Tell Eugene to be nice to Vice President Coolidge—he will be president before long." Two days later he telephoned to say that the symptoms reported made him believe a sharp secondary thrombosis had occurred and that the president would not live forty-eight hours. As Libman remembered, Harding died within twenty-four hours (Libman to Ray Lyman Wilbur, January 9, 1940, "President Harding's Death," box 19, Wilbur Papers).

62. Sullivan, diary, November 18. The journalist evidently did not hear or recall Wilbur's enlargement of the description of chest pain, which the physician set down in a private memorandum at the time and published many years later in his memoirs, that the chest pain was "radiating down the arms, particularly the left arm" (Robinson and Edwards, *Memoirs,* 379). In the memoirs written in the 1940s, Wilbur was uncertain whether Harding's death was from apoplexy or a heart attack. "With the history of cardiovascular disturbance the sudden death could also have been of the heart type." And again: Because of Florence Harding's refusal to allow an autopsy "there was no way of final determination as to whether it was a heart attack or cerebral apoplexy" (ibid., 384).

63. Letter of August 13, 1923, in ibid.

64. Boone autobiography, ch. 20, pp. 199–201, box 45, Boone Papers.

Chapter 2

1. E. Ross Bartley to Boone, April 28, 1930, "Daugherty," box 29, Boone Papers.

2. Frederick Lewis Allen, *Only Yesterday: An Informal History of the Nineteen-Twenties,* 129, 135.

3. Samuel Hopkins Adams, *Revelry,* 80.

4. Ibid., 107.

5. Ibid., 236–37. For the account of Harding shaking Forbes, "That episode is authentic. The witness was a confidential reporter for Adolph Ochs, who had sent him down to the White House on some private mission, and who, mistaking his direction, had stumbled accidentally into this room. He reported it to Ochs, and Ochs told me" (Will Irwin to Samuel Hopkins Adams, undated [c. 1936], Samuel Hopkins Adams Papers).

6. For the following, see Adams, *Revelry*, 301–2, 311.

7. William R. Castle Jr., diary, October 4, 1926: "But the author, he says, is not a big enough man to make of it the tragedy he should have made. The real tragedy consists in the background, the Greek chorus so to speak, of the army of honest government officials to whom the whole affair was horrible."

8. Gaston B. Means, *The Strange Death of President Harding: From the Diaries of Gaston B. Means, a Department of Justice Investigator*, 21.

9. Ibid., 113.

10. Ibid., 53, 55.

11. Ibid., 81–82.

12. Ibid., 82.

13. Ibid., 95–96.

14. Ibid., 111–12.

15. Ibid., 242.

16. Ibid., 180–81.

17. Ibid., 249.

18. Ibid., 260, 263.

19. Paul A. Carter, "Samuel Hopkins Adams," *Dictionary of American Biography: Supplement Six, 1956–1960* (New York: Scribner's, 1980), 6–7.

20. Stanley J. Kunitz and Howard Haycraft, eds., *Twentieth Century Authors* (New York: H. W. Wilson, 1942), 7–8.

21. Serrell Hillman, "Samuel Hopkins Adams, 1871–1958," 15.

22. J. Edgar Hoover with Courtney Ryley Cooper, "The Amazing Mr. Means," 24.

23. Edwin P. Hoyt, *Spectacular Rogue: Gaston B. Means*, 15–16.

24. Ibid., 291–92. A different story, without any physical consequences, is in Hoover with Cooper, "Amazing Mr. Means," 25, according to which Means sent a block of wood by express, claiming it was currency and insuring it for fifty-seven thousand dollars. The consignee suspected a trick and opened the box in the presence of witnesses.

25. An excellent account of Means, based on newspaper files (for he was rarely out of the newspapers), is Louis M. Starr, "Gaston B. Means," *Dictionary of American Biography: Supplement Two* (New York: Scribner's, 1958), 444–46.

26. Hoyt, *Spectacular Rogue*, 167.

27. Ibid., 188.

28. May Dixon Thacker, "Debunking 'The Strange Death of President Harding': A Complete Repudiation of a Sensational Book by Its Author," 10, 12.

29. Ibid., 10.

30. Ibid., 12.

31. To Evalyn McLean, October 31, 1920, frame 85, roll 242, F. K. Harding Papers; to Mrs. Pardee, October 31, frame 88, roll 242, F. K. Harding Papers; to Miss Phelps, November 11, frame 103, roll 242, F. K. Harding Papers; to Grace Coolidge, November 11, frame 108, roll 242, F. K. Harding Papers; to unidentified, frame 154, roll 242,

F. K. Harding Papers; to "Dear Louise," January 3, 1921, frames 202–3, roll 242, F. K. Harding Papers.

32. To George B. Christian Sr. and wife, December 24, 1907, frame 31, roll 249, Christian Sr. Papers; to Mrs. Christian, December 25, 1920, frame 22, roll 249, Christian Sr. Papers; Lillian Rogers Parks and Frances Spatz Leighton, *My Thirty Years Backstairs at the White House,* 164.

33. Boone autobiography, ch. 17, pp. 111–12, box 45, Boone Papers.

34. Ibid., p. 112.

35. Ibid., p. 63–63a; Boone oral history, 22. For days Mrs. Harding's situation was touch and go. Secretary of the Navy Edwin N. Denby and Theodore Roosevelt Jr. "called at the White House and went up and saw the President. I had not realized that it was so serious but apparently the President felt Mrs. Harding would die during the night. As I was leaving Harry Daugherty got my telephone number, because, as he said, he might want me to come down at any time. . . . At eleven-thirty I went down with [Secretary of War] John Weeks again to the White House. The President sent down word for us to come up and sit with him for an hour or so. Mrs. Harding seemed to be resting a little more comfortably than she had in the afternoon early. Dr. Mayo had been sent for" (Theodore Roosevelt Jr., diary, September 8, 1922, box 1, Roosevelt Papers).

36. Robinson and Edwards, *Memoirs,* 382; Boone autobiography, ch. 20, pp. 54–55, box 45, Boone Papers.

37. Dauser to Boone, summer 1964, Boone autobiography, ch. 21, p. 275, box 46, Boone Papers; *San Diego Union,* May 13, 1966, frame 2, roll 237, W. G. Harding Papers. Captain Dauser had written Mont Reily more than thirty years earlier (January 22, 1932) and said the same thing: "When it comes to arguing that President Harding was poisoned by Mrs. Harding, I cannot even comprehend the possibility, no matter what idea is advanced. Where and how could Mrs. Harding have procured the poison; what could she have given that would have killed so instantly, long after it had been given, without producing pain in the meantime, and when could she have given it? As for Mrs. Harding ever being alone with the president during his illness, I am sure that never occurred, and I feel sure that I was the only person ever absolutely alone with him during his last illness. Doctor Boone was supposed to be on the night shift only, but he was constantly called during the day for conferences with the other doctors. His sleep was thus broken, and in the wee hours of the morning, if the president rested, Doctor Boone would lie on a couch in an adjoining room and rest, while I sat by the bedside. I am sure that Mrs. Harding never so much as gave her husband a glass of water during the stay in the room at the Palace Hotel. Either the nurses or the doctors always attended to that" ("The Years of Confusion," 366, E. Mont Reily Papers).

38. Letter of October 2, 1924, "Sawyer," box 29, Boone Papers.

39. Boone autobiography, ch. 21, p. 185, box 46, Boone Papers.

40. Frelinghuysen to Coolidge, September 9, 1924, P.P.F. 26, reel 3, Calvin Coolidge Papers; Florence Harding to Boone, "Harding," box 29, Boone Papers; Robinson and Edwards, *Memoirs,* 382. Mrs. Harding knew about her heart condition, as the following illustrates: "Mr. Harding is recovering from an attack of grippe, but I am thankful to say is all right again, and I am about the room, and am gaining strength, and am doing very well with the exception of my heart" (letter to "Aunt Carrie," January 29, 1923, frames 820–21, roll 242, F. K. Harding Papers). And again, to Evalyn McLean, she wrote: "I am much stronger but my heart is still very uncertain" (February 5, frame 1060, roll 242, F. K. Harding Papers).

Chapter 3

1. The book is in the rare books division of the Library of Congress. It was donated to the library in 1973 by Mrs. Frank P. Atkins of Cincinnati.

2. Nan Britton, *The President's Daughter*, 74. All citations are to a printing in which each illustration counts as a page; in another printing the illustrations did not count.

3. Ibid., 136.

4. Ibid., 234, 237.

5. Ibid., 268.

6. Nan Britton, *Honesty or Politics*, 3.

7. Ibid., 7.

8. Ibid., 32.

9. *New York American*, December 11, 1927; *New York Telegram*, January 3, 1928.

10. Britton, *Honesty or Politics*, 160.

11. Ibid., ix–x.

12. Ibid., 162–63.

13. E. Mont Reily, "The Years of Confusion," 371–72, Reily Papers.

14. Ibid., 379.

15. "There were queer ones like Coolidge, sad ones like McKinley, wise ones like Wilson or Hoover, sporty ones like Harding, sincere ones like Cleveland or Hoover. In fact all kinds of ones" (reel 9, I. Hoover Papers. Hoover's testimony to Reily is in "Years of Confusion," 385, Reily Papers).

16. Britton, *The President's Daughter*, 132, 199.

17. Ibid., 52, 253.

18. Smith, *"Dear Mr. President . . .",* 112–14. In later years Ms. Britton was apparently uneasy about whatever she had sent the president, and observed that she lost a letter during the first month of Harding's term and that it contained many snapshots of Elizabeth Ann and some of herself with their daughter. A friend, a Secret Service man, had assisted Christian until the latter "got onto things," but someone else had opened the president's mail at the time (Britton, *The President's Daughter*, 320). She may have been concerned that in 1927, with a president of the same political party in the White House, the Coolidge administration might have arranged an examination of unanswered mail in 1921 and discovered blackmail letters. In actual fact the Harding executive office files were then in the basement of the White House (see Chapter 5). But, as mentioned, Christian and Smith had destroyed the blackmail letters.

19. When she interviewed Dr. Harding in 1926 she informed him she possessed a watch given her by the physician's brother in 1917, purchased at Galt's, the well-known Washington jeweler (President Wilson's second wife was Edith Bolling Galt, widow of the store's owner). She told Dr. Harding she could trace the watch's purchase. In January 1930 she noticed the watch had disappeared from her jewel case and never discovered who took it, although she suspected Gaston Means whom she recently had met (Britton, *Honesty or Politics*, 321). Here again she failed to take the most elementary measures to protect herself—she could have asked Galt's to search their records and identify the watch's purchaser, and if the search identified Senator Harding she would have had a prime piece of evidence of an affair to display to Harding's brother.

20. Britton, *The President's Daughter*, 325.

21. To Samuel Hopkins Adams, May 23, 1939, Adams Papers.

22. Britton, *The President's Daughter*, 404–5.

23. Ibid., 409.

24. Ibid., 408.

25. Ibid., 375, 379.

26. Britton, *Honesty or Politics,* 57–59.

27. Ibid., 290.

28. *New York Daily News,* November 14, 1927.

29. Loc. cit.

30. Ibid., November 13, 1927.

31. Edgar I. Stewart, ed., *The Life and Adventures of Frank Grouard.* It is difficult to discover information on De Barthe. A letter to the University of Oklahoma Press revealed that De Barthe's editor, Stewart, died in 1971, and the press had no records of the book's reprinting.

32. "In our interview you stated that you possessed medical proof that the President was physically unable to be the father of children. If my memory serves me correctly, you also said that you would be willing to provide scientific evidence of this to a serious researcher" (Downes to Warren G. Harding II, May 9, 1960, folder 82, box 5, Downes Papers).

33. "The Years of Confusion," 381–82, Reily Papers. The governor added that "Close friends of Warren G. Harding have confirmed the fact of his sterility. . . . So Nan Britton was very unwise in the choice of her child's alleged father" (382). In a letter from Reily to Daugherty is a statement that Harding "told me about Nan Britton," with an explanation that "I expect to tell the story in my book" (letter of January 15, 1932, Harding Papers, copy in "Harding 1926–1933," box 21, Albertson Papers). This probably meant the account of sterility.

34. Britton, *Honesty or Politics,* 60–61. The Boone autobiography is explicit about Harding's hemorrhoids. In an effort to deny the sterility issue she might have been referring to the nervous breakdown accompanied by a fever, mentioned by Harding's father to the San Francisco physicians, or generally to the visits to the Battle Creek Sanitarium.

35. September 25, 1931, box MS 402, Albertson Papers.

36. *Toledo Blade,* October 30, 1931.

37. Britton, *The President's Daughter,* 48–50.

38. Weinberg to the author, May 10, 1996. Duckett described his contrary view in detail: "As I turned to look at the xerox copy I was somehow thinking 'Harvey' was the name of the second hotel, and as I glanced at the document my eye was immediately caught—I said to myself 'What is this that Harding has signed.' To my mind's eye it was so unmistakenly WGH's handwriting that at first glance I thought it was signed W. G. Harding, and only on looking again did I see it was signed Harvey. What I am trying to explain is that I didn't start studying the document with the view to finding his handwriting, it just leaped out at me. I do not profess to be a graphologist or a handwriting expert of any sort, but I have spent my professional life reading other people's letters, including perhaps thousands of WGH's, and I would stake whatever small reputation I have that 'Harvey' was signed by the old philanderer himself" (letter to the author, October 14, 1995).

39. *Toledo Blade,* October 28, 1931.

40. Ibid., October 29. The witness said that six years before *The President's Daughter* appeared she heard from a maid in the Mouser house, Maggie Poindexter, that Ms. Britton was not fit company for Annabelle Mouser, the judge's daughter and a former schoolmate and friend.

41. *Britton v. Klunk.* The fact that these quotations from Marsteller's summation were in the case file says that a stenographic record may have existed. Judge Killits quoted Marsteller when he overruled the latter's motion for a new trial.

42. Frames 1026–27, 1031, roll 248, Sawyer Papers.

43. Frame 1033, roll 248, Sawyer Papers.

44. "We secured a section to Chicago. The remembrance of that trip from Connersville to Chicago is very beautiful although it, too, was free from complete embraces. . . . We were both dressed the next morning before we reached the Englewood Station, about nine minutes from the downtown station, and I remarked to Mr. Harding that he looked a bit tired. 'God sweetheart! What do you expect? I'm a man, you know' " (Britton, *The President's Daughter,* 42).

45. *Britton v. Klunk.*

46. Ibid.

47. Both collections are sizable, twenty-one linear feet of Downes's papers, twelve of Albertson's. A doctoral student at the University of Toledo, Tana Mosier Porter, is undertaking a study of Downes as a scholar. The archivist at the University of Massachusetts told the present writer that in her twelve years at Amherst no one had asked to see the Albertson Papers.

48. Nan Britton to Downes, July 23, 1963, folder 23, box 6, Downes Papers. In 1930 Florida philanthropist and world traveler Alden Freeman gave Elizabeth Ann and her mother a vacation in France, after he had gone to Marion to investigate Ms. Britton. His will, dated June 20, 1930, arranged for Elizabeth Ann to have twenty-five hundred dollars a year (Britton, *Honesty and Politics,* 329–33). In an announcement two years later the philanthropist said that "Miss Britton is a most devoted mother and one of the noblest and most unselfish of women" (*New York Herald Tribune,* March 12, 1932). Evidently by 1938 the bequest had come to an end.

49. In an article Downes had written that "Hence she wrote the book, presumably for the income involved, which was considerable" (Randolph C. Downes, "Wanted: A Scholarly Appraisal of Warren G. Harding," 19).

50. *New York Times,* July 15, 1964. Apple spoke with Gertrude Davis (Jane Schermerhorn to Francis Russell, March 1, 1965, Francis Russell Papers).

51. Leech to Downes, June 16, 1960, folder 25, box 6, Downes Papers.

52. Baughman to Downes, June 8, 1960, folder 25, box 6, Downes Papers; Downes to Baughman, June 13, folder 25, box 6, Downes Papers; Baughman to Downes, June 21, folder 25, box 6, Downes Papers. The Harding biographer Francis Russell wrote Baughman's successor, James J. Rowley, who responded September 2, 1964: "This is in reply to your letter of August 22 requesting information on Nan Britton. The Secret Service has no information in its files on Nan Britton." Russell sent the letter to Downes with a notation, "Dear Randolph: At least that settles that! F.R." (folder 25, box 6, Downes Papers).

53. Starling and Sugrue, *Starling,* 170–71.

54. Folder 26, box 6, Downes Papers.

55. *Congressional Record,* 70th Cong., 1st sess., 1928, 69, pt. 2:2077–79; Britton, *Honesty or Politics,* 261; *Toledo Blade,* January 24, 1971.

56. Albertson to Britton, April 10, 1964, box MS 402, Albertson Papers.

57. Ibid.

58. Albertson to Howell, July 1, 1964, box MS 402, Albertson Papers; Howell to Albertson, July 7, box MS 402, Albertson Papers.

59. Box MS 402, Albertson Papers.

60. Undated telephone interview, "Walter Trohan," box 24, Albertson Papers; Trohan to Albertson, September 16, 1964, "Walter Trohan," box 24, Albertson Papers. Trohan's memory was questionable. In the telephone interview he told Albertson that in June 1964 he had spoken with the Chicago bookman Ralph Newman, who had seen the Phillips letters in Marion as an appraiser, and that Newman said one letter indicated that Harding had slept with Carrie Phillips in the morning and Nan Britton the same afternoon. Neither the Phillips letters nor the perhaps fifty pages of notes Ms. Phillips kept for composing her letters to Harding mention Nan Britton. There is no mention of Sloan, Harding, or the others in Walter Trohan's *Political Animals: Memoirs of a Sentimental Cynic* (Garden City, N.Y.: Doubleday, 1975).

61. Notes of telephone conversation, September 2 (3?), 1964, "Jay G. Hayden," box 23, Albertson Papers.

62. *New York Times,* June 23, August 1, and December 27, 1945.

63. Nan Britton to Albertson, September 15, 1964, box MS 402, Albertson Papers; Britton, *The President's Daughter,* 187–88, 191, 228.

64. Stephenson to Albertson, August 11, 1964, box MS 402, Albertson Papers.

65. Letter of September 15, 1964. Sloan, she wrote, had spoken to Dawes about her predicament. She had addressed a brief note to Dawes, which he did not answer.

Chapter 4

1. Harry M. Daugherty, *The Inside Story of the Harding Tragedy,* 256.

2. Walsh to Butler, April 3, 1924, and Butler to Walsh, April 7, both in "Bu-Bz," box 210, Thomas J. Walsh Papers.

3. M. L. Requa in U.S. Senate, *Leases upon Naval Oil Reserves,* 1:59. Senator Walsh who was attempting to prevent private exploitation of the reserves wrote former secretary of the navy Josephus Daniels that "I am struggling along with little help from any sources . . . I have been sorely disappointed at the apparent apathy of the higher officers of the Navy to the whole thing. I imagined they, at least, would exhibit some solicitude about the preservation of these valuable Reserves of the Navy. In my desperation, I tried vainly to arouse the interest of the Navy League, but am confirmed by its indifference in the view that it can see no good in any act of a Democratic administration, nor any possible ill in a Republican administration" (Walsh to Daniels, November 5, 1923, "Da-Dh," box 210, Walsh Papers).

4. U.S. Senate, *Leases,* 2:2123–24.

5. Ibid., 1780.

6. Some months after the initial Teapot Dome hearings Theodore Roosevelt Jr. discussed Doheny and Sinclair with the two lawyers appointed by President Coolidge to look into the oil scandal, Owen J. Roberts and former senator Atlee Pomerene. "Doheny we all agreed was a man who excites a certain amount of sympathy in us. We feel he is an old-timer who plays the game on a rule long since discarded. He has generous impulses. He does things with a gesture, and as a result he has lots of friends in the country. On the other hand there isn't anybody to say a good word for Harry Sinclair. He apparently is a crook from way back. They told me they had something worse than anything we had intimated before on Sinclair. They know he did it but they could not legally prove it. They are trying to work it out now" (Theodore Roosevelt Jr., diary, September 12, 1924, box 2, Roosevelt Papers).

7. The former secretary also accepted a five-thousand-dollar loan from Doheny.

8. Calder to Ray Baker Harris, August 2, 1933, copy in "Harding 1926–1933," box 21, Albertson Papers; Wadsworth to Harris, April 2, 1934, copy in "Harding 1934–1938," box 21, Albertson Papers.

9. Daugherty, *Inside Story*, 82–83.

10. Sullivan, diary, November 24, 1923.

11. Burl Noggle, *Teapot Dome: Oil and Politics in the 1920's*, 53; Daugherty, *Inside Story*, 80–81.

12. Letter of May 5, 1939, Adams Papers.

13. Boone autobiography, ch. 20, p. 195, box 45, Boone Papers; for the remark of Christian Sr. see frame 825ff, roll 249, George B. Christian Jr. Papers.

14. For the quotation see Noggle, *Teapot Dome*, 56 n.

15. Murray, *Harding Era*, 446–47.

16. Archie's appearance came because of the alarm of his brother Theodore. "My brother Archie was employed by the Sinclair Company in 1919. He handled mainly their foreign business. On Friday, January 18th, in this year, he called me on the telephone and asked me whether I thought he ought to resign. No facts were in my possession at that time that indicated anything corrupt insofar as the oil matters were concerned. I told him, therefore, that I saw no reason for him resigning. I felt, however, that he had more on his mind than he told me over the telephone, so I took the night train to New York and saw him there the next morning. He told me of the conversation he had had with Mr. Walhberg, Mr. Sinclair's private secretary. At once I said he should resign, come down to Washington with me that night, and place what he had heard before the Committee. After we arrived in Washington on Sunday morning, the 20th, I got in touch with Senators Walsh and Lenroot and arranged that Archie and I should go and see them that afternoon. We gave them the information and they in turn arranged for the hearings before the Committee, which took place the next day" (letter to William W. Campbell, February 15, 1924, unsent, "Teapot Dome investigation," box 39, Roosevelt Papers).

17. There is reason to believe that McAdoo was trimming when he said his retainer was only half what Doheny said it was. He carefully spoke of the past two years. He had been in an earlier Mexican negotiation involving Doheny that might have brought a larger retainer. The chairman of the committee, Sen. Irvine L. Lenroot of Wisconsin (Senator Smoot of Utah stepped down from the chairmanship early in 1924 in order to accept another Senate chairmanship, but remained on the committee), made a distinction between "the former retainer and not the present retainer, as I understand you." McAdoo responded that "it was under the old matter. The present retainer was only $25,000 a year." In favor of an earlier retainer of $50,000 was the fact that former secretary of the interior Lane was paid that sum, and Doheny would hardly have paid McAdoo less. Thereafter the subject drifted away from retainers. Earlier Sen. Clarence C. Dill of Washington had inquired, "Did Mr. Doheny deliver that money to you in a satchel?" The response was that it always came in the form of a check. McAdoo was asked what he did for a retainer, and he answered with lawyerlike obscurity: "Well, I do not know how much time it has taken. I do not keep a diary of these things, but I am accessible to a client when I am under retainer, as any other lawyer is, for advice and consultation when he wants it" (U.S. Senate, *Leases*, 2:2069–70).

18. J. Leonard Bates, "The Teapot Dome Scandal and the Election of 1924," 306.

19. James W. Wadsworth oral history, 1950–1952, by Owen W. Bombard, Wendell H. Link, and Dean Albertson, 295.

20. Reed Smoot, diary, December 29 and 31, 1922. In the Teapot Dome hearings Senator Smoot's successor as chairman, Lenroot, questioned Doheny in detail as to whether the oilman had lent money to any public official and the answer was no, with hedging—Doheny testified that he might fail to remember, even if the sum was (Lenroot asked) more than ten thousand dollars (U.S. Senate, *Leases*, 2:1936). Technically he was correct, for he had lent the money to Harold Smoot, not the senator.

21. Smoot, diary, November 30, 1923. Milton R. Merrill, *Reed Smoot: Apostle in Politics* (Logan: Utah State University Press, 1990), copublished by the department of political science at Utah State University, contains nothing on Teapot Dome. It appears to be the author's unrevised doctoral dissertation at Columbia University, accepted in 1950.

22. U.S. Senate, *Investigation of the Honorable Harry M. Daugherty*, 1:53.

23. Wadsworth oral history, 294; Daugherty, *Inside Story*, 181.

24. "Personal Characteristics of Warren G. Harding," frame 318, roll 248, Sawyer Papers.

25. Will Irwin, *The Making of a Reporter*, 401.

26. U.S. Senate, *Investigation of Veterans' Bureau*, 1:200.

27. Ibid., 224–25; ibid., 2:1019.

28. Ibid., 1:237.

29. Ibid., 2:1131.

30. Ibid., 1405.

31. Ibid., 1:249, 255–56.

32. Statement of Sawyer, in ibid., 1:754–55.

33. T.R. Jr. for months had been seeking to get Forbes out, but the reason was not for malfeasance but for inefficiency. He had seen the president during a camp-out at Gettysburg and "In the evening we dined together. We lally-gagged on every conceivable subject. I lived up to my reputation as harbinger of woe by telling the President I felt he should get rid of Forbes. He listened attentively to this and asked me to see him on Sunday when he returned" (diary, July 1, 1922, box 1, Roosevelt Papers). Whatever happened during the forthcoming conference Roosevelt did not record. "Today Bill Deegan arrived from New York," he wrote a week later. "We went over the hospitalization situation thoroughly. Forbes, I am afraid, is no good. There is no question but what we want is action, positive action, unchanging action" (ibid., July 9). And again: "There is no question but that the Veterans' Bureau is rottenly run . . ." (ibid., August 27).

34. Murray, *Harding Era*, 430.

35. See Daugherty's account in *Inside Story*, 29, 32–33.

36. Castle, diary, August 16, 1923.

37. Donovan sent a two-page statement to Wadsworth, and the senator repeated the story in a letter to his father ("Teapot Dome," box 20, James W. Wadsworth Family Papers).

38. U.S. Senate, *Investigation of Daugherty*, 1:53; Burton K. Wheeler, *Yankee from the West*, 220–21.

39. Daugherty, *Inside Story*, 247.

40. Boone autobiography, ch. 18, pp. 13, 31, box 45, Boone Papers.

41. Ibid., p. 62b.

42. Daugherty, *Inside Story*, 247–49.

43. Hoover, *Cabinet*, 49.

44. Boone autobiography, ch. 18, pp. 69–72, box 45, Boone Papers.

45. U.S. Senate, *Investigation of Daugherty,* 1:566.

46. Boone autobiography, ch. 17, pp. 120, 123, box 45, Boone Papers; ibid., ch. 18, pp. 30, 39, 57.

47. Ibid., ch. 21, pp. 94, 145, 502, 1222–23, box 46. Mark Sullivan called on Coolidge to tell him he ought to get rid of Daugherty, and the president told him "In confidence, the trouble with Daugherty is mental. He has a son who is defective. I wouldn't be surprised to see a blowup any time" (Sullivan, diary, March 8, 1924).

48. Boone autobiography, ch. 21, p. 144, box 46, Boone Papers.

49. Ibid., letter of June 22, 1926, "Daugherty," box 29.

50. Daugherty, *Inside Story,* 257.

51. *New York Times,* October 12, 1926. Further investigation of Daugherty's encounter with the Brookhart-Wheeler committee and his indictment and two trials in New York may be impossible because of the disappearance of his papers. He willed them to his daughter in 1937, but they failed to turn up after his death in 1941. By far the best analysis is James N. Giglio's *H. M. Daugherty and the Politics of Expediency,* which places Harding's attorney general within post–Civil War Ohio politics (181–93). While nationally very important (Ohio was "the mother of the presidents") those politics were partisan almost beyond belief. Giglio has much feeling for Daugherty's small-town background and personal quirks and health problems. He concludes that Daugherty was probably illicitly involved in the American Metal Company case, in collusion with his friend Smith (202). With that conclusion there is room for disagreement, as he admits. Less satisfactory in its interpretation of Daugherty is Martin Mayer's *Emory Buckner,* which uses Buckner's papers and law office records. Buckner was U.S. attorney for the southern district of New York and prosecuted the former attorney general during both trials. He was incurably hostile to Daugherty. In the second trial the jury failed to convict Daugherty by a single vote, that of a hat-check concessionaire at the Hotel Astor. The judge in the case, John C. Knox, later wrote that had he been on the jury he would have agreed with the dissenting juror (see Knox's memoirs, *A Judge Comes of Age,* 257–58). Buckner could not prove that Daugherty knew about Smith's acceptance of a bribe. He rested his case on the division of the $391,000 bribe given by the German national seeking reimbursement for the sale of the American Metal Company. He could not account for $5,000. Taking that off and dealing with a figure of $386,000, and subtracting $50,000 for Miller, left $336,000. The Harding supporter John T. King who died in 1926 was proved to have taken one-third, or $112,000. Smith apparently received the balance, $224,000, and the presumption of the arithmetic was that he divided it with Daugherty.

52. Ibid., 262–63.

53. Wheeler, *Yankee,* 229.

54. Murray, *Harding Era,* 433–34.

55. Noggle, *Teapot Dome,* 122–23 n.

56. Murray, *Harding Era,* 433–34; Eugene Meyer oral history, 1952–1953, by Dean Albertson, 450. Indeed the Teapot Dome investigators showed a peculiar misunderstanding of what recently had happened in the oil business and before it in other early developments in American industry. Wrote one astute contemporary observer: "It is not such a big surprise to me. I was in Oklahoma in the Spring of 1914 and saw what wild gamblers the oil men were. I have never had much confidence in any oil company except the Standard as a business proposition and in their early days certainly they were none too pure in their methods. Whenever people make large and unexpected

fortunes without any real background they become dangerous, and when their activities come into contact with the Government there is bound to be trouble. Look at the early days of railroad building and the performances of Gould and Vanderbilt and numerous others. The early days of big money making in the steel business were not much better" (George Emlen Roosevelt to Theodore Roosevelt Jr., February 20, 1924, "George Emlen Roosevelt," box 10, Roosevelt Papers).

57. Alben W. Barkley, *That Reminds Me,* 122–23, 134.

58. Interview, January 31, 1964, copy in "Harding July/1923," box 21, Albertson Papers. The play introduced a giggling flapper, beaded and bespangled, by the name of Laverne, one of the dancing La Reve Sisters whom a fictitious President Griffith P. Hastings pulled onto a poker table, by way of a chair. The president clambered up and danced with her (Jerome Lawrence and Robert E. Lee, *The Gang's All Here,* 87).

Chapter 5

1. Clinton W. Gilbert, *Behind the Mirrors: The Psychology of Disintegration at Washington,* iv.

2. Clinton W. Gilbert, *The Mirrors of Washington,* 3–4.

3. Gilbert, *Behind the Mirrors,* 35.

4. Ibid., 6.

5. Ibid., 102; Gilbert, *Mirrors of Washington,* 12–13.

6. Gilbert, *Behind the Mirrors,* 6.

7. Henry L. Mencken, *Baltimore Sun,* September 9, 1921, in Malcolm Moos, ed., *A Carnival of Buncombe,* 45.

8. Ibid.

9. Ibid., 8 (February 9, 1920); ibid., 16 (July 26, 1920); ibid., 25 (October 4, 1920).

10. Ibid., 19 (July 28, 1920).

11. Ibid., 31 (October 18, 1920).

12. Ibid., 28.

13. Ibid., 15.

14. Ibid., 22–23 (October 4, 1920).

15. Ibid., 32.

16. Ibid., 20 (September 13, 1920); ibid., 38–40 (March 7, 1921).

17. Ibid., 20 (September 13, 1920).

18. Ibid., 26 (October 4, 1920).

19. For the *American Mercury,* I am indebted to Randolph C. Downes's unpublished "The Harding Muckfest," courtesy of Kenneth W. Duckett, to whom Downes gave a copy many years ago. Downes analyzed each issue of the *Mercury* for 1924.

20. Moos, *Carnival,* xvi–xvii.

21. Letter of March 31, 1962, folder 15, box 6, Downes Papers.

22. William Allen White, *Autobiography,* 587.

23. Randolph C. Downes, "The Harding Papers," 5, address to the Society of American Archivists, April 28, 1966, in Cincinnati. Copy in the Downes Papers.

24. William Allen White, *Masks in a Pageant,* 425, 433–34.

25. Ibid., 432.

26. Ibid., 424–30.

27. Andrew Sinclair, *The Available Man: The Life behind the Masks of Warren Gamaliel Harding,* 297.

28. He would have liked to have written more than the Harding chapter in *Masks*, and the year after the book appeared was either considering a book entirely on Harding or recommending the project to a friend. "What about Harding? There's a beautiful story . . . No one less than Voltaire or Carlyle should do it. Yet for five years my poor typewriter has had a deep dirty suppressed desire to click it out" (letter to Allan Nevins, July 27, 1929, copy in "Harding 1926–1933," box 21, Albertson Papers).

29. Murray, *Harding Era*, 519–20.

30. Allan Nevins, "Warren G. Harding," 252–57.

31. Alice Roosevelt Longworth, *Crowded Hours*, 324–25; Murray, *Harding Era*, 521.

32. When Alice Longworth's husband was running for the majority leadership of the House his brother-in-law recorded that his drinking was hurting his race: " . . . I am afraid you can't teach an old dog new tricks. Nick has been a hard drinker for years so I don't think you can change him" (Theodore Roosevelt Jr., diary, May 28, 1923, box 1, Roosevelt Papers).

33. Letter of March 31, 1962, folder 15, box 6, Downes Papers.

34. Because of his Republican contacts, Sullivan picked up gossip of interesting sorts. The story concerned a Mrs. Cross, about whom he learned from President Wilson's erstwhile private secretary, Joseph P. Tumulty. Reportedly, the woman had been a Harding intimate, and according to Tumulty the then senator once suffered a heart attack walking up the stairs of her apartment. Mrs. Cross sought to profit from the association, and the Wilson administration in the person of Attorney General Palmer arranged for her to leave Washington. During the Harding administration Attorney General Daugherty embarrassed the Democratic Party by moving against certain Democratic figures, including Palmer. The lawyer Frank J. Hogan was involved in some way; he was attorney for Doheny, and the involvement might have been the imminence of Senate hearings over Teapot Dome. Hogan saw the president, mentioned Democratic behavior over the Mrs. Cross affair, and Harding immediately called off Daugherty (Sullivan, diary, August 2, 1923).

After listening to this story, Sullivan asked Tumulty about Mrs. Peck, a woman with whom President Wilson had been linked by gossip. Many years later, on October 2, 1964, a one-time reporter for the *Washington Post*, Vylla Poe Wilson, spoke with Dean Albertson and identified the Harding friend as Grace Cross, a "tall, beautiful blonde—exceptionally beautiful," who worked in Harding's Senate office. Vylla Wilson told of Harding letters in the possession of Mrs. Cross, which a mutual friend, Bertha Martin, literally snatched from Mrs. Cross during a luncheon on March 4, 1921, and that in a week Bertha Martin became society editor of the *Post*, through arrangement made by Jess Smith ("Vylla Poe Wilson," box 24, Albertson Papers). But then Vylla Wilson told Albertson that Ike Hoover told her he had seen Nan Britton several times leave the White House after visiting the president and that during a *Mayflower* outing for the women of the press corps, Ms. Britton had appeared and the captain had escorted her off the ship.

35. Murray, *Harding Era*, 457–58; Sullivan, diary, November 18, 1923.

36. Mark Sullivan, *The Twenties*, 356 n, 364 n. On the second page, in a note following the first, Sullivan took back the accusation of murder.

37. Ibid., 244. The *Oxford English Dictionary* cites use of normalcy in a mathematical dictionary of 1857.

38. Samuel Hopkins Adams, *Incredible Era: The Life and Times of Warren Gamaliel Harding*, 80.

39. Ibid., 155; Murray, *Harding Era*, 523.

40. Greenslet to Daugherty, October 18, 1939, copy in "Harding—1939–1967," box 21, Albertson Papers.

41. Wolff to Boone, January 10, 1963, "Harding," box 29, Boone Papers. Boone excerpted this line from Alice Longworth's book: "He was just a slob," as well as the passage that "He had discovered what was going on around him, and that knowledge, the worry, the thought of the disclosures and shame that were bound to come, undoubtedly undermined his health—one might say actually killed him" (Longworth, *Crowded Hours*, 325). Beside these quotations he penciled question marks and "Do not believe this so." In response to Wolff's letter he wrote, "If the distortions as I recognize them in Mr. Adams' book, wherein he mentions my name, are indicative of the lack of factuality of other portions of his book, *Incredible Era*, I would be compelled to discount many of the references to other people and events to be found in his book." And again, "Too many so-called historians' writings . . . are based on hearsay and without personal knowledge of the period or people about whom they write" (Boone to Wolff, February 20, 1963, "Harding," box 29, Boone Papers).

42. Kenneth W. Duckett, "The Harding Papers: How Some Were Burned . . . ," 29–30.

43. Britton, *The President's Daughter*, 102, 351; White, *Masks*, 409, 413; Means, *Strange Death*, 56–57; Adams, *Incredible Era*, 101.

44. *Cleveland Plain Dealer*, July 31, 1964, folder 90, box 5, Downes Papers.

45. Randolph C. Downes, "The Harding Papers," 15, Downes Papers.

46. Francis Russell, *The Shadow of Blooming Grove: Warren G. Harding and His Times*, 165–68; *Columbus Citizen Journal Dispatch*, January 20, 1972, folder 90, box 5, Downes Papers.

47. *Columbus Citizen Journal Dispatch*, January 20, 1972.

48. William Estabrook Chancellor, *Warren Gamaliel Harding: President of the United States*, 109. Chancellor wrote that former governor Herrick made the offer of the trip to Japan, together with the cash payment and monthly income. The Myron T. Herrick Papers offer nothing on this subject. Indeed, the formality of a letter from Herrick to Harding congratulating him on his nomination for the presidency makes the possibility unlikely. In folder 148, roll 3, are undated memoranda and notes of private remarks and conversations in 1928–1929 when Herrick was ambassador to France; a friend wrote them down. Herrick died in 1929. He told amusing stories and once asked his friend what was the similarity between the daughter of Alice and Nick Longworth, born in the mid-1920s, and a new golf ball. (Answer: "Neither has a nick in it.") The stories and remarks did not mention Mrs. Phillips. Herrick was in France and England during most of the summer of 1920.

49. The interview appeared in the issue of July 18, 1964.

50. A reporter published an interview with Ms. Britton some months later in which the author of *The President's Daughter* spoke kindly of Mrs. Phillips and her daughter, Isabelle, with whom she had gone to school. She said the Phillipses were neighbors, that she possessed a photograph of Isabelle's pet bulldog, and she wished she would have opportunity to see Isabelle and sit down and have a long visit with her. The interviewer did not mention to her the references to Mrs. Arnold in the book but quoted them extensively in the resultant article (Jane Schermerhorn, "The Love Affair That Never Died: Exclusive Interview with Nan Britton," *Detroit News*, February 24, 1965). The reporter wrote the biographer Francis Russell, who evidently inquired, that

the interview was difficult. "She didn't talk much but I think she was rather stung by the Phillips love letters and there was something like defiance in her manner when she blurted, 'Indeed I have Harding papers and they are safe—under lock and key—in a bank.' A second visit to her was prevented by her attorney . . ." (letter of March 1, 1965, Russell Papers).

51. Sinclair, one might add, was irritable on that point, and published an essay in the *New York Times Book Review* castigating his fellow biographers who had criticized him, remarking that it was possible to obtain enough Xerox copies of the Harding Papers in six days to equal six months of research in the pre-Xerox era.

He also was thankful for Xerox because he detested Columbus, Ohio. In his essay he wrote that Columbus doubtless was "bonny" (he was a Scotsman) to the Columbians, "but I feel rather pre-Columbian toward the civilization which has conquered there. . . . I got my material and got out of town. By August I'd written up my gleanings into the first draft . . ." It was necessary to return to Columbus to check notes, and this involved going into the Ohio Historical Society's search room, the lions' den, where the hostile biographers worked. In accord with Poe's "Purloined Letter" he left his manuscript in full view, so no one would see it. When he submitted it to his publisher, one of the biographers wrote the editor of the series in which it was to appear, advising of the little time Sinclair spent in Columbus. The editor previously had approved the manuscript, but withdrew his approval. Fortunately, the Macmillan house editor refused to be frightened. "It no longer puzzles me," Sinclair concluded, "that some historians have beome Presidents; if you finagle your way in the first profession, the second is a joy ride" (Andrew Sinclair, "The Dear Departed," 2, 28). The only historian to become president was Woodrow Wilson. For a short time John Quincy Adams held the title of Boylston Professor of Rhetoric at Harvard University.

52. Sinclair, *Available Man*, 44, 277–78, 297–98.

53. Ibid., 284, 286, 295, 324.

54. Ibid., 99, 274–77.

55. Ibid., 293.

56. Francis Russell, "The Four Mysteries of Warren Harding."

57. Ibid., 83.

58. Russell, *Shadow of Blooming Grove*, 161.

59. *Dayton Journal Herald*, February 1, 1971, folder 89, box 5, Downes Papers.

60. Sinclair, *Available Man*, 95.

61. The best source for the first five polls is Robert K. Murray and Tim H. Blessing's *Greatness in the White House: Rating the Presidents, Washington through Carter*, 6–9, 16–17. For the William Ridings Jr. and Stuart B. McIver poll, see "1990's Presidential Poll"; the Neal poll is in the *Chicago Sun-Times*, November 19, 1995.

Bibliography

Manuscripts

Adams, Samuel Hopkins. Papers. Hamilton College, Clinton, N.Y.

Albertson, Dean. Papers. University of Massachusetts, Amherst.

Boone, Joel T. Papers. Library of Congress, Washington, D.C.

Castle, William R., Jr. Diary. Houghton Library, Harvard University, Cambridge, Mass.

Christian, George B., Jr. Papers. Ohio Historical Society, Columbus (microfilm).

Christian, George B., Sr. Papers. Ohio Historical Society (microfilm).

Coolidge, Calvin. Papers. Forbes Library, Northampton, Mass. (microfilm).

Downes, Randolph C. Papers. University of Toledo.

Early, Stephen T. Papers. Franklin D. Roosevelt Library, Hyde Park, N.Y.

Fletcher, Henry P. Papers. Library of Congress.

Hard, Charles E. Papers. Ohio Historical Society (microfilm).

Harding, Florence Kling. Papers. Ohio Historical Society (microfilm).

Harding, Warren G. Papers. Ohio Historical Society (microfilm).

Hays, Will H. Papers. Indiana State Library, Indianapolis.

Herrick, Myron T. Papers. Western Reserve Historical Society, Cleveland.

Hoover, Herbert. Papers. Herbert Hoover Library, West Branch, Iowa.

Hoover, Irwin H. (Ike). Papers. Library of Congress (microfilm).

Jennings, Malcolm. Papers. Ohio Historical Society (microfilm).

Reily, E. Mont. Papers. Ohio Historical Society.

Roosevelt, Theodore, Jr. Papers and diary. Library of Congress.

Russell, Francis. Papers. University of Wyoming, Laramie.

Sawyer, Charles E. Papers. Ohio Historical Society (microfilm).

Scobey, Frank E. Papers. Ohio Historical Society (microfilm).

Smoot, Reed. Diary. Courtesy of Jan Shipps, Bloomington, Ind.

Sullivan, Mark. Diary. Herbert Hoover Library.

United States Senate. 1923. Investigation of Veterans' Bureau. Center for Legislative Archives, National Archives, Washington, D.C.

Wadsworth, James W. Family Papers. Library of Congress.

Walsh, Thomas J. Papers. Library of Congress.

Wilbur, Ray Lyman. Papers. Hoover Institution, Stanford, Calif.

The papers of Nan Britton, twelve archival boxes and one flat box, are in the library of the University of California at Los Angeles and are closed until the year 2000.

The archivist arranging the papers of Hubert Work, Dolores C. Renze, assures me that none of Dr. Work's papers deals with Harding's illness.

Records of the special Senate committee investigating the conduct of Attorney General Daugherty as well as the records of the committee on public lands and surveys pertaining to Teapot Dome, save only for a small collection of the latter, have disappeared and almost certainly were destroyed.

Oral Histories

Boone, Joel T., by Raymond Henle. Herbert Hoover Library. 1967.

Jones, Marvin. Oral History Collection, Oral History Research Office, Butler Library, Columbia University, New York. 1953.

Lasker, Albert Davis, by Allan Nevins and Dean Albertson. Oral History Collection, Oral History Research Office, Butler Library, Columbia University, New York. 1949–1950.

Meyer, Eugene, by Dean Albertson. Oral History Collection, Oral History Research Office, Butler Library, Columbia University, New York. 1952–1953.

Wadsworth, James W., by Owen W. Bombard, Wendell H. Link, and Dean Albertson. Oral History Collection, Oral History Research Office, Butler Library, Columbia University, New York. 1950–1952.

Williams, James T., Jr. Oral History Collection, Oral History Research Office, Butler Library, Columbia University, New York. 1953.

Books, Articles, Documents

Adams, Samuel Hopkins. *Incredible Era: The Life and Times of Warren Gamaliel Harding.* Boston: Houghton Mifflin, 1939.

———. *Revelry.* New York: Boni and Liveright, 1926.

Agar, Herbert. *The People's Choice: From Washington to Harding.* Boston: Houghton Mifflin, 1933.

Allen, Frederick Lewis. *Only Yesterday: An Informal History of the Nineteen-Twenties.* New York: Harper, 1931.

Barkley, Alben W. *That Reminds Me.* Garden City, N.Y.: Doubleday, 1954.

Bates, J. Leonard. *The Origins of Teapot Dome: Progressives, Parties, and Petroleum, 1909–1921.* Urbana: University of Illinois Press, 1963.

————. "The Teapot Dome Scandal and the Election of 1924." *American Historical Review* 60 (1954–1955): 303–22.

Behrman, Samuel Nathaniel. "Hyper or Hypo?" *New Yorker* 15 (April 8, 1939): 24.

Blythe, Samuel G. "A Calm Review of a Calm Man." *Saturday Evening Post* 196 (July 28, 1923): 3–4, 73–74, 76.

Britton, Nan. "A Day with Papa." *Today's Health* 44 (February 1966): 30–33, 90–91.

————. *Honesty or Politics.* New York: Elizabeth Ann Guild, 1932.

————. *The President's Daughter.* New York: Elizabeth Ann Guild, 1927.

Britton v. Klunk. Case no. 3476. National Archives, Great Lakes Region, Chicago.

Chancellor, William Estabrook. *Warren Gamaliel Harding: President of the United States.* Dayton, Ohio: Sentinal Press, 1922.

Daugherty, Harry M. *The Inside Story of the Harding Tragedy.* New York: Churchill, 1932.

De Barthe, Joseph. *The Answer.* Marion, Ohio: "The Answer," 1928.

————, ed. *The Life and Adventures of Frank Grouard.* Norman: University of Oklahoma Press, 1958.

Downes, Randolph C. *The Rise of Warren Gamaliel Harding: 1865–1920.* Columbus: Ohio State University Press, 1970.

————. "Wanted: A Scholarly Appraisal of Warren G. Harding." *Ohioana: Of Ohio and Ohioans* 2 (spring 1959).

Duckett, Kenneth W. "The Harding Papers: How Some Were Burned . . ." *American Heritage* 16 (February 1965): 25–31, 102–9.

Farrar, Ronald T. *Reluctant Servant: The Story of Charles G. Ross.* Columbia: University of Missouri Press, 1969.

Ficken, Robert E. "President Harding Visits Seattle." *Pacific Northwest Quarterly* 66 (1975): 105–14.

Fontaine, Roger, and Peter Hannaford. "Warren Remembrance." *American Spectator* 26 (January 1993): 56, 58–60.

Frederick, Richard G., comp. *Warren G. Harding: A Bibliography.* Westport, Conn.: Greenwood, 1992.

Giglio, James N. *H. M. Daugherty and the Politics of Expediency.* Kent, Ohio: Kent State University Press, 1978.

Gilbert, Clinton W. *Behind the Mirrors: The Psychology of Disintegration at Washington.* New York: Putnam's, 1922.

————. *The Mirrors of Washington.* New York: Putnam's, 1921.

Green, Horace. *The Life of Calvin Coolidge.* New York: Duffield, 1924.

Gross, Edwin K. *Vindication for Mr. Normalcy: A 100th-Birthday Memorial.* Buffalo: American Society for the Faithful Recording of History, 1965.

Harding, Warren G. *Speeches and Addresses . . . Delivered during the Course of His Tour from Washington, D.C., to Alaska and Return to San Francisco, June 20 to August 2, 1923*. Washington, D.C.: n.p., 1923.

Harding, Warren G., II, and J. Mark Stewart. *Mere Mortals: The Lives and Health Histories of American Presidents*. Worthington, Ohio: Renaissance Publications, 1992.

Herrick, James B. "Clinical Features of Sudden Obstruction of the Coronary Arteries." *Journal of the American Medical Association* 59 (December 7, 1912): 2015–20.

Hillman, Serrell. "Samuel Hopkins Adams, 1871–1958." *Saturday Review* 41 (December 20, 1958): 15, 37.

Hoover, Herbert. *The Cabinet and the Presidency, 1920–1933*. Vol. 2 of *The Memoirs of Herbert Hoover*. New York: Macmillan, 1952.

Hoover, Irwin H. *Forty-Two Years in the White House*. Boston: Houghton Mifflin, 1934.

Hoover, J. Edgar, with Courtney Ryley Cooper. "The Amazing Mr. Means." *American Magazine* 122 (December 1936): 24–25, 80, 82, 84.

Hoyt, Edwin P. *Spectacular Rogue: Gaston B. Means*. Indianapolis: Bobbs-Merrill, 1963.

Irwin, Will. *The Making of a Reporter*. New York: Putnam's, 1942.

Jenks, Anton Shrewsbury. *A Dead President Makes Answer to The President's Daughter*. New York: Golden Hind, 1928.

Jennings, Malcolm. "Washington-Alaska-Marion." *Rotarian* 23 (November 1923): 13–15, 44–46.

Knox, John C. *A Judge Comes of Age*. New York: Scribner's, 1940.

Lawrence, Jerome, and Robert E. Lee. *The Gang's All Here*. Cleveland: World, 1960.

Lentz, Andrea D., ed. *The Warren G. Harding Papers: An Inventory to the Microfilm Edition*. Columbus: Ohio Historical Society, 1970.

Longworth, Alice Roosevelt. *Crowded Hours*. New York: Scribner's, 1933.

Luce, Clare Boothe. "All for the Love of a Day." *McCall's* 91 (November 1963): 20, 178, 180.

MacMahon, Edward B., and Leonard Curry. *Medical Cover-ups in the White House*. Washington, D.C.: Farragut, 1987.

Mayer, Martin. *Emory Buckner*. New York: Harper and Row, 1968.

McLean, Evalyn Walsh. *Father Struck It Rich*. Boston: Little, Brown, 1936.

Means, Gaston B. *The Strange Death of President Harding: From the Diaries of Gaston B. Means, a Department of Justice Investigator*. New York: Guild Publishing, 1930.

Mee, Charles L. *The Ohio Gang: The World of Warren G. Harding, an Historical Entertainment*. New York: Evans, 1981.

Moos, Malcolm, ed. *A Carnival of Buncombe*. Baltimore: Johns Hopkins University Press, 1956.

Murray, Robert K. *The Harding Era: Warren G. Harding and His Administration.* Minneapolis: University of Minnesota Press, 1969.

————. *The 103rd Ballot: Democrats and the Disaster in Madison Square Garden.* New York: Harper and Row, 1976.

————. *The Politics of Normalcy: Governmental Theory and Practice in the Harding-Coolidge Era.* New York: Norton, 1973.

Murray, Robert K., and Tim H. Blessing. *Greatness in the White House: Rating the Presidents, Washington through Carter.* University Park: Pennsylvania State University Press, 1988.

Myers, Charlton. *Tales from the Sage of Salt Rock of Marion County, Ohio.* Marion, Ohio: Marion County Historical Society, 1996.

Nevins, Allan. "Warren G. Harding." In *Dictionary of American Biography.* Vol. 8. New York: Scribner's, 1932.

Noggle, Burl. *Teapot Dome: Oil and Politics in the 1920's.* Baton Rouge: Louisiana State University Press, 1962.

Parks, Lillian Rogers, and Frances Spatz Leighton. *My Thirty Years Backstairs at the White House.* New York: Fleet, 1961.

Pitzer, Donald E. "An Introduction to the Harding Papers." *Ohio History* 75 (1966): 76–84.

Plunket, Robert. *My Search for Warren Harding.* New York: Knopf, 1983.

Potts, Louis W. "Who Was Warren G. Harding?" *Historian* 36 (August 1975): 621–45.

Ridings, William, Jr., and Stuart B. McIver. "1990's Presidential Poll." *Presidential Studies Quarterly* 25 (1994–1995): 375–77.

Robinson, Edgar E., and Paul C. Edwards, eds. *The Memoirs of Ray Lyman Wilbur: 1875–1949.* Stanford: Stanford University Press, 1960.

Romine, Trella Hemmerly. *Day Before Yesterday: A Collection of Marion, Ohio, Vignettes.* Caledonia, Ohio: Terradise Press, 1994.

————, ed. *Marion County 1979 History.* Marion, Ohio: Marion County Historical Society, 1979.

Russell, Francis. "The Four Mysteries of Warren Harding." *American Heritage* 14 (April 1963): 4–10, 81–86.

————. "The Harding Papers . . . and Some Were Saved." *American Heritage* 16 (February 1965): 25–31, 102–10.

————. *The Shadow of Blooming Grove: Warren G. Harding and His Times.* New York: McGraw-Hill, 1968.

Sampson, John J. "Changing Conception of Coronary Artery Disease." *California and Western Medicine* 54 (January 1941): 6–10.

Sawyer, Charles E., Ray Lyman Wilbur, Charles M. Cooper, Joel T. Boone, and Hubert Work. "President Harding's Last Illness: Official Bulletins of Attending Physicians." *Journal of the American Medical Association* 81 (July–September 1923): 603.

Schruben, Francis W. "An Even Stranger Death of President Harding." *Southern California Quarterly* 48 (March 1966): 57–84.

Sinclair, Andrew. *The Available Man: The Life behind the Masks of Warren Gamaliel Harding.* New York: Macmillan, 1965.

———. "The Dear Departed." *New York Times Book Review* (January 22, 1967): 2, 38.

Smith, Ira R. T. *"Dear Mr. President . . .": The Story of Fifty Years in the White House Mail Room.* New York: Messner, 1959.

Socolofsky, Homer E. *Arthur Capper: Publisher, Politician, and Philanthropist.* Lawrence: University Press of Kansas, 1962.

Starling, Edmund W., and Thomas Sugrue. *Starling of the White House.* New York: Simon and Schuster, 1946.

Stewart, Edgar I., ed. *The Life and Adventures of Frank Grouard,* by Joseph De Barthe. Norman: University of Oklahoma Press, 1958.

Stratton, David H. "Behind Teapot Dome: Some Personal Insights." *Business History Review* 31 (winter 1957): 385–402.

———. "New Mexican Machiavellian?: The Story of Albert B. Fall." *Montana: The Magazine of Western History* 7 (November 1957): 2–14.

Sullivan, Mark. *The Twenties.* Vol. 6 of *Our Times: The United States, 1900–1925.* New York: Scribner's, 1935.

Thacker, May Dixon. "Debunking 'The Strange Death of President Harding': A Complete Repudiation of a Sensational Book by Its Author." *Liberty* 8 (November 7, 1931): 8–12.

Trani, Eugene P., and David L. Wilson. *The Presidency of Warren G. Harding.* Lawrence: University Press of Kansas, 1977.

Underdal, Stanley J. "Warren G. Harding, the Politics of Normalcy, and the West." *Journal of the American West* 34 (April 1995): 24–35.

United States Senate. *Investigation of the Honorable Harry M. Daugherty.* 3 vols. 68th Cong., 1st sess. Washington, D.C.: Government Printing Office, 1924.

United States Senate. *Investigation of Veterans' Bureau.* 2 vols. 67th Cong., 4th sess. and 68th Cong., 1st sess. Washington, D.C.: Government Printing Office, 1923.

United States Senate. *Leases upon Naval Oil Reserves.* 3 vols. 67th Cong., 4th sess. and 68th Cong., 1st sess. Washington, D.C.: Government Printing Office, 1924.

Walker, Kenneth R., and Randolph C. Downes. "The Death of Warren G. Harding." *Northwest Ohio Quarterly* 35 (1962–1963): 7–17.

Ware, Jane. "Marion Loves Warren." *Ohio* (December 1988): 18–24.

Wheeler, Burton K. *Yankee from the West.* Garden City, N.Y.: Doubleday, 1962.

White, William Allen. *Autobiography.* New York: Macmillan, 1946.

———. *Masks in a Pageant.* New York: Macmillan, 1928.

Wightman, Richard. *Ashes and Sparks.* New York: Century, 1915.

———. *Soul-Spur.* New York: Century, 1914.

———. *The Things He Wrote to Her.* New York: Century, 1914.

Wikander, Lawrence E., ed. *A Guide to the Personal Files of President Calvin Coolidge.* Northampton, Mass.: Forbes Library, 1986.

Wilbur, Ray Lyman. "The Last Illness of a Calm Man." *Saturday Evening Post* 196 (October 13, 1923): 64.

Index

Abraham Lincoln Book Shop and Gallery, 73
Adams, Samuel Hopkins, 31, 43–44, 63, 110–11, 134, 149–52, 154, 164; sketch, 38–40
Agriculture, Department of, 107
Alaska, 9–13, 37, 57, 67, 110–11, 123, 126, 130, 144–45, 147
Albertson, Dean, 76, 80–84; sketch, 80–81
Alderfer, Harold F., 151
Alexander, H. F., 118
Alexander Steamship Company, 118
Allen, Frederick Lewis, 31, 145–46, 149–50, 164
American Express Company, 54
American Heritage, 155, 161
American Historical Association, 146
American Language, The (Mencken), 140
American Legion, 115, 122
American Medical Association, 16, 38. *See also Journal of the American Medical Association*
American Medical Directory, 69
American Mercury, 142
American Metal Company, 106, 122, 128
American Red Cross, 120
Anderson, William F., 142
Answer, The (De Barthe). *See Britton v. Klunk*
Anti-Saloon League, 139
Apple, R. W., 78, 158
Armstrong Tour, 53
Army, U.S., 52; Eleventh Cavalry, 22–23; Thirtieth Infantry, 23. *See also* National Guard

Asia Banking Corporation, 65
Associated Press, 20–21
Available Man: The Life behind the Masks of Warren Gamaliel Harding, The (Sinclair), 159–61

Baldinger, Ora M., 152
Ballinger, Richard A., 107
Baltimore and Ohio Railroad, 10–11
Baltimore Sun, 142–43
Baptist Church, 25; in Marion, 26; in San Francisco, 22; in Washington, D.C., 8–9
Barkley, Alben W., 133
Bartley, E. Ross, 20–21, 30
Battle Creek Sanitarium, 2, 157, 160
Baughman, U. E., 78–79
Behind the Mirrors: The Psychology of Disintegration at Washington (Gilbert), 136–38
Bethlehem Steel Corporation, 122
Bible Corporation of America. *See* Wightman, Richard
Blackstone Hotel, 123
Blaesing, Elizabeth Ann. *See* Harding, Elizabeth Ann
Blaesing, Henry E., 77
Blessing, Tim H., 165
Boni and Liveright, 56
Bookman, 142
Boone, Daniel, 6
Boone, Joel T., 2, 7–10, 12, 14–20, 28–30, 40, 46, 111, 125–28, 131, 133, 148, 151; sketch, 5–6
Borah, William E., 146
Boston police strike, 162

Bowers, Claude G., 150
Bowman Company, 51
Brisbane, Arthur, 38
Britton, Dr., 50–51
Britton, Jeannette, 67–68
Britton, Mary, 50
Britton, Nanna P. (Nan), 31, 33–36,
    50–84, 129–30, 149, 158, 161–63,
    165; sketch, 51–52. *See also President's
    Daughter, The*
Britton v. Klunk, 68–76
Brobst, Bryntav H., 73
Brookhart, Smith W., 42
Brookhart-Wheeler Committee, 106,
    121–32, 134
Brooklyn College, 81
Brooks, Arthur, 8, 12, 15, 28, 47, 60
Brown, Walter F., 10
Buchanan, James, 165
Budget Bureau, viii, 146
Bull Moose Party. *See* Progressive Party
Bureau of Investigation, 33–34, 41. *See
    also* Federal Bureau of Investigation
Burns, William J., 33–34, 40–41
Butler, Nicholas Murray, 63, 107, 130
Butler, William M., 128

Calder, William M., 109, 120
Cambridge University, 159
Capper, Arthur, 110–11, 147
Carson, Pirie, and Scott, 51
Catholic Church, 30
CBS News, 151
Chancellor, William Estabrook, 150–53,
    157–58, 161
Chapman, Ernest, 11
Chautauqua, 162, 165
Chicago American, 158
Chicago Sun-Times, 165
Chicago Tribune, 82, 165
Chicago World's Fair, 77
Children's Society, 68
Christian, Elizabeth Ann. *See* Harding,
    Elizabeth Ann
Christian, George B., Jr., 14–15, 23,
    60–61, 79, 111, 153
Christian, George B., Sr., 3, 8, 25–26, 46
Cincinnati Conservatory of Music, 45

City in Terror, A (Russell), 162
Civil War, 23, 123, 160, 167
Clansman, The (Dixon), 33
Clarke, William R., 9–10
Clay, Cassius M., 71
Cleveland, Grover, 159
Close, C. L., 51
Colbert, Claudette, 39
Cole, Mr., 51
College of Wooster, 150
Collier's, 38
Columbia University, 54, 63, 80–81, 107,
    146
Columbus Circle Hotel, 73
Communists, 43
Comstock, Anthony, 56, 68
Congress, 140. *See also* House of
    Representatives; Senate
Congress Hotel, 84
Conservation, 107. *See also* Ballinger,
    Richard A.; Pinchot, Gifford; Teapot
    Dome
Coolidge, Calvin, viii, 6, 18, 21, 25, 48,
    71, 74, 83, 109, 128, 132, 143, 162, 164
Coolidge, Grace, 129
Coolidge, John, 18
Cooper, Charles M., 16, 22, 26, 28–29, 40
Cornell University, 146
Cowles, Paul, 21
Cox, James M., 144, 146
Cramer, Charles F., 116, 121
Creel, George, 108, 112
Cricken, Magnus, 54
Crowded Hours (Longworth), 147–48
Cumming, Hugh S., 120
Curtis, Charles, 83–84
Cushing, Harvey, 27–29

Dana, Charles A., 38
Daniels, Jonathan, 150
Daniels, Josephus, 108, 112
Dartmouth College, 76
Daugherty, Draper, 128
Daugherty, Harry M., 7, 23, 32, 37,
    41–42, 59, 106, 110, 114–15, 130–32,
    141, 144, 147, 149, 151, 158; sketch,
    122–24. *See also* Brookhart-Wheeler
    Committee

Daugherty, Mally S., 106, 127–28, 129
Daugherty, Mrs. Harry M., 125
Dauser, Sue S., 47
Davis, Gertrude G., 77
Davis, John W., 142–43
Davis, Richard Harding, 38
Davis Personnel, 77
Dawes, Charles G., 83–84
Dayton Journal Herald, 156
Dearborn Independent, 19
De Barthe, Joseph, 35, 69. *See also Britton
    v. Klunk*
Debs, Eugene, 141
Debunking, 134–43
Democratic Party, 34, 112–13, 129, 137,
    139, 142–44, 162, 164
Denby, Edwin L., 105, 108, 132, 145
Destroyers-bases agreement, 165
De Wolfe, Henry, 45
Dictionary of American Biography, 146–47
Dixon, Thomas, 33
Dodge, 11
Doheny, Edward L., 108–9, 111–14, 121
Donovan, William J., 124
Doubleday, Frank N., 152
Downes, Randolph C., 27–28, 70, 76–80,
    135, 143, 148, 162–63; sketch, 76–77
Drake Hotel, 117
Duckett, Kenneth W., 73, 154–57, 159,
    163
Dutton, Edna, 74
Dutton and Company, 113

Early, Stephen T., 20–21, 30
Edison, Thomas A., 131–32
Ed Sullivan Show, The, 133
Elizabeth Ann Guild, 33, 56–57, 64–68,
    158
Elizabeth Ann League, 57–58, 64, 68, 79
Elks, Benevolent and Protective Order of,
    142
Emerson, Ralph W., 65–66
"End of a Perfect Day, The," 45–46
Episcopal Church, 122

Fabian, Warner. *See* Adams, Samuel
    Hopkins
Fairmont Hotel, 117

Fall, Albert B., 105, 108–9, 111–13, 115,
    121–22, 124, 130, 133, 144–45
Fall, Emma, 110–11, 147
Federal Bureau of Investigation, 44. *See
    also* Bureau of Investigation
Ferguson, Walter, 83–84
Fess, Lehr, 155
Fess, Simeon D., 155
Fink, A. L., 124
Fishbein, Meyer H., 80
Fitzgibbons, Officer, 162
Flamingo Hotel, 125
Flaming Youth (Fabian), 39
Fletcher, Henry P., 3
Forbes, Charles R., 32, 105, 111, 124,
    130, 132. *See also* Veterans' Bureau
Forbes, Kate, 117
Ford, 108, 136
Ford, Henry, 19, 108
Forest Service, 107
Forever Amber (Winsor), 150
Forster, Rudolph, 2–3
Forty-Two Years in the White House
    (Hoover), 3
France, 164
Franklin, Benjamin, 159
Fraser, Malcolm A., 4
Frelinghuysen, Joseph S., 48
Fryefield, Maurice, 33
"Funeral March," 22
Furman, Bess, 151

Gable, Clark, 39
Gang's All Here, The, 133
Garfield, James G., 26, 148
Garrison, Lindley M., 112
Gary, Elbert H., 51
"Genevieve," 12
George Washington University, 81
Germany, 41, 122, 137, 139, 145–46, 157,
    160
Gibbs, W. Frank, 58, 60
Gilbert, Clinton W., 135–38, 164
Glass-casket case, 42
Globe Hotel, 123
Gould, Jay, 43
Grant, Ulysses S., 148, 165
Grayson, Cary T., 5

Great Britain, 137
Great Depression, 164
Greenslet, Ferris, 151
Gregory, Thomas W., 112
Grouard, Frank, 69
Guaranty Trust Company, 65
Guggenheim Foundation, 162
Guild Publishing Corporation, 33

H. F. Alexander, 118
Hague Peace Conference (First), 161
Hahnemann Medical College, 6
Haiti, 6
Hallelujah, 11
Halpin, Maria, 159
Hamilton, Alexander, 159
Hamilton College, 38
Hane, Mary Catherine, 74
Harding, Abigail Victoria (Daisy), 54,
    62–64, 66
Harding, Caroline. *See* Votaw, Caroline
    Harding
Harding, Charity. *See* Remsberg, Charity
    Harding
Harding, Elizabeth Ann, 33, 36, 52–55,
    59–64, 68, 71–72, 74, 77, 161. *See also*
    Britton, Nanna P. (Nan); Elizabeth
    Ann Guild; Elizabeth Ann League;
    President's Daughter, The
Harding, Florence, 5–9, 11–15, 17–20,
    22–25, 31, 34–38, 43, 52–53, 70,
    83, 114, 130, 135, 151–53, 157, 159,
    161–62, 165; sketch, 44–49
Harding, George T., 26, 28
Harding, George T., II, 1–2, 54, 62–63, 70
Harding, George T., III, 155–57, 162–63
Harding, Warren G.: illnesses: 1–9;
    Alaska, 7–12; San Francisco, 12–20, 22;
    funeral, 21–26; cause of death, 26–29;
    poison theory, 30–49; Nan P. Britton,
    50–84; Teapot Dome, 105–14; Veterans'
    Bureau, 114–21; Brookhart-Wheeler
    Committee, 121–30; scandals, 130–33;
    debunking, 134–43; and journalists,
    143–51; papers, 151–54, 159, 163,
    165; and Carrie Phillips, 153–59;
    biographers, 159–65; appraisal, 166–67
Harding, Warren G., II, 70

*Harding Era: Warren G. Harding and His
    Administration, The* (Murray), 164–65
Harding Memorial, vii, 71, 73–74, 167
Harding Memorial Association, 55, 142,
    152–54, 163
Harding scandals. *See* Scandals
Harlan, Laura, 152
Harper Brothers, 151
Harper's, 145
Harrison, Benjamin, 59, 143
Harvard University, 33, 146
Hawaiian Islands, 107, 114
Hayden, Jay G., 82
Hayes, Rutherford B., 148
Hays, Will H., 67, 115
Henderson, 8, 10–12, 14, 144–45
Herrick, James B., 27–28
Herrick, Myron T., 123–24
Hollenden Hotel, 124
Honesty or Politics (Britton), 56, 79
Hoover, Herbert, viii, 3, 6, 13–15, 20, 28,
    33, 40, 71, 83, 110–11, 126, 131, 148,
    161, 164
Hoover, Irwin H. (Ike), 3, 6, 59
Hoover, J. Edgar, 40
Hopkins, Stephen U., 56, 67
Houghton Mifflin, 151
House, Edward M., 123
House of Representatives, 80, 122, 147
Howell, W. H., Jr., 81
Hughes, Charles Evans, 21, 65, 149
Hurley, Charles F., 114
Hurley-Mason Company, 114, 116–17
Hynicka, Rudolph, 123

Imperial Hotel, 72–74
*Incredible Era: The Life and Times of
    Warren Gamaliel Harding* (Adams),
    39–40
Interior, Department of the, 108–10, 115
Internal Revenue Bureau, 42, 58
Irving-Bank Columbia Trust Company,
    79
Irwin, Will, 38, 116
It Happened One Night, 39

Jackson, Andrew, 140, 150
James, Marquis, 150

Japan, 153, 157
Jarnecke, Elmer, 41
Jefferson, Thomas, 150
Jennings, Malcolm, 9–10, 19
Jensen, Oliver, 155
Johns Hopkins University, 125, 141–42
Johnson, Andrew, 165
Johnson and Johnson, 120
Jones, W. T., 74
Journal of the American Medical Association, 27
Justice, Department of, 31, 33–34.
    See also Bureau of Investigation;
    Daugherty, Harry M.; Federal Bureau
    of Investigation

Kefauver, Weldon A., 163
Kellogg, Frank B., 137
Kenney, Patrick, 58–59
Kenwood School, 77
Killits, John M., 71–76
King, Maude (Mrs. James C.), 40–41
Kiwanis Club, 142
Kling, Florence. *See* Harding, Florence
Klunk, Charles A. *See Britton v. Klunk*
Knopf, Alfred A., 142
Ku Klux Klan, 41

LaFollette, Robert M., 143
Lake Forest College, 77
Lane, Franklin K., 112
League of Nations, 132, 137, 141–42, 146,
    161, 164–65
Leech, Wilmer R., 78
Lend-lease, 165
Levine, Samuel A., 27–29
Lewis, Abigail Victoria Harding. *See*
    Harding, Abigail Victoria (Daisy)
Liberty, 43
Libman, Emanuel, 4
Library of Congress, 152–53, 156, 158
Lincoln, Abraham, viii, 23, 26, 144
Lindbergh, Anne Morrow, 43–44
Lindbergh, Charles A., 43–44
Lodge, Henry Cabot, 109, 131, 146
Longworth, Alice Roosevelt, 147–49, 151,
    164
Longworth, Nicholas, 147–48

Lowden, Frank O., 123

Macmillan, 151, 160
"Maggie," 12
Manhattan Hotel, 51
Marietta College, 11
Marines, U.S., 45–46. *See also* Navy, U.S.
Marion County Historical Society,
    166–67
Marion High School, 51, 54
Marion Hotel, 70, 76
Marion Star, 2, 26, 45, 50, 74, 130,
    152–53, 167
Marion Tribune, 26
Marsdon, Edward, 11
Marsdon, Marietta, 11
Marsteller, William Fish, 71–76
Martin, Warren G., 126
Martin, William R., 74
Masks in a Pageant (White), 110–11,
    143–46, 153
Mason, Ben H., 143–44, 148
Mathee, Isabelle, 156
Mayflower, 5, 7–8, 144
Mayo, Charles, 46
McAdoo, William G., 112–13
McAlpin Hotel, 21
McClure, S. S., 38
McClure's, 38
McCormick, Medill, 137
McCumber, Porter J., 137
McGraw-Hill, 156
McIver, Stuart B., 165
McKenzie, Roger B., 29
McKinley, William, 2–3, 26, 60, 148, 166
McLean, Edward (Ned), 7, 113, 125, 147,
    152
McLean, Evalyn, 7, 43–45, 125, 147, 152
Means, Gaston B., 31, 33–38, 48, 149,
    153–54, 158; sketch, 40–44. *See also*
    Guild Publishing Corporation
Means, Julie, 41
Mearns, David C., 156
Melhorn, Donald D., 74
Mencken, Henry L., 138–43, 149, 164
Methodist Church, 65
Meyer, Agnes, 4
Meyer, Eugene, 4, 133

Midland National Bank, 106, 122, 129
Miller, Thomas W., 106, 122, 129
Milligan, Fred J., 154
Mirrors of Washington, The (Gilbert), 136–38
Montague, H. B., 80
Montmartre, 21
Moody, Dwight L., 167
Moore, Charles, 152
Mormon Church, 113
Mortimer, Elias H., 116–19, 121–22, 132
Mortimer, Katherine, 116–19
Moses, George H., 137
Motion Picture Producers and Distributors of America, 67
Mouser, Grant E., Sr., 71, 73–75
Muehlebach Hotel, 110–11
Murray, Robert K., 9, 131, 133, 135, 145–46, 150, 162, 164–65
Muzzey, David S., 150

N. Gray and Company, 22
Nathan, George Jean, 142
National Archives, 71, 79–80
National Civil Federation, 43
National Guard, 118
Nationalizing of Business, The (Tarbell), 39
Navy, U.S., 12, 22, 47, 107–8, 112. *See also* Boone, Joel T.; Denby, Edwin L.; Marines, U.S.; Roosevelt, Theodore, Jr.
Neal, Steve, 165
Nevins, Allan, 80–81, 146–47, 149, 151, 164
New York Daily News, 64–65, 68, 83–84, 158
New-York Historical Society, 78
New York Public Library, 158
New York Sun, 38
New York Times, 4, 16–18, 21–22, 32, 55–56, 78, 121, 155–59, 161
New York University, 81
New York World, 66
New York World Telegram, 71
New Zealand, 57, 67
Nixon, Richard M., 165
Northwestern University, 54

Ochs, Adolph, 32

O'Donnell, John, 64–65, 67–68, 158
Ohio Central College, 2, 160
Ohio Gang, 35, 131, 144, 147
Ohio Historical Society, 73, 135, 153–54, 156, 158–59, 163
Ohio State University, 76
Ohio State University Press, 163
O'Leary, C. R., 119
Only Yesterday: An Informal History of the Nineteen-Twenties (Allen), 31, 145–46
O'Ryan, John F., 118–19
Our Common Country (Harding), 58
Our Times: The United States, 1900–1925 (Sullivan), 148–49

Palace Hotel, 1, 15–23, 30, 49
Palmer, A. Mitchell, 113, 141
Pearl Harbor, 165
Pennsylvania State College, 151
Pershing, John J., 19, 23
Peter Bent Brigham Hospital, 27
Philippine Islands, 57, 67, 107
Phillips, Carrie, 81–82, 130, 135, 149, 153–59, 161–63, 165
Phillips, David Graham, 38
Phillips, James E., 130, 153, 157, 160
Pinchot, Gifford, 107
Pioneer, 7
Plaza Hotel, 113
Poindexter, Miles, 114–15
Polygraphic Company of America, 64–65
Ponce de Leon Hotel, 125
Porter, David L., 165
Post Office Department, 79–80
Powderly, Ruth, 19, 47
Presbyterian Church, 38, 65
Presidential Studies Quarterly, 165
President's Daughter, The (Britton), 31, 134, 145, 147, 150, 153, 158, 161. *See also* Britton, Nanna P. (Nan); *Britton v. Klunk*; Harding, Elizabeth Ann
Princeton University, 146
Procter, William C., 123
Progressive Course in English, 50–51
Progressive Party, 107, 143–44
Prohibition, 136. *See also* Anti-Saloon League
Prudential Life Insurance Company, 53

Psychopathia Sexualis (von Krafft-Ebing), 69
Public Health Service, 120
Puerto Rico, 58
Pullman Company, 40
Pure Food and Drug Act, 38
Putnam's, 135

Raleigh News and Observer, 108
Red Cross. *See* American Red Cross
Reed, David A., 118
Reily, E. Mont, 58, 60, 70
Remsberg, Charity Harding, 1–2, 4, 19, 63
Republican Party, 3–4, 41, 45, 52, 56–57, 59, 67, 82, 107–8, 112–13, 115, 122–24, 129, 132, 134, 136–37, 139, 143, 146, 148, 150, 153
Revelry (Adams), 31–33, 38–40, 56, 62, 64, 134, 145
Ridings, William J., 165
Riis, Jacob, 38
Rise of Warren Gamaliel Harding: 1865–1920, The (Downes), 162–63
Roberts, Mildred Christian, 74
Rockefeller, John D., 38
Rogers, L. Harding, 57, 65, 68
Rogers, Margaret E., 68
Roosevelt, Archibald, 112
Roosevelt, Franklin D., 4, 6, 20, 81, 150, 164–65, 167
Roosevelt, Theodore, 82, 107, 110, 134, 136–38, 140, 143–48, 152, 164
Roosevelt, Theodore, Jr., 25, 112, 121
Roosevelt Hospital, 143
Ross, Charles G., 3
Russell, Francis, 153–56, 158, 161–64
Ruzzo, Edward J., 155–56

Sacco and Vanzetti trial, 162
Samoan Islands, 107
Sampson, John J., 27–28
Samuel Ungerleider and Company, 62–63, 82–83, 128
San Diego Union, 47
Sankey, Ira D., 167
Saturday Evening Post, 17, 82
Sawyer, Carl, 48, 74

Sawyer, Charles E., 1, 7–9, 12–20, 27–28, 30–31, 37, 40, 48, 115–16, 120, 142, 161; sketch, 4–5
Sawyer, Mandy, 12
Sawyer, Warren, 5
Scandals. *See* Brookhart-Wheeler Committee; Daugherty, Harry M.; Teapot Dome; Veterans' Bureau
Schlesinger, Arthur M., Sr., 165
Scribner's, 151
Sears, Richard H., 57, 65, 67
Secret Service, 78–79
Senate, 2, 42–43, 45, 52, 59–60, 72, 84, 134, 137, 147, 153, 157, 160–61. *See also* Brookhart-Wheeler Committee; Congress; Daugherty, Harry M.; House of Representatives; Teapot Dome; Veterans' Bureau
Sentinal Press, 153
Shadow of Blooming Grove: Warren G. Harding and His Times, The (Russell), 161–62, 165
Shaughnessy Heights Golf Club, 12
Shelton Hotel, 65–66
Shepard, Mrs. Finley, 43
Shipping Board, 82–83, 115
Shoreham Hotel, 149
Sinclair, Andrew, 159–65
Sinclair, Harry F., 109, 111–12, 121
Sinclair, Upton, 38
Sindelar, Ann K., 73
Slade, Tim. *See* Sloan, James, Jr.
Sloan, James, Jr., 60, 62–63, 78–79, 82–84; sketch, 82–83
Slye, John (Jack), 78–79
Smith, Earl Hauser, 65–66, 158
Smith, Frederick C., 120
Smith, Ira R. T., 60–61, 64, 79
Smith, Jess W., 32, 37, 106, 130–31, 145, 147, 149, 154, 158. *See also* Brookhart-Wheeler Committee
Smith, Robert Freeman, 163
Smith, Xenophon P., 80
Smoot, Harold, 113–14
Smoot, Reed, 10, 112–14
Society for the Suppression of Vice, 56–57
Southern Pacific Railroad, 23

Spanish-American War, 3
St. Louis Post-Dispatch, 3
Standard Oil Company, 38
Stanford University, 3, 16, 40
Stark County Historical Society, 166
Starling, Edmund W., 8–9, 46, 79
Stearns, Frank W., viii
Steffens, Lincoln, 38
Stephenson, Francis M., 83–84
Stern, Henry, 124
Stevenson, Adlai E., 150
Stinson, Roxie R., 32, 106, 124, 127–28
Stowe, Harriet Beecher, 57
*Strange Death of President Harding:
    From the Diaries of Gaston B. Means,
    a Department of Justice Investigator,
    The* (Means), viii, 31. *See also* Means,
    Gaston B.
Sullivan, Ed, 133
Sullivan, Mark, 28, 110, 134, 148–51, 164
Sullivan High School, 77
Superb, 10
Supreme Court, 138
Sweet Act, 116
Syria, 57–67

Taft, William H., 3, 25, 107, 136–37, 143,
    148
Tarbell, Ida M., 38–39
Taylor, Joseph, 65
Teapot Dome, 31, 33, 62, 122, 131–34,
    142, 144–45, 147–49, 158
Tenderloin (Adams), 39
Thacker, May Dixon, 33–35, 37, 42–43
Thompson, Glenn, 156
Thompson, John W., 114, 121
Thompson-Black Construction
    Company, 114, 116–18, 121
Thomson and Kelly, 119–21
Through the Looking Glass (Carroll), 135
Tillman, John N., 80
Time, 133, 151
Toledo and Ohio Central Railroad, 1–2
Toledo Blade, 80
Town Hall Club, 54–55
Treasury Department, 78. *See also*
    Internal Revenue Bureau; Secret
    Service

Trible, George B., 48
Trohan, Walter, 82–83
True Confessions, 34, 37
Truman, Harry S., 3, 60–61, 150, 160

Uhler-Phillips Company, 153
Uncle Tom's Cabin (Stowe), 57
Union League Club, 122
United States Steel Corporation, 51
University of California, 27
University of Illinois, 146
University of Massachusetts, 76, 81
University of Michigan, 47
University of Oklahoma Press, 69
University of Pittsburgh, 76
University of Toledo, 76, 163
University of Washington, 13
University of Wisconsin, 76

Vanderbilt Hotel, 41
Versailles, Treaty of, 45, 132, 134, 137,
    161
Veterans' Bureau, viii, 105, 111, 114–22,
    131–32, 134, 161. *See also* Forbes,
    Charles R.
Votaw, Caroline Harding, 59, 63–64
Votaw, Heber H., 3, 64

W. B. Conkey Company, 57
Wadsworth, James W., 25, 109, 113, 115,
    124
Waldorf=Astoria Hotel, 78
Walsh, David I., 119
Walsh, Thomas J., 107, 109–10, 112, 122
Wardman Park Hotel, 37, 106, 116,
    125–26, 128
Washington, George, 51, 150
Washington Naval Conference, viii, 162
Washington Post, 4, 7
Webster, Daniel, 39
Weinberg, Daniel R., 73
Welliver, Judson C., 21
Werblow, Henry, 64–65
Werblow, Robert M., 64–65, 67
Western Reserve Historical Society, 73
Wheeler, Burton K., 131. *See also*
    Brookhart-Wheeler Committee
White, William Allen, 63, 110, 134,
    143–45, 147, 149, 151, 164

White House Profile: A Social History of the White House, Its Occupants and Its Festivities (Furman), 151

Whitlock, Brand, 145

Wickard, Claude R., 81

Wightman, Patricia Margaret Street, 56, 65–67, 158

Wightman, Richard, 54–55, 64, 66–68, 158; sketch, 65

Wilbur, Ray Lyman, 3–4, 16–17, 22, 26, 28, 40, 47, 49, 148–49

Wiley, Harvey, 38

William Penn College, 165

Williamson, Donald, 154–55

Willits, Elizabeth, 36, 52–54, 59, 62–64, 66, 74

Willits, Scott A., 36, 52–54, 59, 62–64, 66, 74

Wilson, Charles H., 57

Wilson, Woodrow, vii, 25, 34, 45, 78, 107–8, 112–13, 123, 132, 134, 136–40, 143, 146, 160–61, 164

Winslow, Francis A., 57

Winsor, Kathleen, 150

Witherill Hotel, 81

Wolff, Perry, 151

Women's Missionary Society, 40

Wood, Leonard, 107, 123

Wooster, College of. *See* College of Wooster

Work, Hubert, 11–16, 30, 40, 48

World Court, 142, 161

World War I, 39, 41, 106–7, 122, 139, 146, 164

World War II, 6, 39, 80, 164–65

Yale University, 122

Young Women's Christian Association (YWCA), 51

Zion National Park, 10

About the Author

Robert H. Ferrell is one of the leading scholars of the American presidency and is the author of numerous books, including *The Dying President: Franklin D. Roosevelt, 1944–1945, Ill-Advised: Presidential Health and Public Trust, Harry S. Truman: A Life,* and *Choosing Truman: The Democratic Convention of 1944.* Ferrell is Distinguished Professor of History Emeritus at Indiana University in Bloomington.